AN INTRODUCTION TO JOURNALISM

AN INTRODUCTION TO JOURNALISM

CAROLE FLEMING,
EMMA HEMMINGWAY,
GILLIAN MOORE
AND
DAVE WELFORD

SAGE Publications
London ● Thousand Oaks ● New Delhi

SAGE Publications Ltd
1 Oliver's Yard
55 City Road
London EC1Y 1SP

SAGE Publications Inc.
2455 Teller Road
Thousand Oaks, California 91320

SAGE Publications India Pvt Ltd
B-42, Panchsheel Enclave
Post Box 4109
New Delhi 110 017

British Library Cataloguing in Publication data

A catalogue record for this book is available
from the British Library

ISBN 0-7619-4181-9
ISBN 0-7619 4182-7 (pbk)

Library of Congress Control Number available

Typeset by C&M Digitals (P) Ltd., Chennai, India

CONTENTS

ACKNOWLEDGEMENTS

This book would not have been possible without the generous help given to the authors by people working in newspapers, radio, television and online. Their contributions will hopefully give readers an insight into how the skills and theories outlined in the book are put into practice in newsrooms across the country every day. The authors would like to thank the following people for the time they gave to provide an insight into their professions. From newspapers: Caroline Smith, Kevin Palmer, Tim Jones, Bob Jones, Paul Linford, Rebecca Sherdley, Rod Malcolm, Stuart Ellis, Sean Kirby, Simon Irwin, Richard Taylor, Martin Wells, Mark Tattersall, Jerome Quinn, Elaine Pritchard. From radio: John Atkin, Mike Young, Tim John, Ryan Martinez, Phil Dixon, Barnie Choudhury, Lisa Teanby. From television: Neil Manship, Nick Kehoe, Simon Hare, John Hemmingway, Mike Blair, Chris Mills, Geoff Byrne, Rob Pittam, John Boileau, James Robeson. From online: Terri Sweeney, Nigel Bell.

The authors would also like to thank staff at the Centre for Broadcasting and Journalism for their support during the writing of this book and for their useful advice, in particular, Amanda Ball, Jo Matthews and Richard Ventre.

INTRODUCTION

At the beginning of the last century the job of a journalist was quite simple to define: it was someone – usually male – who earned their living by writing for a newspaper or periodical. No formal qualifications were required and many people agreed with the description of legendary newspaperman of the time H.L. Mencken that journalism was 'a craft to be mastered in four days and abandoned at the first sign of a better job' (Delano, 2000: 262).

Since then the job itself has diversified to cover radio, television and online, and as its popularity as a career has grown, its status has changed from a craft to a profession, with a subsequent change in entry requirements. In 1965 only 6 per cent of journalists entering local evening newspapers held a degree. Five years later the first postgraduate qualification in journalism in the UK began at University College, Cardiff. By the mid-1990s, two-thirds of journalists had a university education (Delano, 2000: 267), and in 2004 there were 658 courses on offer at universities in the UK covering every aspect of the profession (UCAS).

Many of the changes in journalism have come about because of changes in technology, from the invention of the telegraph to satellite links that connect different continents at the flick of a switch. The emphasis in the 21st century is on immediacy with live radio and television reports, Internet chats with world leaders, and news flashes delivered to mobile phones. Technological changes have also required changes in the working practices of journalists who are now expected to be multiskilled. Newspaper journalists must also provide material for the online edition of their paper, while broadcast journalists are increasingly expected to supply material for radio, television and online services. But despite these changes, the fundaments of journalism remain the same: to report events that affect society in an accurate and balanced way so that some understanding of the world we live in can be gained.

The aim of this book is to try to show how journalists in newspapers, radio, television and online do their job, not only by explaining the process but also by hearing from those who do it on a daily basis. Of course, whole libraries are devoted to every aspect of journalism, and this text is not exhaustive, but an introduction to the techniques used and skills required to be a journalist. It is designed for those who have an interest in the production of news but who have little or no knowledge of the process. Through the interviews with practitioners in each chapter, it is also hoped that even those already embarked on a career in journalism will find some useful tips.

News is a multi-million pound business, but for all that, it tends to be taken for granted by the consumers of newspapers, radio, television and the Internet. In many ways it is the ultimate consumer product – out of date almost as soon as it is reported, with a constant demand for the 'latest' story. But despite the pro-liferation of news outlets over the past decade, the range of stories covered by mainstream media is surprisingly similar. For this reason Chapter 1 examines news as a commodity, showing where news comes from, and how it is selected and used by different media. The chapter ends with an analysis of the news from a particular day to illustrate the similarities and differences between media.

But no matter which medium news is produced for, the basic approach to researching it is similar, and this is explored in Chapter 2. This chapter exam-ines various news sources in detail and shows how reporters verify sources. Turning to localised research, the chapter discusses local publications, press releases, PR agencies, local PR officers, councillors, local organisations, the police and other emergency services, community media, and how to accrue a network of personal contacts. Further comment and analysis are provided by working journalists from both radio and TV media.

Having identified and sourced a story, the next job is to write it, and Chapter 3 outlines the basics of writing a story starting from the intro – the first paragraph of a news story – through to the type of language that should be used. It also looks at story construction and how student journalists should approach differ-ent types of story, including sport and features. It investigates the different ways of writing for newspapers, radio, television and the Internet.

The interview is a key tool for any journalist and Chapter 4 explores the inter-view and its place in newspaper and broadcast journalism. The chapter explains what steps should be taken in order to conduct a successful interview, from finding the right interviewees to formulating effective questions. It outlines in detail how an interview is best conducted for different media, concentrating on the technical and practical aspects as well as the journalist's own skills of inter-acting with an interviewee.

Chapter 5 then takes a look at the skills needed to be a broadcast journalist – from finding the best location for an interview, to recording and editing a news package. This is not a technical manual, but it outlines what needs to be con-sidered at each step of developing a story for broadcast. The chapter ends with an account of the work of an online journalist that shows how the skills of print and broadcast are combined.

Journalists are necessarily constrained by the law, which is designed to pro-tect both those being reported on and journalists themselves. For this reason the next two chapters look at the law and journalism. Chapter 6 provides an intro-duction to the English legal system, and considers a range of legal sources. It introduces the reader to the difference between civil and criminal law, outlines the court structure, and provides a useful list of key legal personnel. In Chapter 7 there is an examination of the range of legal provisions that influence and constrain journalists. A single chapter cannot provide a detailed consideration of the provisions, but by summarising key areas, it supplies a useful snapshot of the subject. The chapter includes an introduction to the laws relating to privacy, reporting elections, protecting sources and copyright. It also explores the complex areas of contempt and defamation law in more detail.

Having provided an introduction to the court system and what can and cannot be reported, the text then in Chapter 8 examines court reporting. This chapter focuses on the basics of what you must have in your story and what you should do before going to court for the first time. It looks at the ways you should approach Magistrates' Court, Crown Court, inquests and tribunals. It investigates the different ways courts are covered by newspaper, radio, television and online journalists.

An equally important source of news for journalists is Government, and Chapter 9 looks at the changing shape of local government from the environment department to the main parts and roles of the local government system. It outlines what sort of stories should be looked for and how to get them. It investigates how to get the best out of councillors and council officers, plus how to bust the jargon and avoid political bias. It also has an extensive section on how regional journalists should aim to cover Westminster.

The day-to-day activities of working journalists are determined by laws, regulations and the practicalities associated with producing news and attracting an audience. However, the nature of the work also raises a number of moral and ethical considerations with which the journalist must grapple. The final chapter considers the role of regulation, with particular attention given to the conduct of journalists and journalism content. The chapter considers different regulatory bodies and the rationales that support such regulation, and the complex interplay between law, regulation and ethics through the exploration of a number of moral dilemmas that working journalists may face on a regular basis.

The final sections of the book provide a Glossary of Legal Terms followed by a Glossary of Journalism Terms, which it is hoped will prove useful to those new to these areas.

WHAT IS NEWS?

'The news' is an integral part of life in the 21st century. Once a discrete category available only in certain formats at certain times, news is now available around the clock on radio, television, the Internet, sent via text to your phone, as well as in its traditional paper form. What is surprising is that despite the proliferation of news outlets, and the advances in technology that have altered the way it is gathered, processed and received, the product itself has barely changed since the emergence of a mass circulation popular press in the second half of the 19th century. Then, as now, different news outlets catered to different audiences and so gave greater or lesser prominence to different types of stories all under the heading of 'the news'. And then, as now, cultural commentators criticised journalism for debasing cultural standards as 'politics and opinion began to be supplemented, if not replaced, with material of a "human note", crime, sexual violence and human oddities' (Williams, 1998: 51).

A single definition for the news is problematic because so many different factors influence its selection and production. There are also many different approaches to analysing news selection whereby each views the news from a different theoretical perspective.[1] This chapter examines news as a product and discusses organisational influences on its production. It then examines how news is used by different media, and within each medium how it is used to target specific audiences.

Technology has played a major part in the way news is gathered and disseminated. Advances in printing technology towards the end of the 19th century allowed for cheaper newspapers to be produced; better systems of roads and rail allowed for mass circulation; and the invention of the telegraph opened the area able to be reported upon and the style in which it was written (cf. Allan, 1999; Williams, 1998). More recent technological advances have made communication across the world faster and easier, and for that reason the impact of technology on news, and global influences on news, will also be discussed. The chapter ends with an examination of the news taken from newspapers, radio and television, which illustrates how and why different media use the news.

SELECTING THE NEWS

At its simplest, the news is the reporting of events to an audience, but as Stuart Hall comments, 'Of the millions of events which occur every day in the world, only a tiny proportion ever become visible as "potential news stories": and of this proportion only a small fraction are actually produced as the day's news in the news media' (Hall, 1981: 234).

Given that almost any event has the potential to be news – from a local mugging to a terrorist attack – it might be surprising that on any given day, the majority of stories reported in one news outlet are also covered by every other outlet, albeit to a greater or lesser extent, as the analysis at the end of this chapter shows. Journalistic myth would have us believe that this is because all journalists have an instinctive 'nose for news' that alerts them to newsworthy stories. However, an analysis of what actually becomes the news shows that there are certain factors that consistently influence whether or not an event is deemed newsworthy. This is not to suggest that every news story will have all, or even any, of these factors, or that journalists consciously select stories on this basis. However, research, most notably by Galtung and Ruge (1981), indicates that the following characteristics are consistently evident in most news stories.

- **Relevance:** For an event to be reported, it must be seen to affect, however indirectly, the lives of the audience. This accounts for one of the biggest differences between national and local news: a mugging in Manchester would most likely go unreported outside that area, unless it were linked to a series of attacks around the country.
- **Timeliness:** Stories tend to stress what is happening now rather than reflect past events. Events that take place at times when they can be easily monitored are favoured, hence the tendency for press conferences to take place at times that allow it to be reported in the main broadcast news bulletins, and in time for the next day's national newspapers.
- **Simplification:** Stories that can be told in straightforward, unambiguous terms that are easy to understand. This is particularly important for broadcast news bulletins, which are constrained by time limitations.
- **Predictability:** Stories that deal with events known about in advance like anniversaries, the release of the latest unemployment figures, or state occasions (diary jobs).
- **Unexpectedness:** Something that is unusual or rarely happens, for example when Mars became visible from earth by the naked eye in the summer of 2003 for the first time in almost 700 years.

- **Continuity:** Stories where the initial event has repercussions that affect people. These are stories when there is seen to be a need for regular updates, as in the coverage of major court stories, or, notably, the war in Iraq in 2003.
- **Composition:** News editors like to provide a range of different types of stories: serious political news as well as lighter, human interest stories.
- **Elite people:** A woman caught shop-lifting is unlikely to make the news. But if she is a well-known Hollywood star, the story is covered across the globe.
- **Elite nations:** Events in 'first world' countries, especially the USA and Europe, are favoured over those in developing nations.
- **Negativity:** 'Bad news' is generally deemed more interesting than 'good news', so stories about disasters, crime and scandal feature highly.

What eventually ends up as the news is further influenced by the way the news is gathered. Ultimately the news is a business and as such it is highly organised. The detailed structure of a news organisation may vary from one outlet to another, but to a large extent every news organisation uses the same sources to get the news. Editors cannot rely on events just happening in order to fill their paper or bulletin, so the vast majority of stories are not spontaneous but planned. As Paul Manning points out, 'The production of news each day, each week or on a rolling 24-hour basis, involves the routine gathering and assembling of certain constituent elements which are then fashioned to construct or fabricate an account of the particular news event' (Manning, 2001: 50). In other words, in order to satisfy the increasing demand for news, reporters tend to access similar sources that traditionally provide material.

This can be problematic, as Gay Tuchman (1975) has shown. She coined the phrase 'the news net' to describe the way news outlets organise their news gathering using reporters, freelances ('stringers') and wire services (for example, Associated Press or Reuters) to create a 'news blanket' that will cover all potential news stories. However, in practice there is a huge amount of duplication. Stringers might tip off a newsroom that a celebrity is planning a remote Highland wedding, but it is likely the news organisation will then send their own staff to cover the event in order to make it 'their' story, and also because it is cheaper to send staff than to pay a freelance. Similarly, the wire services may cover an anti-war demonstration in London, but news organisations will send their own staff to develop a local angle on it. The resulting story would then combine the broader wire service coverage, for example reaction to the demonstration from abroad or from official Government spokesmen, with more specific reporting about families from their area and their experience of the demonstration. In this way, says Tuchman, 'Instead of blanketing the world by their joint efforts, the news media and the news services leave the same sort of holes justified by a professionally shared notion of news judgement' (1978: 295).

Rebekah Wade, the editor of the *Sun*, has defined journalism as 'an ability to meet the challenge of filling space',[2] and to be able to do that, journalists have to order the world and make it manageable. What is interesting to note is how the 'ordering' of the world links to the characteristics researchers have identified as common to most news stories, as discussed above.

One of the primary ways of organising news gathering is on a geographical basis, thereby making sure that stories are 'relevant' to particular audiences. National news media tend to cover stories within the UK, and often only within a particular area of the UK. Unless a big story breaks, like September 11th or the Bali bombing, international news is provided by freelances based abroad, the wire services and, for larger organisations, foreign correspondents. Similarly, local and regional media have clearly defined geographical areas with news from outside the area provided from elsewhere.

The news media are further organised on the basis of specific 'territories' that regularly provide stories, like government (both local and national), courts, the police and other emergency services. These news beats tend to be covered by specialist correspondents who build up a range of contacts who will readily speak to them, and sometimes provide stories to be followed up. Larger news organisations have further specialisations in areas like industrial relations, health, education and the environment. As Manning points out, the popularity of various specialist areas tends to reflect the wider political and economic environment: 'For example, during the last decade the fortunes of British financial, health and education correspondents have all prospered, while the labour and industrial beat enjoyed a "golden age" during the 1960s and 1970s but is now in almost terminal decline' (Manning, 2001: 74).

Areas that have specialist correspondents are those that regularly provide stories, and often they are running stories that require 'continuity'. This could be the passage of a controversial bill through Parliament, a high-profile court case, or the hunt for a missing teenager. By covering these stories with specialists who have not only built up a lot of knowledge about a particular area, but also have a range of contacts they can use, news media are able to convey the story more readily.

A further way that the news is organised is on the basis of topic. At its simplest this could be a division between news and sport, although, particularly in newspapers, there are often further divisions that provide 'variety' in the kind of stories covered. For example, many newspapers have a features department that does not deal with day-to-day news, but produces stories of general human interest from articles about school truancy, to reports on environmentally friendly homes. Further divisions can include business and financial news, fashion and lifestyle, and celebrity or entertainment news.

Of course, any newsroom's main source of stories should be its own staff. This is particularly true for regional and local newsrooms, where the staff live in the area that they are reporting about. Staff should be alert to the potential for any event to become a story, from noticing an unexpected school closure that turns out to have been caused by the discovery of dangerous wiring in the building, to hearing in the newsagents that local shops are closing because of the level of vandalism. Everyone is a potential contact for a reporter, and it is just as important for a general reporter to cultivate contacts as it is for the specialist who gets tipped off about Government corruption. These are the kind of stories that might easily slip through the news net, and to some extent it is the job of a reporter to make sure they get covered.

But with the best will in the world, it would be difficult to fill every newspaper and news bulletin with wholly original stories, and this is where the more routine aspects of reporting take over. These include newsroom diaries, press releases, the emergency services and other sources of news detailed in Chapter 2. But the stories chosen by news organisations are also influenced by the particular deadlines and requirements of each medium, as the following examination of newspapers, radio, television and online explores.

NEWSPAPERS

The majority of a daily newspaper's content is prepared in advance of the day's edition, with only the front page and a few inside pages filled as close to the deadline as possible. Newspapers cannot compete with electronic media in speed, so their approach has to be to find something different to tempt people to buy them. National tabloids tend to rely on brash headlines and large, dramatic pictures to hook their readers. They are written in simple and direct language to appeal to as wide a readership as possible, and beyond the front page, they tend to focus on human interest stories with a lot of celebrity gossip and show business news. By contrast, the front pages of broadsheets still tend to be dominated by 'serious' news from major institutions, although increasingly even more staid papers like the *Daily Telegraph* have a lighter item somewhere on the front page, and front page pictures are more prominent than in the past.

However, the definition of a tabloid may be changing. In September 2003 the broadsheet the *Independent* launched a tabloid or 'compact' version of its paper in the London area, designed to appeal to commuters who found the broadsheet format difficult to handle. While the move to tabloid format was widely regarded as a last-ditch attempt to boost the paper's ailing circulation, it proved such a success that the tabloid edition went national four months later. By March 2004 the paper's circulation showed a 15 per cent increase, and two months later in May 2004 the paper went completely tabloid, ending two decades as a broadsheet newspaper.

Even before the increase in sales was established, *The Times* retaliated and launched its tabloid version in November 2003 in the London area, extending its availability over the country over the next four months. Newspaper analysts had a mixed reaction to the changes, with most fearing that the compact format would mean less in-depth reporting of serious news. The *Independent* carried all its broadsheet material in the tabloid version, but as analyst Roy Greenslade noted, this was not true for the *Times*, with many broadsheet versions of stories either truncated or omitted:

> A detailed study comparing the broadsheet and compact editions reveals a pattern in which the editorial content of the former is vastly superior to that of the latter ... scores of stories were far shorter in the tabloid. Many stories were cut back to news-in-briefs. (*Guardian*, January 19 2004)

But despite a less positive reaction to the compact *Times* than to that of the *Independent* (which won the national Newspaper of the Year award at the British Press Awards in March 2004), the *Times* suddenly stopped production of its 216-year-old broadsheet at the end of October 2004. Although other broadsheets currently have no plans to go tabloid, the changes could mean that tabloid newspapers in the future are defined purely by their format rather than their content.

The move by the *Independent* and the *Times* to tabloid can be viewed as the latest reaction to a general decline in newspaper sales since the mid-1950s. Over the years, various tactics have been used in an attempt to reverse the trend. These range from changing the editorial stance, as the *Mirror* did for a short time post September 11th, to price-cutting wars, and even giving them away free to try to tempt a new readership to buy them in the future.

Newspapers, like all media except the BBC, depend on advertising for their survival. They use their content to attract a readership which is then 'sold' to advertisers, and this has had an effect on their content, as papers strive to target specific sections of society. The *Guardian*, for example, has a different supplement every day aimed at different professions, while the *Daily Mirror* in part attributed its return to sales over the 2 million mark in August 2003 to the introduction of a Saturday supplement, 'We Love Telly'.[3] As Linda Christmas comments:

> The feature content of all national daily and Sunday newspapers has increased in the last 15 years – much of it has been devoted to areas which attract advertising, like leisure activities and supplements listing what's on and where to go, plus health and fitness. There has also been a huge increase in human interest stories, tales of triumph over tragedy, and advice on how to handle relationships. (Christmas, 1997: 3)

The regional press is following a similar trend with local evening papers typically bulked out by supplements on property, motoring and sport on different days of the week. Despite this, regional dailies and evening papers are struggling to maintain their readers, although local weekly newspaper sales are increasing.

An examination of three national newspapers from November 13 2003 reveals how different newspapers use the news to appeal to different readerships. The *Sun* is the UK's biggest-selling daily newspaper, registering a circulation of 3,363,612 for August 2004 (source: Audit Bureau of Circulation). The paper has a populist approach to news, and tends to attract more male than female readers, not just because of its trademark 'page three girl', but also because it has very good sports coverage. In the first year of Rebekah Wade becoming editor in January 2003 with a promise to 'inject more fun into the *Sun*',[4] the paper increased its show business and television coverage, launched attacks on asylum seekers urging readers to 'read this and get angry',[5] and, in what could be seen as an attempt to woo more women readers, launched a campaign to highlight the victims of domestic abuse.

The *Daily Mail*, with a circulation of 2,310,532 for the same month, is the *Sun*'s nearest rival in terms of circulation, but it targets quite a different market. It regards itself as a 'quality tabloid', and its editor Paul Dacre says the secret of its success is knowing its audience. 'I think some newspapers and a lot of the radio and television media are now run by liberal, politically correct consensors who just talk to each other and forget that in the real world there are people who feel differently' (*Guardian*, July 7 2003). However, newspaper analyst Roy Greenslade says that under Paul Dacre, the paper has become a 'middle class bible', since by 'playing to the fears and narrow-mindedness of its audience, it magnifies their xenophobia and hypochondria, panders to their envy and, despite its vaunted image as a paper sympathetic to women, disparages feminism' (*Media Guardian*, September 2 2002).

The *Guardian*, with a circulation of 338,323 for the same month, is at the opposite end of the political spectrum from the *Daily Mail*. A serious broadsheet newspaper, it is unique among British newspapers because it is owned by The Scott Trust, rather than a media tycoon or shareholders. It describes itself thus: 'Free from the influence of a proprietor, shareholders or any political allegiance, the *Guardian* is able to report on news stories unhindered and conduct serious investigative reporting in the public interest. The paper consistently breaks stories and sets the news agenda' (*Education Guardian*, April 29 2003). Among national broadsheet newspapers, it has a high proportion of 18–24-year-old readers, particularly students, and this may contribute to its reputation as a haven for ineffectual left-wing liberals.

On the day being examined, the Soham murder trial[6] dominated the news. Both tabloid papers devoted the whole of their front page to the latest in the trial. The *Sun* featured the headline 'The Panic' above pictures of the anguished faces of the mothers of Holly Wells and Jessica Chapman. Inside the paper devoted six pages to the court case, going into detail about what each witness had said the previous day. The *Daily Mail* took a slightly different focus on the court case, with its front page featuring pictures of Ian Huntley, who was accused, and later found guilty, of the girls' murders, and Holly Wells's father Kevin. Between the photographs is the headline, which is a quote from Ian Huntley to Mr Wells: 'I am so sorry I didn't realise she was your daughter'. The story is continued on page two of the paper, with further coverage of the court case on four more pages. In contrast to the tabloid papers, the *Guardian* relegates the story to 300 words in the bottom right-hand corner of the front page. Its story, headlined 'Huntley comforted by Holly's father, court told', takes a similar line to the *Daily Mail's* front page, but has no accompanying pictures. Inside the paper a half page is devoted to the previous day's court hearing.

That all the papers cover the trial of Ian Huntley is no surprise: the story had dominated the news ever since the two ten-year-old girls went missing in August 2002, to their bodies being found two weeks later, the murder investigation, and the subsequent arrest and trial of Ian Huntley and his girlfriend Maxine Carr. Neither is it surprising that each paper provided the same information, given that it all derived from the court case at the Old Bailey. But the way that each paper deals with the story shows the different market each targets.

By focusing on the anguish the mothers felt when they realised their daughters were missing, the *Sun* is appealing to the parents of every young child to empathise with them. The angle taken by the *Daily Mail*, however, tends to demonise Huntley (at this point still not found guilty), by portraying him as a callous hypocrite offering his condolences to the father of the girl he had murdered. By devoting just 300 words on the front page to the Soham trial, the *Guardian* acknowledges the importance of the story but places it within a global context. Its main front-page story was headlined 'We could lose this situation' and featured a picture of the devastation caused by suicide bombers in Nassiriya in Iraq, where 18 Italian soldiers had been killed the previous day. The other front-page story is about a £100,000 settlement being made by the Metropolitan Police Force to a police officer alleging racial discrimination in an employment tribunal. Neither of the tabloid papers ran this story, while the story of the suicide bombing was given half a page, with no pictures, on page 2 of the *Daily Mail*, and two columns, with two pictures, on page 22 of the *Sun.*

In order to get a clearer picture of the content of the newspapers under examination, their content has been broken down into various categories in Table 1.1. 'Celebrity reports' are those that are only there because they feature a celebrity. 'Business news' and 'Women's pages' are those tagged that way in the paper. 'Features' are stories that are topical but not news. 'Comment/columnist' pages are opinion pieces, not including celebrity or television topics. As can be seen, the broadsheet *Guardian* has the highest news content, with the *Sun* and the *Mail* roughly the same. Within that category, the only foreign news in the tabloid papers was a report on the Nassiriya bombing featured on the *Guardian*'s front page, although the *Sun* gave a page to a report about orang-utans being used for boxing matches in Thailand. The *Guardian*, however, had five pages of international news. It should also be noted that although the *Guardian* has no features, women's pages or television in its main paper, all these categories are covered in its tabloid supplement 'G2', and on a Thursday it also has a 'Life' supplement which covers medical, science and environmental issues.

The *Mail* has the highest content of women's pages, and this reflects the fact that it has the highest number of female readers among national newspapers. Despite this, it regularly runs features that attack women, and in the issue examined there was a two-page feature about Britain's first female Law Lord, Dame Brenda Hale, headlined 'The Marriage Wrecker'. It detailed the 'controversial' views of Dame Brenda, as well as revealing how she had remarried nine days after her divorce.

Predictably, the *Sun* has the most celebrity and television news with just over 15 per cent of the paper devoted to those topics, compared to just over 7 per cent in the *Mail*.

Table 1.1   Breakdown of newspaper content

No. of pages on each topic	Sun	Mail	Guardian
Total pages	72	96	36
News	18 (25%)	23 (23.9%)	17 (47.2%)
Celebrity reports	6	3	0
TV news and listings	5	4	0
Business news	1	5 (inc. Career Mail)	6
Women's pages	4 ('Health' pages)	16 (Femail magazine)	0
Reviews	0	1	1
Sport	11	13	6
Features	1	2	0
Comment/columnists	Double column p. 8	4	2

RADIO NEWS

Radio journalists will argue that local radio news is *the* most important element of local radio – and that's because for the most part it is. For some smaller independent commercial stations it almost defines them ... and for some larger ones it is one of the main things that keeps them local. For many listeners, it is an essential part of their daily lives – they love knowing what's going on where they live. Whether it's unpleasant things like a fatal accident on a major road, a murder or a stabbing, or something lighter like a report on local fundraising or a pop concert, people will listen because they want to know about it. It's the most immediate form of broadcasting and when listeners tune in, they expect it to be there. That said, it's important to remember the role of news within the wider station. Particularly in a commercial market, news is one of the few departments that doesn't make a radio station any money because under current rules it's unable to attract things like sponsorship. Also, whilst listeners like getting their news, many don't want it all the time. So, you need things like music, weather, travel, showbiz, competitions, sports and features to be played around the ads to get people to listen to your station. The more people who listen the more money the station will make. If a commercial station didn't make money, then it simply wouldn't exist, meaning no news and ultimately no jobs.

Tim John[7]
newsreader/reporter
106 Century FM

The growth of radio in the UK can be traced to the 1990 Broadcasting Act, which allowed commercial radio to target a specific audience for the first time.

Prior to this, commercial radio stations were obliged to provide programming for everyone in their transmission area. This made radio stations less attractive to advertisers, who wanted to target specific demographics. Following the 1990 Act, radio stations began to tailor their output to attract specific audiences that could be delivered to advertisers. The most attractive audience for advertisers is the 24–35 year old woman, as they are regarded as having the largest disposable income, and tend to be responsible for the purchase of fast-moving consumer goods. Unsurprisingly, this was the audience that most commercial stations targeted, tailoring their programmes, including the news, to this sector. As more radio stations came on air, they began to target different audiences in order to attract a wider range of advertisers.

The success of radio in attracting advertisers is shown by the fact that in 1990 radio had a 2 per cent share of all advertising revenue, but by mid-2004 it had increased its share to 7 per cent (Radio Advertising Bureau). Moreover, as radio critic Maggie Brown has reported,[8] local advertising on radio is growing twice as fast as national advertising. In commercial terms, this means that radio is a thriving industry, with fierce competition for the limited FM bandwidth. For example, the last franchise awarded by the Radio Authority before it became part of the super-regulator Ofcom, was for the Glasgow area. This attracted 13 different applications, each targeting a slightly different audience. Unlike television licences, radio franchises do not cost anything, but the Glasgow licence, finally awarded to Saga Radio, has the potential to be worth 'upwards of £20m in advertising and commercial opportunities as it broadcasts across an area with an adult population of around 1.6 million' (*Guardian*, November 6 2003).

Although the BBC does not compete for advertising in the way that commercial radio does, it does compete for audiences. Hence, within the BBC each station is aimed at a different audience in the hope that overall they can attract different audiences within the BBC 'family'. For example, Radio 1 is obviously aimed at a young audience, typically 15–25 year olds, while the Radio 4 audience is typically older (40+) and attracts people interested in news and current affairs. The BBC's most popular radio station, Radio 2, is aimed at the middle ground of people between 25 and 40, which is also the audience most commercial stations target. By contrast, BBC local radio aims at older audiences who share an interest in the community in which they live.

What this means is that in order to have a consistent brand identity, radio stations now tailor their news to the audience they are serving. They do this by making the news relevant to this audience, not only in the selection of stories, but also in the way they cover them. Hence, stations aimed at younger audiences tend to have short news bulletins read over a music bed so that the bulletins sound lively and in keeping with the pop music output of their programmes. By contrast, those aimed at an older audience tend to be longer bulletins delivered in a more serious and measured way.

News is very important to an older audience – 40 plus – but I believe younger people are not so concerned about 'news every hour' and would be content with their favourite station producing news bulletins a few times a day rather than regularly. It's crucial to target news to the audience. If every other aspect of a station's output is targeting a specific demographic, it is pointless the newsroom having its own agenda. News must fit in with the programming style of the station.

Phil Dixon[9]
managing director
Saga 106.6 FM

The different way news is covered by particular stations can be seen from an examination of bulletins on two local radio stations on Thursday, November 13 2003. Trent FM, which is part of the GWR group, is a local commercial station covering Nottingham and Mansfield. Its target audience is the 25–34 year old, who is more likely to be a woman than a man, although the station is aware that it should not alienate men. According to the GWR brand document, the station's listeners can be described as 'everyday, up-for-it people, in touch with where they live', with many of them having young families. BBC Radio Nottingham, in line with all BBC local radio stations, caters for a much older audience of around 50+. The station has a slightly wider transmission area than Trent FM, taking in the rural areas around Nottingham as well as the city and surrounding towns. Typically, its listeners will have strong ties with the local community, and know and care about its history and culture. Many of them will be retired. The different audiences of these two stations are reflected in the stories and style of stories, as seen in Table 1.2.

As can be seen, the BBC Radio Nottingham bulletin is twice as long as that of Trent FM, and consequently on average the BBC bulletin spends twice as long on each story. In the Trent FM bulletin, although the bulletin's top story has no local connection, it is the sort of story that would appeal to the station's 24–35 year old, mainly female, audience, many of whom have children of their own. The audio for this story would have been provided by IRN. The next two stories are relevant because they concern local people, and both are follow-up stories: the first providing the end of a previously reported court case, and the second referring to the previously reported fatal accident. The story about four men being charged in connection with the Birmingham New Year shootings,[10] including the half-brother of one of the victims, is a follow-up of a high-profile national story. It can also be regarded as of interest to Nottingham listeners because of the city's gun-crime problem. In light of its target audience, Trent FM does not routinely cover sport, but the station makes a point of linking itself to all local sports teams, and keeps its audience in touch with the main sports stories. The Paul Hart[11] story fits this category because even people who do not follow Nottingham Forest would want to know about any major changes at the club. Finally, the chocolate bar warning story, with audio again from IRN, is the

Table 1.2   Radio bulletins 96 Trent FM: November 13 2003 – 5pm. Bulletin duration: 3.05 minutes

Story	Treatment
Weather headline.	Copy.
Hunt for missing teenager in Devon.	Clip from police officer.
Nottinghamshire headteacher cleared of indecent assault on pupil 15 years ago.	Copy.
Three Nottingham men charged in connection with hit and run fatal accident.	Copy.
Four charged with New Year shooting in Birmingham.	Copy.
Forest Manager Paul Hart favourite to take over at Leeds United.	Copy.
Cadbury's may put warning on chocolate bars to avoid overweight people suing them.	Clip from solicitor.
Traffic news.	Live report + phone update from listener.
Traffic hotline phone number.	Copy.
Weather in more detail.	Copy.

sort of quirky tale the GWR group refer to as 'water cooler gossip': a light story that people tend to chat about socially.

In contrast, the BBC Radio Nottingham bulletin does not mention the missing teenager story, perhaps rationalising that it has no local relevance, and also aware that it is covered in national BBC bulletins. This also explains the emphasis on local stories in the Radio Nottingham bulletin: national and international news are provided in more depth by other BBC stations. The inclusion of the Soham court case and the latest developments in Iraq are justified because they are major news stories regarded as being of interest to everyone. Their top story has more relevance to their audience not only because it is local, but also because many of their listeners will be a similar age to the headteacher, and will empathise with his case. Other local stories in the bulletin reflect the station's mission to cover the whole of its transmission area: those in rural areas, and also those in Mansfield. It is also most likely that the potato ring-rot story, which was covered nationally by the BBC, was the result of a local follow-up sparked by the national story being included in network news. Another example of Radio Nottingham aiming to include the whole of its transmission area comes in its sports coverage, which mentioned all three local football teams.

A striking difference between the bulletins is the amount of local audio they feature. The Trent FM bulletin has no local audio, while all the audio in the Radio Nottingham bulletin, with the exception of Soham and Iraq, comes from their own reporters. This reflects the size of the newsrooms. Because BBC local radio has a high speech content, including news magazine programmes, they need many more reporters and so are able to cover a wider range of stories. Most commercial radio newsrooms operate with a staff of three or four people, including newsreaders, making it difficult to get a wide range of local audio other than telephone interviews.

Table 1.3   BBC Radio Nottingham: November 13 2003 – 5pm. Bulletin duration 6.10 minutes

Story	Treatment
Nottinghamshire headteacher cleared of sexual assault on pupil 15 years ago.	Voice piece.
Soham murder trial update.	Voice piece.
Nottingham solicitor found guilty of stealing cash from clients.	Voice piece.
President Bush wants a fast hand-over to Iraqis.	Clip from George Bush.
Nottingham police search for 59 year old missing for six weeks.	Copy.
Notts farmers meet to discuss discovery of potato ring-rot.	Clip from National Farmers' Union.
Notts MP moves to save wildlife charity in Mansfield faced with closure.	Clip from man who runs the charity.
Sport:	Copy read by sports reporter.
• Derby mid-fielder may go to Notts County. • Mansfield Town reject offer from Rotherham. • David O'Leary denies interest in Leeds job – Forest manager now the favourite. • Steven Gerrard out of England squad with injury.	
Weather.	Copy.

Finally, the style of the bulletins is quite different. The Trent FM bulletin is read at a much faster pace than that of Radio Nottingham, with the stories brief and direct. This reflects the perceived lifestyle of their audience, who have neither the time nor the interest to listen to detail, but want to be kept up to date with major stories and what might affect them. Radio Nottingham listeners are perceived as having more interest in the news in general, and local news in particular, so their bulletins provide more detail and tend to be read at a more measured pace.

Just because bulletins are different it doesn't make them either better or worse than each other – they merely reflect their audience. As the take-up of digital radio increases, and more stations find different niche audiences to cater to, it is increasingly likely that radio news will continue to refine itself to reflect those audiences. Detractors claim this is dumbing-down news, but those in the business feel differently, as Tim John of 106 Century FM, makes clear:

I feel that writing the news to suit your target audience isn't dumbing down. In fact, it can often have the reverse effect. A well-written story can actually hook the listener in, keeping them with something that they would have ignored otherwise. I would also reject the argument that for lighter stories, the selection process means that news is automatically dumbed down. Breaking stories tend to be run, but for diary items, in every newsroom that I've worked in, we usually discuss as a team or at least with the editor what we're going to run and the angle we're going to take. There seems to be a perception that radio journalists often argue the case for not running a story – in fact most would run far more if time allowed. That said, there is still that basic journalistic instinct to be challenging and uncover the truth behind a story (despite what some press officers would prefer you to believe), and as long as that continues, I fail to see how you can actively dumb a story down.

TELEVISION NEWS

I would always say the most important thing for television news is good pictures because that's what plays to television's unique selling point. This is perhaps less true than it was ten years ago because of the advent of so many 'lives', nevertheless, it's still important. The other big element we look for more and more these days is an emotional element. It's considered important that the audience feel involved in the story and care about what they're seeing, whether it's because it's something that affects them personally or because they sympathise with the people involved.

Nick Kehoe
journalist
Central News East

Television news is important not only because it is the medium through which most people get their news, but also because it can enhance the reputation of television companies by showing them providing a public service through their provision of accurate and up-to-the-minute reports. The emphasis for news on television, as Nick Kehoe notes, is for moving pictures that bring the story to life, and live reports that stress its immediacy. But television news programmes are not open-ended: they have a slot in the schedules that dictates when they start and when they end, unless there are exceptional circumstances when programmes are extended to cover events. This means that, generally, television news creates the illusion of being spontaneous while all the time following a carefully planned and timed script. This can be seen in Table 1.4, which examines the BBC's *News at Six* and ITV's *Evening News* at 6.25 pm for November 13 2003.

What is interesting about both programmes is the number of live reports. The BBC particularly emphasises this by showing two of their correspondents on location and waiting to give their reports at the top of the programme. The effect is that this news organisation has correspondents across the world with the very latest news. But as Table 1.5 shows, the reality is that most of the reports, although linked into live by a reporter at the scene, are in fact pre-recorded. Although live links can add drama to a story, there is a widespread belief among television reporters that often they are done just because they *can* be done, and to justify expensive satellite trucks, as Nick Kehoe explains:

Table 1.4   Television news programmes. BBC *News at Six* – November 13 2003: 6 pm

Story	Treatment	Duration
Headlines: • More troops to Iraq. • Four charged with New Year shooting in Birmingham. • Potato 'foot and mouth' in UK.	• Shots of troops in Iraq. • Still picture of dead girls. • Shots of potato harvest.	0.18"
What's coming up: • Live report from Washington. • Live report from Wales. • Fears of new ice age for Britain.	• Video wall shot of Washington reporter. • Video wall shot of reporter in Wales. • Shots of ice breaker in the Arctic.	0.18"
East Midland's headlines: • Mum's campaign to clean up estate. • Kerb crawlers to be phoned at home.	Presenter in front of video screen: • Shots of mothers on patrol. • Shots of warning poster and map.	0.14"
More troops to be sent to Iraq.	Report with night vision raid on Iraq homes/ clips from US ambassador and George Bush.	1.56"
Nassiriya bombing of Italian soldiers.	Report on previous day's bombing and implications for the security of soldiers.	2.15"
Live report from Washington on Jack Straw's visit.	Two-way with reporter in Washington.	1.18"
Four charged with New Year shooting in Birmingham.	Report on court appearance of four charged with murder/some background to the case.	1.50"
Other stories: • Royal Mail back in profit. • Fears for missing student. • Woman charged under official secret's act.	Presenter voice over pictures: • Shots of mail workers. • Still of missing girl. • Shots of GCHQ.	0.42"
Soham trial.	Report including graphic reconstruction of court/library footage of Huntley and Carr.	2.00"
Ken Livingstone to rejoin Labour Party.	Live two-way with reporter outside 10 Downing Street.	1.44"
Potato rot found on Welsh farm.	Live link to reporter in Wales who links into recorded report with interviews with farmers and NFU official.	2.43"
Reminder of top story: More troops to Iraq. Tease for ambulance death story. East Midland's teases: • Cancer girl says thanks. • Meet the oldest driver in the region.	 Shots of UK troops. Clip from family's news conference. East Midland's presenters: • Shots of girl. • Shots of OAP driver.	0.26"
Special report on Italian reaction to suicide bombing in Iraq that killed 18 Italian soldiers.	Report from Italy showing those pro and anti war and tributes to the dead.	2.46"
16 year old dies after falling out of the back of ambulance taking her to hospital.	Report with clips from family news conference/shots of ambulance route/shots of girl's school and family.	1.30"

Table 1.4 (Continued)

Story	Treatment	Duration
Police apologise six years after shooting dead unarmed man.	Report with interviews with dead man's family/police chief constable/shots of crime scene.	2.04"
Britain may face a new ice age.	Reporter in front of video wall showing extreme weather. Promo for *Horizon* programme later that night.	2.45"
Latest on Rio Ferdinand row with FA over failure to take drug test.	Live two-way with reporter at Old Trafford/ clips of Ferdinand training.	1.16"
Severe floods in Southern California.	Presenter voice over pictures of flooding.	0.27"
Weather.	Weather girl in front of maps.	1.25"

In my opinion, the use of so many live links is a policy that comes down to us from head of news level and above. Since the emergence of *Sky News*, there's a received wisdom in the industry, wrong in my view, that live news is automatically more exciting news. Most news programmes now have their own satellite truck. They're very expensive and consequently there's a pressure to use them every day. As there are very few genuine, late-breaking stories, live top and tails or Q&As (reporter two-ways) are bolted on to perfectly good, self-contained packages.

The most obvious difference between the two programmes is that the BBC's top story is about the latest news from Iraq, while ITV lead on the latest from the Soham murder trial. This illustrates a key difference between the stations. The BBC prides itself on its extensive network of correspondents and places a lot of emphasis on international news and political news. ITV, while covering international news and political stories, prefers to emphasise home news, particularly high-profile stories that they know will interest their audience. Another difference between the programmes, at the time in question, is that the BBC national news advertises the regional news that it is sandwiched around, while ITV regional news programmes are quite separate and not acknowledged in their programme. In linking the regional programmes to the national news, the BBC is showing viewers that they can provide all the news anyone would need at national, international and regional levels: there is no need to change to another channel.[12]

Despite these differences, the reports from both stations on the main stories are very similar. Both feature dramatic night vision footage of American soldiers raiding homes in Iraq – footage that would have been supplied from pooled war sources, also used on *Sky News* that night. Moreover, both have live correspondents in Washington covering Jack Straw's visit and his announcement that more British troops will be sent to Iraq. The difference in the reports comes in the BBC's emphasis on *international* news, with its report from Italy on the previous day's suicide bombing which killed 18 Italian soldiers, and ITV's emphasis on *home* news, with a report on a Scottish regiment preparing to go to Iraq. And although the various aspects of the Iraq story are broken into short reports to provide pace to the programme, both stations devote a similar

Table 1.5   *ITV News*, November 13 2003: 6.25 pm

Story	Treatment	Duration
Headlines: • Soham murder trial. • Girl dies after falling from ambulance. • Why we'll be spending less this Christmas. • *Love Actually* – another hit?	ITV 'gongs'. Presenters' voices over: • Library shots of Ian Huntley. • Still of dead girl. Clip of father from news conference. • Christmas shopping scenes. • Clip from the film.	0.30"
Soham murder trial.	Presenter in front of video screen with pictures of Holly and Jessica, then Ian Huntley. Link to live report from outside the Old Bailey. Reporter links into recorded report on day's events, using graphics of the court, the area in Soham, shots of people leaving court. Link back to the studio.	4.56"
16 year old girl dies after falling out of the back of an ambulance.	Report on news conference called by father and brothers of dead girl/shots of where the accident happened and picture of the victim.	2.15"
War in Iraq: Americans step up their search for Sadam sympathisers.	Report from Iraq of night raids by American troops following suicide bombing yesterday.	2.24"
Jack Straw says more UK troops could go to Iraq.	Live report from reporter in Washington who links into recorded report on Straw in the US, then link between studio and Washington reporter.	1.42"
Among troops going from UK is company from Royal Scots Regiment.	Live report from Edinburgh where troops are leaving. Link into recorded report showing them preparing to go.	2.15"
Teases into break: • Will there be less spending this Christmas? • *Love Actually* set to be a smash hit.	Presenters in vision. Voice-over: • Woman in toy shop. • Clip from the film.	0.15"
Four men charged with shooting in Birmingham at New Year.	Live report from Birmingham – link into recorded report on background to the case and day's events in court.	2.08"
Survey says we'll spend less this Christmas.	Live report from Regent Street in London where Christmas lights about to be switched on. Link into recorded package about consumer spending this Christmas.	2.50"
Rugy World Cup.	Report on how the Australians are baiting the English rugby team prior to their match against France at the weekend.	2.16"
Headlines: • Soham trial. • Ambulance death. • More soldiers to Iraq.	Presenter voice over pictures: Still photograph of Ian Huntley. Photograph of victim. Shots of soldiers leaving.	0.26"
And finally – preview of latest Richard Curtis film released this weekend.	Report with interviews with Curtis and stars of new film.	2.16"
Promo for ITV news channel and *News at Ten*.		

amount of time to it: the BBC's three reports take up 5.29 minutes with a further 2.46 on the special report from Italy, while ITV's three reports take 6.21.

The reports on the Soham murder trial are also similar. Court reporting on television can be problematic because cameras are not allowed into the court-room, so pictures tend to be restricted to people arriving at or leaving court. To get around this, television news now uses three-dimensional graphics to recre-ate the courtroom and convey some of the drama of the day's events. Both the BBC and ITV used courtroom graphics for their reports, and ITV emphasised the timeliness of their report with a live link to a reporter outside the Old Bailey, who then linked into a pre-recorded package.

Just as interesting as the stories both programmes covered, are those that were only covered by one of them. Although both programmes are around 25 minutes long, the BBC had 12 news stories and 1 feature story (the ice age in Britain), while ITV covered 6 news stories and 1 feature story (the opening of *Love Actually*). Feature stories are useful in television news programmes because they can be done well in advance of broadcast. In general, the BBC's reports were all shorter than ITV's, and it also used 'OOVs', which are stories read by the out-of-vision presenter over relevant pictures. In this way they were able to cover three stories in 42 seconds. The only story exclusive to the BBC was the dis-covery of potato ring-rot on a farm in Wales: other stories not covered by ITN were covered by *Sky News* that night. This story was covered with a live link to a reporter who linked into a report about the disease and what it could mean for farmers. Meanwhile the only story exclusive to ITN was a report based on a con-sumer survey that predicted lower spending over Christmas. This too was done by a live link to a reporter waiting for the Christmas lights to be switched on in London, who linked into a pre-recorded package. The different exclusives again show the different approach to news by each programme: the BBC reflecting its public service remit to cater to as wide a section of society as possible by report-ing on rural matters, and ITV reflecting its more populist approach by reporting on consumer issues that they feel directly affect their audience.

ONLINE NEWS

The way the Internet is evolving means the quality and speed of watching video or listening to audio have vastly improved. Sound, images and video can add features to your story that you just wouldn't get in print, but they're not essential. The news story is the essential part of the activity of an online journalist. However, as interactivity is the new buzzword across online, there is more of a demand for audio and video.

Sometimes you can utilise the audio and video to give a story more of an edge or the pictures do this for you. For example, if you're covering something like the Soham murders, the Beslan Siege,[13] or a Radio 1 campaign on mental health, just the sound of someone's voice or the moving images taken live as the news unfolds can give your audience more of a sense of involvement in the news. As

(Continued)

(Continued)

people logged on to the Beslan story on September 3 2004, the moving images of children and panic were immediate. They were almost instantly on the web as videophones and other technology allow instant uploads to the net.

Terri Sweeney
interactive content producer
BBC Radio 2/BBC 6 Music

News on the Internet combines print with audio and video as well as offering links to as much detail on stories as the user requires through in-depth background reports, related reports, and, in some cases, even links to source material such as Government reports. Most media outlets have a web presence. In some cases, such as radio stations, this takes the form of 'added value', providing information about presenters, merchandise, what's on in your area, and live streaming of programmes. Indeed, radio listening has increased as the popularity of the Internet has grown because it can be listened to, either through a computer, or in the more conventional way, while online.

The same is not true for all media, and just as newspapers suffered a decline in sales with the advent of television, there is some evidence that the same is happening as more people turn to the Internet for their news. Media analyst Roy Greenslade noted in November 2004 that:

A study of recent declining circulation figures and the statistics which show the increasing use of newspaper websites suggests that the switch from print to screen is happening more swiftly than even many web missionaries might have predicted. ... Just as worrying is the fact that many people get their news from net sources unconnected to newspapers, especially the BBC. (Greenslade, 2004)

The most popular UK website for news is the BBC (www.bbc.co.uk). As early as 2000 it was ranked the most trusted site in the UK, and was the ninth most popular of all UK sites (McIntosh, 2000). Since then it has gone from strength to strength and in October 2004 it was rated the top news website in the UK with 3,527 unique users (Gibson, 2004). Its success is easy to understand because it uses its vast news-gathering operation to service its online presence, combining text and pictures with audio and video supplied by radio and television journalists, and in-depth reports from correspondents across the world.

At times the amount of information offered by the BBC online can be overwhelming, but not all news websites have the same approach. The website of the Press Association (www.pressassociation.co.uk), for example, which is one of the UK's leading news agencies and supplies services to every national and regional daily newspaper, major broadcasters, online publishers and a wide range of commercial organisations, is much simpler. Its website reflects its background as a news wire service, and would appeal to those who simply want the latest news of the day without extra reports. Nonetheless, both websites follow what is now regarded as a conventional approach to news websites. The 'front page' of each site gives a brief paragraph about various stories under different categories such as news, sport and business, and clicking on any particular story takes you into more detail. An examination of these two websites for Thursday, November 13 2003, shows the different approach taken by each.

The BBC News front page online is designed as a shop window advertising all the wares available inside. As well as a ticker-tape providing the latest headlines, a panel on the left side provides access to different categories from World News to Entertainment News, as well as links to other related BBC websites. The main body of the page gives the top stories illustrated with a photograph and a sentence describing the story. This is no more than an extended headline to tempt users to click for more details. The right-hand side has a column listing other 'top stories' in a text headline form, as well as two lighter stories illustrated with a picture and a line of text. A link to BBC Sport online is also provided.

To break the page up, a bar about halfway down the page gives links to feature articles, all illustrated with pictures. Although presented as news, these links actually take users to different sections of BBC online. For example, a feature about whether to have public or private health and education links to the BBC Magazine online, and the third 'feature' is an invitation to 'have your say' by nominating the UK's worst eyesore. These links to other parts of the BBC online are continued in the bottom third of the page, where users can access news around the world and further news categories like business news, political news and entertainment news, as well as the latest BBC radio and television news bulletins.

In line with the BBC national news for this day, the top story online was about Iraq – but this time about Japan's decision not to send their troops there. The headline 'Japan postpones Iraq deployment' was illustrated with a picture of an Italian soldier guarding the site of a suicide bomb attack in Nassiriya the previous day which killed 18 soldiers. Two smaller links take users to stories on the reaction in Italy to the previous day's suicide bombing, and a story about preparations to hand over the governing of Iraq to an interim government. The two second lead stories were about the arrest of a fifth suspect in the Birmingham New Year shooting, and the latest on the Soham murder trial.

Going behind any of the three top stories provides an exhaustive amount of information, including video reports and links to related articles and websites. For example, the page behind the top story not only gives full details of Japan's decision not to send troops to Iraq, including a map of the occupation zones in Iraq, it also features a video report from the BBC's Jonathan Head about Japan being one of the USA's closest military allies. Below that there is a panel headed 'The Struggle for Iraq' which contains 'in-depth' reports on five key stories about Iraq, and a further panel called 'Features and Background' which offers another five related stories.

To a certain extent, all the information presented on this news site is available elsewhere in newspapers and on television and radio – but not in one place. But the biggest difference that the online news site offers is that users can take part in an online discussion about the Iraq situation by clicking on 'Have Your Say' to see what other people think about the Falluja offensive, and post their

Figure 1.1   BBC Online: November 13 2003

own views. There are also two links to other websites: one for the Coalition Provisional Authority site, and another for the US Central Command site.

The Press Association news site could not be more different.[14] Its layout is that of a conventional web news page, with a ticker-tape showing the latest news headlines, and a left-hand panel for PA products and services – from news, sport and television listings, to event guides and archive services. The right-hand panel gives contact details for the Press Association and links to the Scottish PA, other PA services, and the PA publicity picture service. The central panel of the page gives the day's news, but unlike the BBC, there are no pictures to illustrate the stories. Instead the news is divided into seven boxed categories. The top box is 'Live News' and the top story is headlined 'Relative Charged Over New Year Deaths', followed by a short sentence. Links to two other stories – the Soham trial and the Iraq suicide bombing – are also given. Further boxes labelled Football News and Sports News, each have a headline story and two other stories, while boxes labelled Showbiz, Health, Technology and City each have a simple headline.

The biggest difference, however, comes behind the front page. Where the BBC provide extensive background to their stories, the Press Association merely provide a few paragraphs on each story. There are no video, audio, background features, or links to other web pages. The main reason for this is that the PA site is mainly a corporate site, designed to advertise the various services offered by the Press Association. These range from news, sport, business news, photographic services and audio and video that can be bought by news outlets for their own use, therefore are not freely available on their site.

What is interesting about each of the Internet news sites above is that despite being new media, they use the same tactics as traditional media in tailoring the news to their target audience and promoting their brand image. The BBC news site showcases the extensive network of BBC correspondents, and reinforces the Corporation's image as a conveyor of trustworthy, professional news on both the national and international fronts. The site is globally acknowledged as reliable and balanced, and gives the BBC a way to reach audiences unable to access the Corporation on radio or television, further enhancing the BBC brand.

The Press Association site, by contrast, is the no-frills version of the news with its focus on UK national news rather than international events. This is in keeping with its image. The Press Association describes itself as 'the national news agency of the UK and Ireland', and its core business is providing news and pictures to newspapers. According to its website, 'a network of news journalists produce 150,000 words of copy and over 100 photographs each day setting the news agenda minute by minute'. In other words, its key audience is news professionals who are already up to speed with what is happening, and who just want the core latest developments in their simplest form without having to negotiate through various pages. Its simple layout may lack the flashiness of other sites, but it's easy to negotiate and quick to deliver the information.

It is also interesting to note that the PA site does not provide links to other websites. This is in keeping with the practice adopted by most websites to try to keep users on their own site for as long as possible. To a large extent the BBC adopts the same philosophy. Most of its links are to other BBC sites, and the outside links offered are usually to official sites, like those of the Government or other official agencies, which are generally less interesting to the casual browser.

CONCLUSION

What this examination of various news outlets shows is a remarkable consistency between the stories covered by each one. It also shows how each outlet adapts its coverage of stories to emphasise the unique features of its medium, and to appeal to its target audience. But while each medium has a different approach to news, the basic craft of finding a story, researching it, and making sure that it is accurate and balanced, is the same for all reporters, as we shall examine in the next chapter.

NOTES

1 Michael Schudson (1996) usefully identifies the three most common approaches to news analysis in 'The Sociology of News Revisited' in *Mass Media and Society*, 2nd edn, pp. 141–59. See also 'Media Routines and Political Crises' in *The Whole World is Watching* by Todd Gitlin, pp. 249–82 for another approach to news selection.

2 Cited in Boyd, 2001, p. 29.

3 *Media Guardian*, 'Mirror back above 2 million' by Ciar Byrne, September 5 2003, accessed at www.mediaguardian.co.uk.

4 Quoted in the *Guardian*, January 13 2004.

5 Ibid.

6 In August 2002 two 10 year old girls, Holly Wells and Jessica Chapman, went missing from their home in Soham Cambridgeshire, sparking a massive police hunt that lasted 13 days, and dominated the news. The girls had been pupils at Soham school where the caretaker was Ian Huntley, who lived with his girlfriend, Maxine Carr, a teaching assistant known to the girls. During the hunt for the girls, Huntley was interviewed by the media, and appeared to be concerned and helpful. Finally, he was arrested for the girls' murders, just before their bodies were found. Maxine Carr was charged with perverting the course of justice by withholding information about Huntley from the police. It was November 2003 before Huntley came to trial.

7 All quotes from Tim John are taken from author interview, January 2005.

8 *Media Guardian*, January 3 2005.

9 All quotes from Phil Dixon are taken from author interview, January 2005.

10 On New Year's Eve 2002, two girls, Letisha Shakespeare, aged 17, and Charlene Ellis, aged 18, were shot dead in a drive-by shooting outside a party in Aston, Birmingham. Two other girls with them were also wounded. The shooting was part of a battle between two Birmingham drug gangs in a turf war. The shooting of the innocent girls shocked the whole country, and added fuel to calls for a crack-down on the 'gun culture' that was seen to be encouraged by rap music.

11 Paul Hart was the manager of Nottingham Forest FC at the time.

12 Interestingly, a few months after the period being examined here, ITV national news adopted a similar approach to the regions as the BBC, and regional programmes are now integrated with the national news programmes.

13 On September 1 2004, over a thousand children and adults were taken hostage in a Russian primary school in Beslan by 30 armed Chechnyan separatists. The siege lasted two days and ended in chaos when explosions were heard inside the school. Russian troops stormed the building and over 330 of the hostages – mainly children – died.

14 In spring 2005 the Press Association website was redesigned. It is now a corporate website that advertises the services available from the Press Association.

RESEARCHING A STORY

The best news isn't planned … it's just responding to events as they unfold. But no newsroom can operate without some degree of planning. This includes checking important dates for a developing story or finding a follow-up which can help to fill a gap on a quiet day. In television, much of the lighter end-of-programme features can be pre-planned as they can easily be held over to another day if the 'on the day' news agenda changes.

Simon Hare[1]
BBC reporter

One of the most important skills to develop as a journalist is to know the most efficient way to research a possible news story. This may be a short process involving a couple of phone calls to ascertain or clarify facts with which you've already been provided, or it could be a lengthy and difficult task, involving making a series of phone calls over a number of days, conducting interviews in person, attempting to persuade people to provide you with information, and even carrying out surreptitious research to try to find out facts that other people or organisations may not want you to know. However mundane or complex the story, there are a number of ways in which you can make sure that the research process is carried out thoroughly and that the information you gather is accurate and pertinent to the story you want to cover.

This chapter examines the sources of different types of news stories, and how to react to various news situations so as to decide whether or not the information you are receiving is both newsworthy and reliable. It will also look at how to approach researching different types of stories, so that you can be sure you have covered the ground and have your facts straight, before you go out and conduct interviews or gather material.

NEWS SOURCES

As we saw in Chapter 1, news is not easily definable, and there are as many definitions as there are media experts and journalists to make them. Therefore for the purpose of this chapter, rather than negotiating our way through a mine-field of different conceptions of what is news, it will be more helpful to produce our own working definition of what we mean by news. To do this, we'll explore the ways in which a journalist usually accesses information or is made aware of possible newsworthy events. These are known as 'news sources' and there are quite a number of different ones used on a day-to-day basis. Each one requires a slightly different response from the journalist and it's useful to know what they are, and how they impinge on the daily life of any newsroom.

Let us assume that news can be generally defined as an event or series of events that happen somewhere outside the newsroom that may be of interest to the watching, listening or reading public. The journalist's job is to find the news, hunt it down, and gather it into the newsroom so that it can be produced and transmitted to the waiting public. Sometimes that news is waiting to be found, while at other times it may be obscured and may need to be uncovered. News sources usually assist the journalist in finding the news that wants to be found. More difficult stories are tracked down using other tactics that are discussed later in the chapter.

PRESS RELEASES

Most large newsrooms, whether they're for newspapers, radio, television or online, have a forward planning department. In regional newsrooms the planning depart-ment may consist of just one person whose job it is to search for stories, read press releases and filter news access enquiries that are sent to the newsroom every day. A journalist working in news on a daily basis will often be approached by the plan-ning department who have already set up a story for them to cover. If this is the case, much of the hard work will already have been done. The planning journalist or researcher will have made the necessary phone calls and fixed up locations and times for you all to meet. However, this does not mean that you do not have to make at least one phone call to introduce yourself, as well as to make that all-important first contact with the interviewee. As discussed in Chapter 4 on inter-viewing techniques, this first contact with your interviewee is extremely important and could make the difference between a successful or a difficult interview.

If you're approached by the planning department and asked to cover a news story, the chances are that it was first discovered in the form of a press release sent to the newsroom. These make up a large proportion of regional and national news stories, though there is frustration among many experienced journalists that they provide the department with easy stories of little news value and are a lazy way of tracking down news. As Simon Hare comments:

All newsrooms receive dozens of press releases every day through the post, fax and now email. Often you also receive a phone call to check you've got it. Press releases do sometimes produce good stories but there can be a tendency for journalists to rely on them, particularly on a slow day. Young reporters should be encouraged to develop their own stories – and it's much more rewarding than writing something from a press release. Many press releases are often thinly disguised advertising for a company and its products and services. These should be avoided. The maxim 'news is something that someone, somewhere wants to suppress and all the rest is advertising' is very true.

More often than not, press releases are prepared by professional public relations officers with an understanding of the needs of the media and the constraints they operate under. Prior to the 1990s the use of PRPs (Public Relations Professionals) tended to be confined to Government departments and large corporations, but since then their use has spread.

Deacon's (1996) survey of the voluntary sector found that 31 per cent of organisations had press/publicity officers, 43 per cent used external PR agencies and 56 per cent monitored the media. A survey of the trade union sector by Davis (1998) found that two-thirds of unions had at least one part-time press officer, 25 per cent used PR consultancies and 57 per cent used agencies to monitor the media and provide other services. (Davis, 2003: 30)

This means that news organisations are bombarded with potential news events designed to provide easy copy, audio and pictures for hard-pressed newsrooms. Indeed, larger organisations go so far as to provide recorded items ready for transmission in the form of video and audio news releases. As Davis notes, it is no coincidence that 'just as the public relations industry has expanded, so editorial resources have declined' with the number of journalists per news product reduced, or at best only increased slightly (Davis, 2003: 31).

Nonetheless, press releases allow newsrooms to plan the coverage of events in advance and can provide useful contact names for future stories. One of the tricks worth learning when looking for news from press releases is to try to find a story behind what you're being told by the company or organisation.

For example, you are sent a release detailing a new highly automated packaging service that a pharmaceutical company is introducing. At first glance this seems uninteresting – it's not news, it's simply advertising. But if you employ a little lateral thought and try to read between the lines, you may question whether this new service will actually replace people's jobs. You may think that disguised in this piece of information about a new service is a much more important story about a large company, the provider of many local jobs, that's going to make people redundant. Of course, at this stage this is merely your own speculation. But now you may feel that it is worth contacting the company's personnel department to ask some questions along these lines. You may get no official response and your speculation may remain unsubstantiated, but you could be lucky. A couple more phone calls and you could get hold of a union spokesman for the company who is prepared to tell you that the bosses have warned him of possible future job losses. Now you've got a story. Your hunch has been confirmed and you've found someone who will say so. You also have a lever with which you can go back to the management spokesperson who initially refused to give you any information and ask them to comment on what you've been told. If they refuse to comment, you can still interview the union spokesman and some workers from the company, while pointing out that management was approached but refused to give an interview. And if they do accept that there is some truth to the rumour that there may be job losses, you've got another interview for your piece. Either way, you now have a news story that is of interest to your audience.

News is all about information that you as a journalist receive and re-package for public consumption, and press releases are just another source of information. The secret is to use them intelligently. It's not wise to ignore them altogether, just because you think they are pushing some line or other. Even if most of it is advertising or self-promotion, a press release could still contain information that would be of interest to the public. For instance, you could get a press release from a national building firm promoting some of its new builds in your area. You certainly don't want to cover this as a news story. But this company has also carried out original research into house prices and has concluded your area is one of the best places to buy houses as properties here hold their value better than in the surrounding areas. That is suddenly of interest to your readers or listeners, and you are quite within your rights to use the company's research, as long as you credit it, to construct a news story about house prices that does not mention the company's new development at all. This is often the case with press releases from public institutions such as hospitals or universities, where they are hoping to promote some new research carried out by a certain department. The research, which could be into cancer prevention, or new statistics showing that children from single parent families suffer discrimination in the job market, will have wider public appeal. It is up to you to use your judgement and decide what is and is not of interest to your specific audience.

NEWSROOM DIARIES

The news diary is a key tool in every newsroom. It consists of events that are known about in advance, from seasonal happenings like the annual Christmas lights switch-on, to special occasions like a royal visit. Typically it would also include reminders about the start or finish of important court cases or public inquiries, as well as press conferences. The diary provides the basis for the daily news conference where stories are discussed and allocated to reporters. Diary stories remove some of the uncertainty of filling a newspaper or news programme because the coverage of events can be planned in advance. For example, at the end of a high-profile court case, most news outlets will report the outcome of the case along with a background piece, usually prepared weeks in advance, which recounts the story and often includes interviews with either the victims or the family of victims.

News diaries are a way to manage the pressure of daily deadlines. But as the cycle of deadlines increases, driven by technological advances that allow for more editions of newspapers to be published, and rolling 24-hour news channels, there are fears that news organisations are becoming ever more reliant on diary events to manage that pressure (Manning, 2001: 58). The fear is that dependence on diary stories means that those people or organisations that understand the pressure that news organisations work under can exploit the need for managed news by providing the right kind of material at the expense of original stories and investigative reporting.

EMERGENCY SERVICES

One of the most common sources of news is the emergency services. The police, fire brigade and ambulance service all provide information about their work. Most of them have a dedicated press number that usually accesses a taped recording of their most recent incidents and the cover which they provided. This is referred to as the 'voice bank'. Some are more efficient or media friendly than others and may have their own press office with a dedicated press officer in charge of detailing the press. If this is the case, it is well worth getting to know this person. Take time to go and meet them, so that you can establish a good professional relationship. In times of large-scale emergencies or disasters, this may save you valuable time and get you information more quickly when other reporters are also demanding information and interviews.

Many police departments do not allow press interviews to be arranged other than through the press office, so it's really worthwhile establishing a relationship based on mutual trust and professionalism. If there is no press department and you can't get the information you need from the recorded voice bank, then you will need to ask the switchboard to put you through to the control room. Once there, ask for the duty inspector and they should be able to tell you the latest developments. It takes time to learn how to approach and communicate with the emergency service departments. Often they can be brusque or even stand-offish. This is usually due to the pressure that they're working under and the volume of press calls they receive. Don't let obstructive individuals keep you from getting the information you think you need. It is worth remembering that the press also serves the emergency services in terms of putting out information or appeals to the public. There is usually an unspoken understanding of this mutual dependence, but if you're tempted to lose your temper with someone particularly unhelpful, remember that you'll be phoning them tomorrow and the next day and that relations do need to preserved even at times of stress. Many newsroom editors ask reporters to ring round the emergency services on an hourly basis. These are known as 'check calls' and many news stories arise from these enquiries.

CHARITIES AND PRESSURE GROUPS

Pressure groups are a good source of news but you should approach their news releases with the same caution as you would any other press release. As their name implies, they are in the business to promote a certain cause and therefore their information is invariably one-sided. That said, pressure groups and charities do commission original research that can reveal important social or political trends. This could be the number of people sleeping rough every year, or the number of immigrants being employed illegally, or whether passive smoking is a factor in the number of children suffering from cancer. All of these stories have a news element and may be of interest to your audience.

It is well worth familiarising yourself with the local representative of national charities and pressure groups. As well as being a good source of information or news, these people can often be called upon to comment on a related issue, thus providing the reader or viewer with an alternative view. There are far too many grey-suited 'experts' that journalists call upon to comment on political, economic or social issues. It is often more refreshing and more interesting to use someone from a pressure group for this kind of comment. As long as it is clearly stated that this person represents a specific organisation, their views are often very well researched and more accessible to the wider public.

There are hundreds of separate charities and pressure groups, so it's a good idea to build up a list of those in your own area. You should have a contacts book where you write down details of everyone you come across when researching a story, and it is worth having a dedicated section for these organisations. If you need help getting started, go to your local library and ask for a list. If they are unable to provide you with one, the local telephone directories and the Yellow Pages as good a place to start as any. One word of caution – always double-check the status of any organisation when you are researching a story, as it is often quite difficult to ascertain whether or not they are a registered pressure group or charity.

LOCAL GOVERNMENT

About a quarter of total Government expenditure is delivered through elected local councils to provide us with services ranging from community care to highways and schools. Much of this activity is of direct and daily importance to viewers, listeners and readers of the local media. It is their children who suffer if the schools are sub-standard; it is their cars that are damaged by pot-holes in the roads; it is they or their relatives who are at risk if community care services are inadequate; it is their council tax bills that rise if local politicians are corrupt or incompetent.

Mark D'Arcy
producer
BBC Radio 4
(Cited in de Burgh, 2000: 213)

Government at all levels provides a rich source of news, and stories can always be found by attending and reporting on the many council committee meetings held by your local authority. These issues are of direct relevance to your listeners or readers. You need to be familiar with the set-up of your own local government, how it works and what laws are applicable to you as a journalist reporting any proceedings, as discussed in Chapter 9.

It is a good idea to find your way around a town hall, develop some credibility with politicians and officials working there, and be able to decipher reams of council documents in order to identify possible news stories. This all takes time to get to grips with, but it can pay off. Planning applications and developments often make good local news stories, as do applications for licence extensions to public buildings such as pubs and night clubs. Some of the typical issues dealt with by the local authority that can make good news stories include: housing, employment, social services, schools, hospitals, corruption cases, the contracting-out of council services, planning applications and local politics. With so many potential news stories situated in one building, it's certainly worthwhile spending some time getting to know the key players and those who can tip you off with possible story ideas.

Politicians at all levels are usually more than willing to make themselves available to journalists, especially on non-contentious stories. This can keep them in the public eye and help their chances of re-election. But as Andrew Boyd warns, 'this type of reaction can be overdone, lead to accusations of political bias, and leave a bulletin sounding as dull as a party political broadcast' (Boyd, 2001: 34).

The debate over the extent to which politicians manipulate the media is well known. It is one that journalists need to be aware of in order not to fall into the trap of recycling political rhetoric as opposed to legitimate news stories. But this should not rule out politicians as sources of news, no matter how media-savvy they may be. Politicians' actions affect people. Journalists have a duty to report those actions, but they should avoid using politicians as a 'rent-a-quote' resource.

TRADE ORGANISATIONS

Trade organisations look after the interests of certain specific trade workers, such as builders or licensees or factory workers. These organisations may offer updates on the state of the industry from surveys that they carry out from time to time. While most of these surveys may not hold much interest to the general public, it is still worth making periodic checks to see whether there are any news items of wider appeal. These organisations can also be of use when a comment is needed from the industry in light of any changes in law. For example, you might want a comment from the Licensed Victuallers Association if you were doing a story about proposed changes to the licensing laws, or one from the Chamber of Commerce if the story was about a proposed new shopping centre.

CONSUMER GROUPS

Consumer groups look after the rights of the consumer at large and often issue public warnings regarding specific products. As with trade organisations, they may not be a particularly fertile news source most of the time, but may prove useful for an investigation into a new product as part of a more consumer affairs-based programme, or if you want comments on a more general consumer issue. A good example of this would be the introduction of Sunday trading, when consumer groups were called upon to answer criticisms from various religious groups.

INTERNET RESEARCH, WIRES AND EMAIL

Technological developments that have taken place in newsrooms during the last five years have allowed reporters to drastically reduce the time it takes to research a story. In the past, journalists may have had to make several phone calls, visit people in person and kept them on file while they built up a complete picture of the story they were investigating. If the story was on a national or international scale, it could take even longer tracking down the right people to interview and discussing specific issues with them prior to filming or recording material. Access to the computer and the Internet has changed all this. The time it takes to reach people has been drastically reduced by the use of email. More than one person can be targeted at once, saving many hours of precious time to find a spokesperson for a particular line in the story. Email chat rooms and bulletin boards also allow journalists to post up messages saying who they're looking for to illustrate a particular strand of the story. With the ability to access hundreds of people all over the world at any one time, the endless days of painstaking 'phone-bashing' are almost over. However, a word of caution here. Like anything to do with the Internet and computer-based research, it is absolutely imperative that you can identify your source and be able to check its authenticity before you use any of the information that you access. Of course, journalists should always check their sources, as we shall be discussing later on in the chapter, but there is a tendency among students of journalism who are increasingly using the Internet for their research, not to verify the information they find or to identify its origin. Just because information is published on the Internet does not make it reliable. Indeed, it could be entirely fictional and highly inaccurate. If you are unable to check the veracity of information that you find, don't use it in your story.

Good though they may be for indexing the World Wide Web as a whole, the big search engines such as Yahoo! or AltaVista are not necessarily that good for indexing news items as they take too long to visit a site. Often news stories appear and disappear before they get indexed, or they get indexed in one location and then move.

To search for news items, it is best to use specialised databases such as TotalNEWS, News Index, Excite's NewsTracker, Northern Light's Current News and the news sections on Yahoo! and Infoseek. Infoseek news offers several different news databases to news wires, national news and news websites. The news databases include wires such as Reuters, PR Newswire and Business Wire. Wires are electronically available publications of breaking news releases and newsrooms usually have access to the most common wires services. There are Reuters, Associated Press, and PR Newswire, all of which provide both national and international coverage. Local press agencies can also use the system to send out their own news releases to specific newsrooms in their geographical area. Organisations that publish news releases on a wire service have checked the veracity of their stories.

There are literally hundreds of sites that are useful for journalists researching or checking stories over the Internet, and it is beyond the remit of this chapter to provide an exhaustive list. However, it's worth naming just a few to give you a flavour of what's on offer and how you can access more sites through your own research.

- **www.networksolutions.com**   This is a very useful site for verifying the information you get hold of over the web. This site can tell you who runs a particular website that you've found. It may not enable you to check your sources as thoroughly as you need to, but it's a great start. Sometimes it will just provide the address of a particular website but this can be of great value in assessing the independence or accuracy of information.
- **www.facsnet.org**   This site has been created by journalists themselves and gives advice on how to trace sources online as well as advice and tutorials on how best to use the Internet to research stories.
- **InternetNewsBureau.com**   This publishes news press releases from more than 10,000 journalists and business professionals who subscribe to the site. However, the sources of these press releases have not been checked by the bureau and it is clearly stated that the responsibility for checking sources lies with the journalists themselves.
- **Holdthefrontpage.co.uk**   A useful site that has job vacancies in the regional press, story ideas, useful contacts and law updates, as well as lots of information about newspapers across the country.
- **Commercial Radio Companies Association** – **www.crca.co.uk**   The website for the umbrella group that represents all commercial radio stations in the UK. It has information and contact details for every commercial radio station in the country, as well as research carried out by the CRCA into audiences, public service broadcasting and other areas of interest to radio.
- **News and news alerting**   Although there are hundreds of sites you can visit for up-to-date news reports, this would take you forever and you wouldn't have time to actually do any reporting yourself. Therefore it is worth knowing about news alerting. The principle is straightforward. Instead of you having to visit a site, a news gatherer sends you notification of breaking news stories.

These can be sent via email, to your own website, to your mobile phone or to your pager or other hand-held device. Some of these are: Powersize.com, Moreover.com, The House of Commons Weekly Information Bulletin, ScienceDirect and the Publications Resource Group. It is easy to set up your own alerts by visiting the site and following on-screen instructions. Some ask for a small subscription fee, while others are free.

- **Web pictures**   There are many sites that are of use to the newspaper journalist. The *Cyberpix Guide* is a comprehensive reference book with details of the best photo-sample sources on the web. It includes Corbis, George, Eastman House, The International Museum of Photography and Film, Kodak, PhotoDisc, Publisher's Depot and PNI.

MEDIA DIRECTORIES

The *Willings Press Guide* is a comprehensive guide to newspapers and magazines, television and radio, business and specialist publications in the UK and world-wide. *BRAD* (British Rate and Data) is a monthly classified directory of media in the UK and the Republic of Ireland that carries advertising. *The Media Guide* covers most media sectors in the UK with a section for the Republic of Ireland. *The UK Press Directory* gives a complete overview of the newspaper industry, whilst *Media UK Internet Directory* gives a complete listing of online media in the UK to include newspapers, radio, television and magazines. The Commercial Radio Companies Association also produces a Pocket Book that has contact details and information for every commercial radio station in the UK, available from its website (www.crca.co.uk).

CONTACTS BOOK

There is nothing more valuable than an up-to-date and comprehensive contacts book. This is a journalist's most prized possession and should be kept with you at all times. When you start out in the profession, it may only contain a few names of people you've come across in your training who provided you with information, or people you interviewed in connection with certain events. They may not seem useful to you after you've finished with that particular news item, but it's imperative that you keep people's details to hand. You may be covering a separate story that doesn't initially seem to connect with anyone you've interviewed before, but you'll be surprised how many times you draw on names in your contact book either for general advice, or help in tracking down others you need for your particular story. As you get more experienced, your contacts book is your testimony to a history of thorough research and as news stories come round again, even if in slightly different guises, you'll find there are people you can contact quickly by means of keeping them updated in your book.

Never think you won't need to talk to someone again, or that their particular relevance to today's story is too specific to be of future use. Even if you don't need to use an interviewee again, you may be able to help a colleague who's looking for that same Feng Shui expert whom you interviewed two years ago. If you get a new contact from a colleague, write them into your own book so that you can develop your own directory of people from as many different walks of life as you can find. If you have a few particularly useful contacts, go and see them regularly. People will find you more trustworthy if you can show them you've got time for them too. Gratitude is very important here: if a contact has given you a good tip-off, then don't forget to say thank you. It may only take a couple of minutes of your time, but it shows you value the relationship.

You may be out with friends in a pub one evening and overhear something that you think would make a great news story. Often people who don't work in the news industry can't imagine that their own stories are of interest to others. It's up to you to have the flexibility of mind to be able to spot a story, and to approach someone so as to encourage them to tell you more. Often the best stories are revealed through idle chit-chat in an unguarded moment. The best reporter knows how to identify them quickly and to make the individual concerned realise that they've discovered or experienced something important.

RESEARCHING A STORY

There is no substitute for going to talk to someone face to face.

John Hemmingway[2]
freelance television journalist

The first thing to accept when researching any kind of news story is that it could take time. Therefore you'll need to have an idea as to the deadline you're working to. For instance, if you're employed on a weekly news programme, you'll obviously have more leeway than if you're being asked to get a story for the evening news programme. Be realistic about your deadlines. It's no good spending three-quarters of a day on the phone getting to the bottom of the story on overcrowding in prisons, if you've then left yourself only an hour and a half to travel to the location to conduct all your interviews.

To avoid this kind of time mismanagement, make sure you communicate clearly with your editor or producer at the beginning of the day. When do they want the story? How much detail are they looking for? Do they want an evaluative piece or a straight news story? Do they want a three-minute radio package, or if you're working for a newspaper, how many words are they expecting? All of these pragmatic issues have a bearing on the research that you carry out.

The main purpose of any research you carry out is to make sure you've got your facts straight. This is true no matter what story you're covering. Libel suits can be extremely expensive and if you get the story wrong, people will want to know why. Don't be tempted to cut corners and if you're being pressured, be honest about the holes that you may still have in your research. It's far safer to be clear about what you've found out, and what you still need to verify, than to hope it'll be OK once it's all put together and transmitted or published.

You'll need to develop persistence. It isn't easy trying to get information from people within a limited space of time – especially as they may not want you to know it. You must expect to be refused access to people or stalled by receptionists, press officers or secretaries on occasion. This is part of the job. If you give up after you've made one or two phone calls, your editor won't think much of your enquiring nature. Editors want to hear who you have spoken to, not who you can't get hold of. You need to develop a credible and firm telephone manner but remain polite, even when you may feel like losing your temper with someone for being so deliberately obstructive. Be determined at all times, but never lose your cool. You may find that you've hit a brick wall and the person you're talking to, or trying to talk to, just won't help you out. You have to think laterally. How else can you get to the story without having to talk to this particular person? There will be another way round – you've just got to find it. If you're in this position, before you finally end the call, make sure to ask whether you can come back to them if you find out anything else. This will give you a way back in should you find someone to back up your story.

You will need a good deal of lateral thinking even before you start making your phone calls. Sometimes you'll get a few facts that in themselves don't really add up to a story. You need to think around them to spot something there that isn't at first obvious. This may mean taking a couple of pieces of information from one source, and seeing whether or not they relate to another piece of information you've got from someone else. Never assume that one person has the whole story. You'll need to piece the information together, rather like an intricate jigsaw, until you can see what the final version of events might be. And remember, even when you think you've found the final story, you still need someone to verify it. It's no good if the only person who can tell the story is you. You need evidence for your hunches, and people to go on the record.

You also need to be prepared to be unpopular. You may have to hassle a busy manager, or come back to a receptionist who hasn't passed on your message and isn't aware of your pressing deadline. You may also need to go and knock on the door, rather than rely on the telephone, as it's harder to be ignored if you're on the premises. Again, if this is the case, remember to be polite and to make sure you can't be accused of trespass or harassment.

ASKING THE RIGHT QUESTIONS

Obviously this will differ depending on the story you're covering and its audience, but there are a few tips worth remembering that should help you deal effectively with any research situation. The most important thing to do when you're trying to set up any story is to talk to the people involved. It sounds obvious, but too many journalists think they can get away without really tracking down the appropriate people and talking through the issues. We've all seen or heard reports where a lazy journalist has thought they could get away with telling the story themselves, and hasn't managed to interview those directly involved. Those news reports are unsatisfactory for the people who produce them, and they're certainly unsatisfactory for the people listening to or watching the report.

The first question you'll need to ask yourself before picking up the telephone is: 'Is this a story?' You may find this difficult to answer at first, but one of the ways to recognise whether or not the story is newsworthy is to ask yourself if *you* would be interested in it. If you're aware of who your audience is, ask yourself whether or not they'd be interested in it. Would they learn something from hearing this information? Would it be a topic of conversation between them? Would they react to the information that you're going to tell them? All of these questions help you decide whether or not you've got a news story. You might want to talk it through with colleagues who may have a slightly different view to you, or who might have a contact that you hadn't thought about.

Knowing if something is a news story is not an exact science and can change depending on where you work, your target audience, even the journalistic fashion of the times. For instance, in the mid-1990s every local radio and regional television news programme was running stories about killer dogs. There were seemingly hundreds of Doberman pinschers and pit bull terriers mauling small children up and down the country. These stories don't appear any more, but you can be sure that the dogs haven't all gone away, nor that some aren't still mauling children. It's just that this particular story is no longer fashionable. So don't think that there are hard-and-fast rules that govern what is news. Defining what *is* news is an elliptical and often muddled art. It's also something that you'll get used to doing over time, without even noticing you're doing it.

The next question you'll need to ask is: who do I need to talk to? This could be a simple list of three or four main people involved in the story who can be easily identified and contacted. Sometimes it's not that easy and you'll have to think about the possible ramifications of the story in order to know who your best contacts could be. It's always a good idea to share your thoughts with colleagues. They may have a slightly different take on the story, or have covered something similar and can be helpful in identifying the right people. Sometimes you'll phone somebody you think is relevant to the story, but who turns out to be rather peripheral to it. Don't be afraid to ask them for help in contacting those more directly involved. There's nothing worse than reading or listening to a news piece where it's obvious that the 'victim' being interviewed isn't really the best representative of the story. If you can sense this at the research stage, your audience certainly will.

At all times in the research process listen carefully to what you're being told. Often news stories are curled up inside one another and, just as in an interviewing situation, you may hear a better story than the one you've been chasing just by listening to what you're being told. You need to assimilate information quickly so that you can piece together the facts as you're talking to your source and be aware of your source's own limitations. If they can't tell you something you need to know, they may know who might be able to help you. Never push someone too far. You'll only lose the chance to get at that vital piece of information that you need, and by making yourself unpopular you'll lose future opportunities for research.

CONCLUSION

Research isn't easy. It's a skill that comes with time. Don't be put off by your inability to get to the people you need when you first start out. It's just a matter of perseverance, honing your skills as a persistent questioner and a critical thinker. Don't forget that your audience is also a great source of stories. In these days of more sophisticated Internet and email interaction between media and audience, the journalist can use listeners, readers or viewers as very important sources of information. Some of the best stories can come from people following the programme or accessing the news site on their home PC. Remember that if you remain approachable, consistent and encourage people to contact you, some of the best and most exclusive stories could come your way. The best piece of advice is to think of research as a continual process. It isn't just what you do at the beginning of a news day when the editor is clamouring for stories. Reporters should keep their eyes and ears open for news all the time. You never know when that great story will come your way. All you need is the ability to recognise it when it does.

CHECKLIST

✓   Try to identify the type of story you're researching. Is it a diary or planned event, a story you have found from a press release, a story you've heard about from an official contact – for example, a local government spokesperson or a member of the police or a representative from a certain educational establishment – or is it a snippet of information that you've overheard in the pub?

✓ Decide what the story is about. This may not be easy to begin with, but you need to have some idea as to the 'type' of story so that you know who to contact first.

✓ If your story originated in a press release, try to see behind the story presented to you by the organisation. Remember that they are after publicity – you're after news.

✓ Just because you have been sent a press release, this doesn't mean that it is a news story. You have to make that decision through your research.

✓ When you're trying to find out about a story originating from a press release, you need to talk to the individuals involved, not just the press officer. The press officer is your first contact point, but unless you can then talk to specific individuals, it's very difficult to ascertain the news value of the story.

✓ If your story originates from a 'check call', you still need to find out the names of individuals who you will need to interview – don't just rely on making one call to a police or fire service voice bank. You need to follow this up by talking to those involved in the incident. If they can't be reached by phone, be prepared to go to the scene yourself and find them.

✓ Remember that researching by telephone is not the only or necessarily the best option. Try to meet people face to face.

✓ Be aware of your audience. When researching your news story, ask yourself whether or not your audience would be interested in it.

✓ Don't be satisfied with the first interviewee you find. They may not be the best representative of your story and you may need to do further research to find exactly the right people.

✓ Don't ignore any information that you may pick up in the course of your research. Even if you think it is not directly relevant to the story, it may help you find out the information you need, or get to the people you want to interview.

✓ At all times in the research process, listen carefully to what you're being told. You may be able to find out a better story by listening to what your contacts are telling you.

NOTES

1 All quotes from Simon Hare are taken from author interview, September 2004.
2 All quotes from John Hemmingway taken from author interview, September 2004.

WRITING A STORY

So you've carried out all your interviews and done all your research, but how on earth are you going to write the story? This chapter will outline the basics of writing a story starting from the 'intro' – the first paragraph of a news story – through to the type of language that should be used. It will also look at story construction and how student journalists/trainee reporters should approach different types of story. It will investigate the different ways of writing for newspapers – which will be tackled first – then radio, television and the Internet.

WRITING FOR NEWSPAPERS

The hardest nut to crack has got to be the intro. Budding young reporters have historically been told they've got to answer the questions 'who?', 'what?', 'when?', 'where?' and 'why?'. But as Harold Evans points out, 'a great deal of harm has been done by this rule' (1986: 85). He says the five Ws are a rule for the *whole* news story, not an intro. Keeble (2000) believes that 'who?' and 'what?' tend to be the most important.

Let's look at what we might end up with if you did answer all those questions:

A 15 year old schoolboy, Dominic Downey, of 11 Derby Road, Nottingham, who attends St Michael's College, Long Eaton, drowned in a swimming pool while he was on work experience at Ilkeston Leisure Centre. His body was discovered at 11.42 am yesterday.

After reading this, you would have to come up for air (excuse the pun) or would have alternatively (a) fallen asleep; (b) moved on to the next story or (c) thrown the paper in the bin. Unnecessary information in the intro slows down the story; this also applies to other early paragraphs. Do we need to know the schoolboy's name? Do we need to know exactly when this unfortunate incident occurred? Is it vital to discover the name of the leisure centre? Should we be told Dominic's exact address? The answer to all these questions has more often than not got to be 'no'. We don't want to tell the reader when this happened because the chances are this is already 'old' news. Equally, we don't want to give away clues about where the boy is from or which school he attends because we want to keep the reader guessing. We want to keep them reading. So the first three paragraphs of this story might be written as follows:

> A 15 year old schoolboy has drowned in a swimming pool while he was on work experience.
>   Dominic Downey's body was spotted by a lifeguard at the leisure centre where he had just started a two-week placement.
>   The youngster's parents were last night too upset to talk about the tragedy.

Does that give the game away? No, it does not. Dominic *might* have drowned weeks ago but we wouldn't be so stupid as to tell the reader that.

Of course, editors on weekly or daily regional newspapers may argue that it's vital to say where this happened or where the boy was from as early as the intro to stress the local angle. But there are two good reasons why this should not be the case.

- What would be the point in writing a story about someone who isn't from your circulation area? The editor of the *Nottingham Evening Post* wouldn't use the story if the boy was from Leeds or if the story hadn't happened in his 'patch', so why say in the intro that he's a *Nottingham* schoolboy?
- By saying the boy is from Nottingham (or Newark, or Mansfield), this immediately alienates a huge percentage of readers, viewers or listeners whose immediate reaction is likely to be (a) 'Not another Nottingham story – what's in the paper for me?' or (b) 'What am I doing reading about people from Mansfield?'

The moral of the story is to delay the 'when' (and while we're on the subject, count how many times the national newspaper you bought today could have done without using the word 'yesterday' in its intros) and definitely delay the 'where' because it will encourage everyone to read on. The usual exception to this (and there's always one) is in foreign stories in which it's often important to establish where a certain incident has taken place. And the obvious exception to delaying the 'when' is if the news is new. The words 'last night' convey the message that something has just happened. Equally, the word 'today' is also acceptable. As Keeble (2000) comments, the hotter the news, the more saleable it is. Even better than today is 'this afternoon', although why some reporters persist in using the words '*earlier* today' is difficult to gauge. Of course it happened earlier!

Problems arise when reporters try to get the word 'today' in their intros at all costs. The intro 'An investigation was today underway after a 15 year old schoolboy died in a swimming pool' has its merits in that it updates the news. But surely Dominic's death is the most important angle. The best alternatives usually arise with a genuine hard news follow-up, perhaps after the parents have been interviewed. This would lead to intros like 'A heartbroken mum whose teenage son drowned at a leisure centre today told how her son had so much to live for' or 'The parents of a schoolboy who drowned in a swimming pool told today how they are still coming to terms with the tragedy'. Obviously this story would also be ideally accompanied by treasured snaps of tragic Dominic along with a picture of his grieving parents.

HUMAN ANGLES

More and more news stories concentrate on people. Newspapers especially have been repeatedly accused of dumbing down, filling more of their columns with stories about celebrities. Even the esteemed *Financial Times* was caught up in the trend when it featured the demise of 'Nasty Nick' from Channel 4's *Big Brother*, while the *Daily Telegraph* devoted the entire top half of its third page to the MTV awards. But even lesser-known mortals find their names adorning intros. The *Sun* carried the following two intros in the same edition (November 21 2002).

> MADCAP Bryan Fullerton has made his home the Santa of attention – by building a 32ft Father Christmas on the front.

> PUB landlady Gladys Tildsley met her idol Rod Stewart – when he popped into her boozer for a pint of bitter.

The advantage for the reporter is that using someone's name helps to focus the mind on what the news is about. Notice also how those intros use a few other techniques.

- 'Madcap': try to make the first word do some work – it will grab the reader's attention.
- 'The Santa of attention' – puns make you want to read on but, as Bagnall (1994) says, the only sound advice on puns is: don't force them.
- Dashes – a useful intro aid.
- Celebrities – no point in just talking about a pub landlady meeting her idol when you can get the ever newsworthy wrinkly rocker Rod in your intro.

NEWS IN BRIEF

Reporters across all disciplines should be aware that intros need to be short and to the point. Rules are there to be broken, but a maximum of 20 words for the first paragraph of your story is as good a guideline as any. You might get away with a few more on a broadsheet. It's probably also worth thinking along the lines of a maximum of 30 words for subsequent paragraphs. More often than not, those paragraphs will comprise just one sentence, each with no more than one subsidiary clause. This is particularly important in the early paragraphs of your news story, when overloading paragraphs with too much information or too many clauses will slow the story down. So just as we decided that putting dear Dominic's address and the name of the leisure centre in the intro was bad news, we wouldn't really want to do this sort of thing in the second paragraph:

> The body of Dominic Downey, of Derby Road, Nottingham, was spotted by a lifeguard at Ilkeston Leisure Centre, where he had just started a two-week placement.

You might think that this is taking things to extremes, but pick up your local newspaper and count how many times it happens. Information overload and too much punctuation is a big turn-off.

KEEP IT SIMPLE, STUPID

We've seen how it's important to cut out some unnecessary information from intros, but there's more! Don't bore the reader by starting your intro with long titles like Derby City Council environment sub-committee chairman Tommy Trueman, or hit them with abbreviations they won't understand. There are only a handful which are acceptable, such as the BBC and FA. Even during the fire-fighters' strike, plenty of people would have had to think twice if you used the abbreviation FBU in an intro (it stands for Fire Brigades' Union, by the way).

EXPERIMENT

One of the best ways to improve your intros is to read newspapers. Adapt their style and experiment. Bagnall highlights how tabloids deal with a world in which blondes are *stunning*, redheads *vivacious* and dark girls *raven-haired*. Bereaved parents are *tragic*. Villages are *tiny communities*, but subject to *massive upheavals* when developers *send in the bulldozers*. He adds, 'Since its stock of words is small, writing in this way is not hard to pick up. It is merely hard to do well' (Bagnall, 1994: 25).

Evans also adds a note of caution. He says every word should be scrutinised: if it is not a working word, adding sense to a sentence, it should be struck out.

> Some writers think that style means spraying adjectives and adverbs on sentences. These may give a superficial glitter. They often conceal rusty bodywork. (Evans, 1986: 42)

Alternatively, when writing intros, imagine that you are telling your friends the news. In the case of Dominic, you would hardly prop up the bar and tell your mates: 'While I was enjoying my regular post-work dip at the local leisure centre, I was in the unfortunate position of witnessing the discovery of a boy who had suffered an untimely death.' You would probably be more inclined to say something along the lines of: 'A teenager has just drowned at the leisure centre.' Another good rule to force you to be economical might be to imagine you are writing a text message, although hopefully we are still a long way from reading newspapers with intros along the lines of 'Tnagr hs drwnd at swmng pl wl on wk xprns'!

STORY CONSTRUCTION

We've seen how the first three paragraphs of the Dominic story provide the intro and then *explain* the intro. One of the best ways to proceed with the rest of the story is to work chronologically through how the events happened. You will also ideally need a blend of direct quotes and indirect reporting, and to keep your story as logical as possible by writing it in chunks. In Dominic's case, you might have got quotes from his family, the police and the leisure centre boss. He might have been an apprentice with Nottingham Forest Football Club, which as well as giving you the opportunity to ask them for glowing tributes should affect the way you write your story. It would now be more likely to start:

> A promising young footballer has drowned ...
> The body of Dominic Downey, who was on the books of Nottingham Forest, was found ...
> The youngster's parents last night said they were still trying to come to terms with the tragedy.
> And Forest youth team coach Freddie Frost told how Dominic was on the verge of a promising soccer career.
> He said: 'Dominic was a lovely kid with a bright future ahead of him.
> Some more Freddie quotes ...'
> Then chronological details about the drowning tragedy ...
> Then family quotes ...
> Then the police (remembering that *blend* of quotes and indirect reporting) ...
> Then the leisure centre boss ...

Historically, the inverted pyramid is the way of constructing news stories. In a nutshell, that means putting the most important stuff at the top and proceeding in an orderly fashion until you get to the bits that could be cut out if necessary. And that's a good rule for stories that you *can't* write chronologically. Rely on your news values to decide which are the best bits and those that could go by the wayside.

ANSWER ALL THE QUESTIONS

If poor wee Dominic had died in a car crash, the reporter would need chapter and verse about the incident. Readers would want to know what time the accident happened and where it took place, who else was in the vehicle and what injuries they suffered. And while we're on that subject, remember that accident victims never *receive* injuries. It's not their birthday (unless they're really unlucky) and their serious multiple injures don't come gift-wrapped. They *suffer* injuries. If you're looking for an alternative, use *sustained*.

Meanwhile, back at the scene of Dominic's horror smash, you'll want to know the number and type of vehicles involved. You'll want to concentrate on drama as well as the human angle, so if poor Dominic had been decapitated (perish the thought), then the 'news values' alarm bells in your head should start ringing with the message – this should be in the intro. Reporters should be on the look-out for the unexpected. Was this a freak accident, were there any eyewitnesses who might add colour to your story, and was the Nick Bateman who was in the other car (or perhaps – bizarrely – at the wheel in the same vehicle as tragic Dominic) the 'Nasty Nick' of *Big Brother* fame? And was he under the influence of intoxicating liquor? All these – and more – should obviously be answered and reflected in your subsequent piece of award-winning purple prose.

GET THE RHYTHM

Evans highlights how economy as well as rhythm requires all kinds of sentences should be used. But budding journalists should note how, particularly in the national tabloids, we are looking mainly at short sentences that keep a story flowing. Bagnall says a test worth carrying out on one's prose from time to time when it seems to be getting a little too convoluted is that all sentences should be able to be spoken aloud in a single breath. He says sentences should be short but not monotonously so: 'Vary the shape of your sentences. If they all sound the same they may rock the reader to sleep' (Bagnall, 1994: 86).

REMEMBER YOUR AUDIENCE

You are not writing to impress your friends or family. Bagnall says journalists who constantly use big powerful words to do the light work, which could easily be done by smaller words, are slowly bankrupting their vocabulary. He also doubts if the English language would be seriously impoverished if it lost words like ascertain, remunerate, adjacent, emolument and participate. So the apprentice hack should study the language of newspapers and think about who will be reading their copy: 'Journalists must have someone in mind while they are writing. It might be a news editor or it might be Aunt Jobiska. But it shouldn't be no one at all' (Bagnall, 1994: 111).

Wynford Hicks agrees. He says the best advice to a journalist is to write for your reader: 'You should use a clear form of English, avoiding jargon, slang, pomposity, academic complexity, obscurity' (Hicks, 1998: 1). Sellers (1985) adds that it is important to have seen all the top 20 TV programmes at least once, because the people you are writing for will have done so and – professionally at least – you have got to share their lives.

PUNCTUATION

Hicks outlines how grammatical mistakes often appear in broadsheets because their sentences are long and complex. He says it is a fact about language that such sentences are more likely to have mistakes in them. So the moral of the story, as ever, is to keep your sentences short.

Bagnall has an excellent chapter on punctuation, and is particularly good on commas. He says:

> It is hard to makes rules about commas, because there will always be exceptions. But one rule that can usually be followed is: if a dependent clause or phrase in the middle of a sentence has a comma in front of it, it should have one after it too. And vice-versa: if there is a comma after it, there should be one before it. (Bagnall, 1994: 150)

An example:

> Campaigner Lucy Cope, of Mothers Against Murder, demanded tougher sentences and a zero tolerance policy.
> But Lucy, whose 22 year old son Damian was shot dead last year, added: 'There is no quick fix.'

Notice how both sentences make perfect sense if we remove the clauses which are enclosed by commas. Follow that rule and you're on your way. Think of commas hunting in pairs …

Bagnall's final word on commas: they are like children in the kitchen – welcome when they're helping, a pest when they're not (1994: 157).

NAMES

> A blindingly obvious statement is that a news story should be accurate. This is one of the keys to the whole business. This cannot be overstressed. If it's not accurate, then it's not a news story, it's fiction. If it's fiction then it should be in a bookshop with the Harry Potters, not in the news rack. Nothing dismays a reader who knows something about an area more than recognising an inaccuracy.
>
> Simon Irwin[1]
> editorial director
> Kent Messenger Group

Names are a basic building block of news reporting. Get them right, every time. The reporter's most basic tool beyond his or her pen is the voice. If you don't know something, especially how to spell a name or where something is, then ask. Nobody will mind. It's annoying to appear in the local paper and to find your name spelt wrongly. Simon Irwin, editorial director of the Kent Messenger Group, says:

> Spelling 'victims' tell all their friends, who then share their not very high opinion of what has now become for them 'the local rag'. There are enough people who wish to pour scorn on journalists and newspapers without helping them.
>   An in-depth investigation about a scandal involving a headteacher's involvement in illegal dog fights at a local school will be totally compromised if you get the name of the school wrong, the name of the head wrong or the name of the road the school is on wrong. Everyone reading it will assume that if you can't get these basic facts right, then the rest of the story is rubbish too, and who could blame them?

FACTS

Get the facts right. Sometimes this can mean getting the simplest things right, for example, copying figures out of a council report. Just because it is simple does not mean that it's always done correctly. Indeed, because it seems so straight-forward, many reporters do not bother checking what they have done until the fact in question has appeared wrong in the paper. Again this makes the story lose credibility and can potentially be very expensive. Having established that the information you have is a fact, make sure you write it down correctly.

BALANCE

All good, well-written news stories should be balanced. Balance gives the story credibility, helps the reader understand what the issues connected with the story are and, importantly, can make the story a lot better. It is also vital to be able to show balance if you are being sued.

What do we mean by *balance*? Again, this is common sense: balance, put simply, is making sure that, as far as possible, both sides of an argument or issue are represented. It does not mean that both sides should be given equal space: for example, four paragraphs each.

Simon Irwin says it can mean as little as approaching the other side.

> For example, if you have a story from a local headteacher complaining that she has been sacked 'for no good reason', then it is important that you contact the body that sacked her, either the school governors or the local education authority. If they decide to say 'no comment', then simply report this in the story. It shows that the LEA had the opportunity to put their side but chose not to do so. However, the LEA may come up

with some interesting and newsworthy reason for sacking the headteacher that stands the story on its head – so to speak – and makes it a much better story, for example, that she was having an affair with a pupil.

In some cases, approaching the other side for their views may mean that you kill the story altogether. A binman who says he has been sacked for singing at work is a good story. A binman who has really been sacked for not going to work is not a story at all. Getting the other side is really vital.

INACCURACIES

The general public know that it is a news reporter's job to ask questions. So, not surprisingly, when they come up against one they expect to get asked some questions. So do it. Irwin says: 'In news reporting, credibility is everything and it is easy to lose and difficult to get back. Inaccuracies will lose you credibility and readers faster than anything else.' They may also cost you a lot of money. The omission of the word 'not' could cost thousands of pounds in legal fees and damages for defamation. For example, 'The court heard that Mr Bloggs was a paedophile' has a completely different and potentially vastly more expensive meaning than, 'The court heard that Mr Bloggs was not a paedophile'. As Irwin highlights:

> No one is perfect and no news reporter can honestly say that inaccuracies have never crept into their work. The trick is to keep those mistakes to an absolute minimum and to aim for 100 per cent accuracy. No other target will do. If you don't know something is true, or you have no official source to rely on, then don't put it in or, in very rare cases, put it in but make it clear that it is potentially inaccurate.

An example of this might be during a major incident where information is unclear as you are going to press, for example:

> Six inmates were killed during a riot at Pocklington Prison this morning, according to ambulancemen leaving the jail.
>   The number of dead has yet to be confirmed officially by either the prison authorities or the police.

This is not the same as using unattributed sources. An example of this is a chat with the leader of the local council who tells you that central government cutbacks mean that the council will have to cut 1,000 jobs. Unfortunately, he doesn't want to be identified as the source of the information, but you believe what he is saying. In this case it would be fine to write:

> Up to 1,000 jobs will have to go at Cubley Council, according to a senior council insider.

You would, of course, have to approach all the sides concerned for an official comment.

GIVE THE CONTEXT

Set the story in its background in every sense – historically, geographically and, if necessary, how unusual it is. Irwin says:

> If a robbery at a village post office is the third in six weeks, then say so. If the village is isolated and 12 miles from the nearest police station, then say so. Your editor or news editor may remove this if he or she does not wish to be seen as promoting the fourth robbery. If the robbery was done by a man threatening the postmaster with a rubber chicken, then make sure you get this fact in as it is not such a common occurrence.

LOOK TO THE FUTURE

What will happen next to the people or organisation in the story? Will the post office shut, forcing pensioners to go 12 miles to the nearest town for their pension? Irwin says:

> Sometimes the 'what happened' angle is not the best. Information that looks to the future often provides a better introduction or line to a story, especially in areas where the local TV and radio have already told everyone what happened. Look at news stories in your local paper. The good ones will nearly always answer these questions. The poor ones, those that leave you the reader asking your own questions, will not.

EXAMS

> In exams, as in the 'real' newspaper world, the two factors which most frequently sabotage budding reporters' efforts are their lack of comprehension of what they have been told – or even have on paper in front of them – and their inability to express what they want to say in clear, concise English.
>
> Richard Taylor[2]
> NCTJ examinations
> marker and moderator

Newspaper journalism students, and reporters, have to sit practical exams set by the National Council for the Training of Journalists (NCTJ). Richard Taylor, who has spent a lifetime in journalism – mostly in the provinces where he held executive posts on daily, evening and weekly papers – is now a marker and examinations moderator for the NCTJ. He says accuracy, as always, is the watchword:

In an NCTJ exam – especially in the prelims where candidates are usually students who have had little significant newspaper experience – even a dull piece of copy can earn a pass if it covers all the key facts without making any mistakes. Ideally, of course, examiners are seeking what every editor wants of his reporters – a vigorous, well-constructed story which does justice to a strong, local story. A piece of bright writing is more likely to be awarded a credit, but don't jack up the story, generalise or add 'comment' words.

The following 'howlers' are taken from actual exam answers:

'Youths tried to set the fire alight.'
'Paramedics stretched Mr Coombes from his vehicle.'
'... silver worth £15,000 and jewellery belonging to his wife Hilda, valued at £10,000 ...'
'... thin, aged 30, 6ft long arms and legs ...'
'After eating the food and polishing off half a bottle of whisky, DCI Lockhart said the robbers ...' [It was, of course, the villains who had drunk the whisky.]
'The councillor's parents were among the headstones smashed.'
'...in a light-coloured pullover, aged between 20 to 40 years.'

Taylor says that in any story, you hamper your chances of a good mark if you do not include two or three sound quotes:

These need to be full sentence quotes and must punch their weight. A good quote is one which is on a main news point and encapsulates the speaker's intention in a dramatic way and which would be less effective if put into indirect quotes.

FEATURES

Features offer the writer more latitude to delve deeper. Keeble highlights how news features 'tend to contain more comment, analysis, colour, background and a greater diversity of sources than news stories and explore a larger number of issues at greater depth' (Keeble, 2000: 216). Features also offer scope for more flowery writing but you still need to remember your audience. There is no point in producing dazzling prose if your readers won't understand it. And it's worth bearing in mind that in many cases, there is still a story to be told. You need to hold the reader by the hand and guide them through an article which could be thousands of words long. The big difference from writing news is that you need to finish with a bang. As Hennessy says:

The ending should make you feel that the writer has achieved his or her purpose, whatever that was. It should be fulfilling, satisfying in some way, though some articles might tend to raise questions and worries that stem from the raw edges of news. (Hennessy, 1997: 143)

You also need to make the reader sit up with a jolt at two, three or more points during the article. This could be with a startling quote or an important piece of information. But it should still be remembered that the intro is the most important part of the article. As Hennessy says, 'If you find your ending would make a far better intro than the one you've got, transfer it and rewrite the ending' (ibid.: 142). Budding young reporters should also remember that feature writing does not simply mean it's their chance to impress the reader with their amazing thoughts or opinions on world matters. There is a space for that in many newspapers through a variety of personal columns, but for many up-and-coming journalists those heady heights are a long way off.

Features demand the same blend of direct quotes, reported speech and background information seen in news reporting. But because articles tend to be longer, more thought needs to be given to how they will be structured. Hennessy highlights how an outline can help you tackle your worries one at a time: 'Once you've used your analytical powers to think out the overall shape, your creativity can be released' (ibid.: 44). He also argues that it's worth writing a title: 'Even though it might be changed ... it still helps to have a good provisional title. It can provide the controlling idea, it can help give direction' (ibid.: 134).

And in the same way that news writers need to study craftsmen at work in the pages of national and regional newspapers, so aspiring feature writers should read features and copy or adapt their style. Hennessy gives some sound advice for 'interview' features: 'Try to get the following into the piece very early – a strong quote, a topical peg, the setting where the conversation took place, the appearance of the subject, perhaps a distinctive mannerism' (ibid.: 224). There is also the chance to explore the wonders of writing styles. If you haven't received the finest classical education, one of the easiest ways to discover some of these delights is to go on the Google website and search for rhetorical terms. There you will find fairly common terms such as alliteration (the use of words with the same initial letter) but also rhetorical triplets (a series of three items usually arranged so that the last one is somehow climactic) and a host of other ways of potentially turning your feature into a work of art. But don't forget that all this will be wasted if your readers don't understand what on earth you're on about.

Martin Wells, assistant editor of the *South Wales Echo* (and former features editor of the *Derby Evening Telegraph*), says an editor underestimates the power of the feature at his peril. He adds:

> The best features will be considered analyses of events and developments that are still current issues. They will take their lead from stories that have been written straight, untainted by editorialising or explanation.[3]

Thus, if the Government plans a wholesale shake-up of sex discrimination laws, most self-respecting newspapers will devote space to the issue, breaking up their coverage into manageable parts. For example:

- a straightforward outline of the feature – the standfirst;
- a general résumé of the planned legislation, couched in narrative terms;
- a straightforward interview with a politician backing the legislation;
- a recap of events concerning the plight of women at golf clubs, for example, contrasted with the situation at an enlightened establishment;

- a short think piece on the erosion of men's masculinity;
- a first-person account of a woman's visit to a men-only club.

Using this kind of breakdown, feature writers will take a dry news item and introduce real people, real experiences, history, comment, a local angle and plenty of facts.

Wells says the trick is to spot the issue as it breaks, be aware of the issue before it becomes a hot potato, and realise there are questions that remain unanswered and avenues unexplored after the news reporters have had their say.

But where will you get your ideas? Wells says:

> Unless you have access to Government press releases, council reports, minutes and confidential memos, you'll find most of them staring out at you from the pages of the national media – the specialist publications, the trade magazine, the local newspapers, television and radio, the man in the street and the 'word' that goes with him. As the saying goes, if you can spot a bandwagon, it's already too late … which is probably why the best commentators keep at least one eye on events across the Atlantic. A craze in America is almost certain to catch on over here, too.

One good place to look for ideas is holdthefrontpage.co.uk, which has a very useful section on story ideas which is frequently updated.

Some basic ideas include the following.

- TV licences are something we take for granted, but who knows what goes on inside a TV detector van? An afternoon spent inside one of these hi-tech vans, or with an inspector confronting people without a licence, will make a good, informative, fly-on-the-wall feature.
- Public service workers are always hot topics. A day spent with a nurse or a fireman will reveal the true face of the man/woman behind the headlines.
- How switched on is your town to tourism? Playing the innocent abroad for a morning, asking dumb questions of passers-by and retailers, will speak volumes about your polite society, or the angry brigade waiting for the unsuspecting traveller.

Wells adds:

> When putting pen to paper, make sure you don't make the mistake made by many writers who, when faced with the task of writing features, tend to write them in the same style as news stories – punchy, hard-hitting intros, an active verb, capturing the essential facts of a story in a sentence. Then, instead of writing 350 words, they write 1,000.

SPORTS REPORTING

The message from most sports reporters or sports editors is: do news first. News gives you the all-round grounding of writing and interviewing that will put you in a good position when you make the move to sport. There are plenty of people who don't want to jump that hurdle and see themselves covering the Monaco Grand Prix, Ryder Cup, Olympic Games and World Cup, mixing with the stars and travelling the world. But you need plenty of experience before you hit those heady heights. You need to be good and you might need a lot of luck. Not everyone can be Des Lynam; also it's not as glamorous as you might think. Would-be Lynams should remember that their groundwork might involve a trek up to Hartlepool on a cold midweek February night, arriving back home in the wee small hours. Most of their weekends will be written off first covering a match on Saturday, then heading into the office on Sunday to help produce a 12-page supplement for Monday's paper. They will be required to be a jack of all trades, not only covering their favourite sport but also others that are not quite as glamorous and which they are not necessarily too familiar with. They will probably also need to quickly become proficient as a sub-editor, staring at a computer screen and page proofs for hours on end. That task may also include rewriting the work of freelancers whose gifts for the English language are not quite in their league. And before they become the chief football writer for the *Daily Telegraph*, they will need to master a craft that is not as easy as it looks.

Harris and Spark (1997: 167) describe good sports writing as 'a mixture of fact and interpretation spiced with comment'. To achieve that mix, you will need to be a good writer, to be imaginative enough to raise your game so your reports are a cut above the average, and to be able to concentrate hard enough so that you can describe exactly how a goal was scored without the aid of a video rewind button. A lot of that takes practice, and plenty of it should involve learning from the best. Just as with news and features, read and learn …

MATCH REPORTS

> Above all, remember that seat in the press box is a privileged position. You're being paid to watch and comment on an event that most other people have paid their hard-earned cash to see. Get your facts wrong, short-change your reader or spout an ill-founded prejudice and you are abusing that privilege. You won't be popular with your reader or your employer.
>
> Mark Tattersall[4]
> former deputy sports editor
> *Derby Evening Telegraph*

Mark Tattersall, a former senior assistant editor of the *Western Mail* and deputy sports editor of the *Derby Evening Telegraph*, describes a match report as an unavoidably subjective view of an event that any number of other people will also have seen:

It might be two men and a dog at the same local football match that you're describing, or millions that have seen the same FA Cup final on television – probably with a far better view than you. The nearest news equivalent is probably a concert or theatre review. Its main ingredients are accuracy and originality.

Accuracy is important in every area of journalism, but you're much more likely to get found out if you get a fact wrong in reporting a football match. Tattersall says:

If it's a low-level match where you're not familiar with the players, make sure you get an accurate team list. It will probably be the players themselves who read your report and if you spell the hat-trick hero's name wrongly, or attribute an own goal to the wrong defender, you and your paper lose credibility. If it's a Premiership match and you describe a brilliant defence-splitting pass by a player who was substituted 10 minutes earlier, it will be 50,000 spectators and untold millions watching on the telly who will think you don't know what you're talking about.

So the rules for sports reporting are pretty much the same as any other area of journalism: prepare properly (make sure you've got an accurate team sheet); stay awake (concentrate on the game and make accurate notes); and double-check your facts (if you're not sure whose backside deflected the winning goal into their own net, ask afterwards).

Originality is every bit as important as accuracy – and for some of the same reasons. The people most likely to read your match report are those who were at the match, wanting to know what the so-called expert makes of the game they saw. So the last thing they want to read is a simple recitation of the facts. Those facts need to be there – for the record, and for the reader who didn't see the game – but you have to offer a bit more besides. Tattersall says:

It might be a manager or player's view that you have to yourself, it might be a colourful metaphor or humorous slant, or it might be an analysis of one detailed aspect of the game. Whatever it is, it needs to be different to the competition. If you're simply re-hashing the same information the reader might already have, you're short-changing the customer. Do that, and they might not come back.

SPORT STORIES

A sport story is much closer in form to a news story in that you are (hopefully) telling readers something they didn't know and following all the same rules of balance, fairness and so on. Tattersall comments:

It might sound like stating the obvious, but the first requirement is that you tell the reader something they didn't already know. Just like a news reporter, it's your job to find the story and inform the reader. It's only the context that differs.

And whether it's a council story or crime story or cricket story, the rules of fairness, accuracy and so on are just the same. Tattersall says:

Where sport stories can differ is the ease with which you can slide into the clichéd and the arcane. There is, for instance, an aversion these days to 'the groin-strain story'. The hard-core fan may be interested to know that Fred Winger has a slight hamstring strain but should be OK for Saturday. However, that fan – and more importantly a lot of other readers besides – will be talking about your story a lot longer if you tell them that Bill Midfielder is studying to become a monk or that Albert Defender is leaving the club because he doesn't agree with the chairman's involvement in arms sales.

Like all those old definitions of what makes news, a good sport story is about people. If the club is in financial trouble, ask how the player is going to pay his bills. If the club is moving to a new ground, what does the groundsman feel after devoting 50 years to the pitch at Gasworks Road?

CONTACTS

Tattersall says the best way of building and maintaining contacts is honesty. That is the one principle that underpins any successful relationship and the one between sportsman and sports journalist is no different. You have to invest the time and commitment to get to know the contact, to immerse yourself in the manager's football club, to understand the athlete's training schedule. Their job won't be nine till five and yours can't be either. You won't get the county crick-eter's respect and trust if you're not there slogging up and down the motorway with him.

But if the relationship does go completely pear-shaped, don't worry too much, there will be another one along soon. Tattersall says:

> I still treasure the incident, years ago, in which a close colleague claimed a pretty good exclusive with an interview with the disillusioned and dropped goalkeeper of what was then a Division One team. 'Enjoy your exclusive, it'll be your last,' said the manager in a fairly terse telephone call. Sure enough, the manager became an ex-manager and the reporter is now the sports editor.

LEARNING THE LANGUAGE

A sports reporter is a specialist and a specialist, by definition, is expected to know his or her subject. Tattersall explains:

> It is nigh on impossible to bluff it. Try covering a cricket match without knowing the dif-ference between mid-off and long-on and you will be found out as quickly as the health correspondent who can't distinguish between eczema and an enema.

If you know less about the subject than your reader, you won't get very far – and the reader probably won't come back. In reality, of course, the problem shouldn't arise. Nobody is likely to employ a cricket correspondent who hasn't a clue about the game. More likely is the emergency stand-in who has no great knowledge of the subject. Tattersall says: 'If that happens to you, just be honest about it. Explain your shortcomings and ask for advice and help.'

If you do know your subject, you then have to balance the jargon with clarity – and it helps if you know who you are writing for. Tattersall comments:

> They say you should never assume anything, although it's probably safe to say a reader of the sports pages will know what the 4-4-2 formation is. But if you're covering an inquest into the death of a cricketer brained while fielding at silly point, you are more likely to be writing for a wider audience and will need to explain what that means.

The close relative of jargon in sports reporting is the cliché. As the old joke goes, avoid them like the plague. According to Tattersall:

> There isn't a sportsman around these days who isn't 'focused', or a manager who will take anything more than 'one game at a time'. So an intro that begins 'City star Fred Winger is totally focused on Saturday's big game against Rovers ...' is not terribly illuminating.

WRITING FOR RADIO

> The secret of writing for radio is quite simple. Simplicity. It's as if we're having a conversation with a listener.
>
> Barnie Choudhury[5]
> BBC correspondent

One of the strengths of radio is that it talks to the individual rather than a mass audience. In other words, although radio is broadcast to hundreds of people simultaneously, good radio makes each listener feel as if they are being spoken to personally. One of the ways it does this is to *speak* to people, rather than *read* to them, so scripts have to sound as if they are coming from the mind of the broadcaster – like part of a conversation – rather than something that is being read. That sounds straightforward enough, but in practice it is more difficult because writing as we speak involves abandoning a lot of the 'rules' of writing that we've been taught from an early age.

In order to make the written word sound part of a conversation, a useful starting point is to visualise the person you're talking to. All radio stations target specific audiences. Radio 1 sees its audience as 15–25 year olds, while BBC local radio targets an older audience of over 55 year olds, and the majority of commercial radio stations aim their output at 24–35 year olds. Although the target audience may be younger or older than you are, broadly speaking they will be on the same level as you, so there is no need to adapt the language you normally use for writing. What can be useful is to think of a typical member of the station's audience and talk to them. So if the station targets older people, think about how you would tell the story to your grandmother. If it targets younger people, think about how you would tell the story to your best friend. There is no need to use special language to try to impress them, which might come across as pompous, or to take a simplistic approach which might be heard as patronising. Use everyday language.

Visualising who you are writing for can also help you to write in a way that exploits the intimacy of radio and involves each listener personally in what is being said. One way to do this is to include them in the story by using words like 'us' and 'we' rather than the more impersonal 'listeners' or 'the audience'. For example, a story about rogue traders in a local market might begin: 'We all like a bargain – but police are warning shoppers not to be taken in by cheap DVDs in Everytown market'. This immediately includes the listeners in what is being said and is more effective than 'Police are warning shoppers in Everytown market to be on the look-out for pirate DVDs.'

> The key to good writing is simple thoughts simply expressed. Use short sentences and short words. Anything which is confused, complicated, poorly written or capable of being misunderstood risks losing the listener ... and once you have done that, you might just as well not have come to work.
>
> *The BBC News Style Guide*

The key difference between writing for print and writing for radio is that in radio you have one chance to get your story across. Listeners cannot rewind the broadcast to work out what you are saying, or ask questions about something they do not quite understand. For those reasons it is important that your writing is logical and progresses at an even pace. Work out what points you need to make, then connect them in a way that makes sense. As BBC correspondent Barnie Choudhury explains, 'What is the story? Get that right in your own mind and the rest falls into place.'

As with writing for print, the first line is vitally important. This is the 'hook' that will keep people listening, or if it is badly written, cause them to switch off either mentally or physically. Ideally the first line should get to the point of the story immediately but avoid details. It needs to be relevant and direct but at the same time be intriguing enough to make people want to know more. For example, in a story about the introduction of a law to make driving while talking on mobile phones illegal, it is more effective to say: 'We all do it – but from today it'll cost us a fine and points on our licence' than 'A new law's being introduced today to make it illegal to drive while talking on a mobile phone.' The first version includes the audience and draws them into the story. The first words are intriguing enough to make most people stick with the story, and the reference to 'points on our licence' makes it clear that the story has something to do with driving which most people do. The second version is accurate but quite uninteresting, and essentially the whole story is summed up in that sentence so there is no need for listeners to hear any more.

Another way that writing for radio can connect with the audience is for it to start with the *effect* of the story rather than the cause. It is more effective to say 'Cigarettes are going up by five pence a pack from midnight' rather than start that story by saying 'The Chancellor of the Exchequer has announced that the duty on cigarettes will rise by five pence from midnight tonight.' The first version goes straight to the way the Chancellor's action will affect people, and so is immediately more interesting. It is also an immediate turn-off for most people if a story begins with the name of an official organisation. By the time most people hear 'Edinburgh City Council says it's cutting back on refuse collections from next month', they have mentally switched off. Focus on how the story affects people: 'Our bins aren't going to be emptied so.often starting next month'. The same rule applies for police forces, health authorities and government bodies. The top line needs to say how the story affects people.

Radio lovers often say that you get the best pictures on radio. In other words, what is being said on radio allows the audience to create pictures in their minds about what is happening, and because of this, the best writing for radio allows people to visualise what is being described. Too many facts packed together will cause confusion rather than pictures, so spread out the facts. A rough rule of thumb is to cover one point per sentence. After the first line, the second sentence should explain the story and lead logically to the next sentence. Writing for radio is not just a matter of imparting information – it's about telling stories and keeping the audience with you every step of the way. Use short sentences, simple language, and wherever possible concrete images to help create the picture. For example, instead of giving the physical dimensions of a new shopping mall, relate it to the size of an existing shopping centre. 'The new mall will be twice as big as the Chillwell Centre' creates an instant picture, whereas 'The new mall will cover 15 square miles' is meaningless to most people.

Of course, the listener could always work out what was meant by '15 square miles', but the key to good writing for radio is that listeners should not have to work things out. Your job is to write so that the story is clear at first hearing. For that reason you need to be careful with the use of abbreviations and acronyms because only a few are well enough known to be instantly understood. While it is acceptable to use short forms like NATO, BBC or AIDS, other abbreviations need to be explained the first time they are used. This does not mean that they have to be spelled out in full, but you do need to explain what they are. For example, in a story about teaching you might refer to 'Peter Smith from the teaching union, the NUT ...' but later in the story simply say 'the NUT says it fully backs the action' because you have already explained what NUT means.

Dealing with statistics involving numbers and measures in radio writing can be tricky because they are difficult to visualise. A story on job losses can easily become a meaningless jumble of numbers unless it is carefully written. Generally it is better to round figures up or down to the nearest whole figure. So rather than saying '1,487 clerical staff at insurance offices across the country will lose their jobs', it is better to say 'nearly fifteen hundred clerical staff'. Try to interpret statistics as simply as possible. Say 'nearly half' rather than '49.8 per cent', but do not mix decimals, fractions and percentages in the same story, and make sure you compare like with like. It is confusing to hear that nurses are angry at being offered a 2 per cent increase in pay when firemen are being given an average increase of £150 each.

Another way that listeners can be confused by what is being said is through the use of jargon. This is used by groups of people working in the same field to unite them through language that is common to them alone. It can also be used to disguise the true meaning of what is being said. In either case, it needs to be translated into straightforward English. As discussed in Chapter 1, a lot of news comes from press releases sent to newsrooms. These tend to be riddled with jargon. For example, the ambulance officers will often refer to an accident victim being 'fatally injured' rather than saying the victim was killed. Hospital press officers say the patient is 'undergoing surgery' rather than having an operation. The police often refer to 'two white males' being sought, rather than two white men.

Your language needs to be colloquial – which is not the same as sloppy. What it means is that your writing needs to sound like ordinary conversation. Wherever possible you need to use contractions, so that 'it is' becomes 'it's', and 'would not' becomes 'wouldn't'. The use of slang in radio writing varies from one station to another. Generally speaking, the BBC avoids slang, while many commercial stations, especially those targeting a younger audience, fully embrace it. For example, in reporting the story about a British pensioner suing the FBI for being falsely arrested, one station referred to 'that old geezer arrested by the FBI last week', which is a term unlikely to be used on a BBC station.

Radio is an immediate medium so wherever possible you should write in the present/active tense rather than the past/passive, which is used more for print writing. For example, write 'The Archbishop of Canterbury is calling for more religious tolerance' rather than 'The Archbishop of Canterbury has called for more religious tolerance'. Similarly, use 'says' rather than 'said', as in 'Tony Blair says he's determined to win'.

FORMS OF RADIO WRITING

I cannot stress the importance of learning from others. Never miss the opportunity to listen, watch, learn and adapt their style. The listener has just one chance to hear the news, and you have just one chance to get it right.

Barnie Choudhury
BBC correspondent

The simplest form of radio news writing is a copy line. This is a news story written for broadcast as part of a news bulletin. Copy tells the whole story without any audio to illustrate it. Copy lines can vary in duration from 8 seconds to 35 seconds in greater or less detail, but in every case they stand alone as a complete story.

Most stations have an on-screen proforma for writing copy, cues and scripts. This will contain information about who has written the copy, what bulletin it was prepared for, and a 'slug' or 'catchline' to identify the story. All this information is important to whoever is compiling the bulletin. They need to know who has written it in case there is a query, and when it was written in case it needs to be updated. Broadcast speech is calculated at three words per second, and it is vital that the duration of copy is included so that the bulletin can be compiled to a specific time.

Where audio is used to tell the story, it needs to be introduced so that listeners know who is talking and what they are talking about. For that reason every piece of audio on radio needs to have a cue. The cue has two main functions. In the first place it should 'hook' the audience so that they want to hear the following audio. In the second place, it should explain what the story is about and introduce the person talking on the audio. This might be a sound-bite from a politician, the eye witness to a fire, a reporter doing a voice report, or a reporter leading into a package that has several sound-bites from different people on the same story.

In all cases the cue should not repeat what is being said in the audio. Instead it should set the story up and the audio should then explain and/or illustrate the information in the cue. For example, the cue into a sound-bite with someone taking part in an anti-war demonstration might say:

> Over ninety thousand people took to the streets of London this afternoon to demonstrate against the war in Iraq. Police say the event was peaceful and good humoured with families and old age pensioners taking part. The protesters arrived by car, bus, and train. Charley Farley from Leeds says the trip was well worth it.

The audio would then have Charley Farley saying 'It's important that all those of us who are against this war make our views known. Tony Blair needs to realise this war isn't wanted by the vast majority of the country – and we're going to make sure he gets the message.' What is important here is that the cue did not say 'Charley Farley says it's important for people to demonstrate' because that repeats his first words.

Like copy, cues need to have details of the story slug, reporter's name, date and time of bulletin. However, they also need details about the audio so that the news editor knows the total duration of the piece to compile the bulletin, and the newsreader knows what to expect. At the end of the cue, the slug used on the audio needs to be given, as well as the duration of the audio, the 'out words' which are the last few words on the audio clip, and the total duration of the piece, which is the duration of the audio plus the duration of the cue.

Where a story is too complicated for a simple copy line and there is no audio available to illustrate it, the story is often done as a voice piece. This is a voice report by a reporter. It consists of a cue to be read by the news reader that introduces a report that is either live or recorded from the reporter. Voice pieces are most effective when they are done at the scene of a story when background noise can add atmosphere to the report. For example, a reporter covering the anti-war demonstration used above might do a voice piece with the demonstration in the background via telephone. This could then be used as a 'holding piece' until the reporter gets back to the studio with audio from the demonstrators.

Cues are also needed for more complex audio pieces like news packages. A news package is a fuller look at a story, and usually involves linking more than one audio clip on the same story. Because packages deal with stories in more depth than a single audio clip, the cues are generally shorter, but they still need the same technical details at the end. For example, the cue for a news package about the anti-war demonstration might simply say, 'Over ninety thousand people took to the streets of London this afternoon to demonstrate against the war in Iraq. Reporter Jane Smith was with them.' The package would then begin with the chanting of the demonstrators, which would fade under the voice of the reporter who would introduce a pensioner on the demonstration, then back to the reporter who would link into a policeman's comments on the demonstration, back to the reporter who would link into a pro-war person, back to the reporter who would round the story up.

A good cue for a package should set it up in such a way that listeners want to hear it, but which also prepares them for the audio that follows. This means that if the package starts with sound effects, the listener is prepared for them. If the above cue had not explained that the reporter was with the demonstration, then the following chanting might not have made much sense. The cue also needs to introduce the reporter, otherwise they remain anonymous.

The key rule about writing for radio is that there are no rules – just more or less effective ways of doing it. Listen to a wide range of radio and work out why the news is written in that particular style, and whether or not it is effective in telling the story in an engaging way. Each radio station, or at least group of radio stations, has its own style that should reflect the audience they are targeting. But allowing for differences in style, the general aims of writing for radio are the same: talk to people, don't read to them. The best way to make sure you write as you talk is to start by telling the story aloud to yourself, and writing that down. You can always make it more polished once you have the basis down. Once you have the finished piece, read it aloud. This not only helps you to hear how it sounds, it also shows up tongue twisters and words that are awkward to pronounce. Reading in your head does not work: it always comes out perfect.

The best radio writing is direct, logical, and makes the listener feel they are being spoken to individually. Master that and the rest is easy.

WRITING FOR TELEVISION

> You do not want the viewer to realise that you are actually *reading* the words from the autocue, so it's best to keep the script as conversational as possible. Short sentences, simple words and informal asides are all important ingredients in a good script.
>
> Jerome Quinn[6]
> BBC Northern Ireland

A lot of what has been said before about writing for newspapers and radio applies here as well. Use short sentences, avoid abbreviations unless you're absolutely sure everyone will know what you're talking about; in general, keep it simple.

BBC Northern Ireland sports presenter Jerome Quinn says:

> Some sports writers on high-brow newspapers can regurgitate the Oxford dictionary in their analysis of the same sporting event, and indeed they may pour scorn upon the relatively simple, basic language used by the television presenter, but the latter style is a skill all in itself.

There are, however, separate points that you need to remember when you are writing a TV script which are to do with the sometimes complex relationship between words and pictures. Writing must enhance the visual image that you see, not explain it. Therefore, don't be too literal. You don't need to describe what the viewer is seeing. The viewer can see this for themselves.

So how does the writing best enhance the image? It does just that by telling us more than we can see, and by acting as an audible pathway through the images – leading the viewer by the hand, as it were, though the images. The words should be clear and simple but they should always be related to the pictures in some way. It is no good rushing ahead of your pictures, or lagging behind. So you must pace your script to the images that you have on the screen.

Pictures and words should always be partners, never rivals. Your script should be talking about either what is on the screen or what is about to come up on the screen. For instance the script should not be saying 'Mr Blair, who was addressing the Labour Party conference …' over shots of him leaving Number Ten to attend the conference. Sound and pictures always work in harmony. Because the words need time to be understood, it is often necessary for them to slightly precede the pictures, which can be understood at once if we know what we are supposed to see. When the visual interest of one picture has been exhausted, the viewer can then pay attention to words preparing the way to the next picture. But again, try not to be too literal.

However, when you have a graphic or map on the screen, the words must reiterate whatever words are shown on the screen. Remember that the viewer can't take in too much. They can't read the screen and listen to words separately.

Therefore they have to be exactly the same. Quinn spells out how it works for him:

> The process goes something like this: first, collect your material, view it carefully and make notes. Second, decide upon the most interesting line of news and the most original pictures. Third, try to match the two together. From there, knit the story together throughout the package, building on the opening gambit to enforce the point. This ensures that the viewer is encouraged to watch the full report, rather than switching channel half-way through.

You may want to use a musical sequence. When editing music you must fade out at the end of a musical cadence, never in the middle. It is extremely irritating to the ear for the music to stop before the cadence has been completed. The two exceptions to this rule are:

1   where the music is faded out so gently and gradually under dialogue or some other sound that one is not aware of its going or of its end;
2   where the music is immediately swamped by another more forceful and much louder sound.

In your writing you must introduce one idea at a time. Make sure that you don't pack too much into one sentence or into one paragraph. Make sure that there is a logical development from one paragraph to the next so that there's a thread the listener can follow. Remember, you are telling a story.

Another very important thing to consider is that you have to keep the audience's attention all the way through and the piece that you're writing can be anything from 2 minutes up to 30. Therefore you have to have titbits with which to pepper your piece as you go along. What this means is that it's not good enough to save all your most important or shocking or controversial elements for the beginning and the end of your script. You need some good stuff at suitable intervals to keep them interested, just as you would in a newspaper feature or a long radio package.

Always read what you have written aloud to yourself. What looks beautifully crafted on the page may well sound complicated, convoluted, or out of breath when it's read aloud. Also, when you read something aloud – especially to another person – you will be able to tell whether or not you have answered all the questions that you may have posed in the minds of the listener.

If you're making a longer piece of television, you will need to think of several different ways to introduce your interviewees. In terms of the writing, you will want to avoid using the same cue as it can become irritating to the viewer. Try to avoid using the term *Mr White explains*. It is a lazy method of getting into an interview. The best way is to give the viewer some kind of a hint as to what the interviewee will say, without giving everything away. Be careful that your cues do not sound like a reiteration of what we are about to hear, just in different words. It may sound like common sense, but it is also a very common mistake. For instance:

> CUE: Lisa described her feelings of shame and anger at discovering the situation ...
> START OF INTERVIEW: 'I felt angry and I was ashamed ...'

This way the interviewee has provided nothing for the viewer.

Quinn provides some sound guidance for people wanting to succeed as a broadcaster:

> My advice to anyone interested in writing for radio and television is simply to listen to as much of the experts as possible and study their varied styles. Take the best bits and develop a style that you are comfortable with. One of my personal favourites is Kevin Gearey from BBC News. With a colourful script, entertaining asides and sometimes caustic comments, he succeeds in making cricket reports on television sound lively to *all* viewers.

WRITING FOR THE INTERNET

There are three major differences between writing for the Internet and writing for newspapers or magazines.

1 Anyone can be an 'online writer'. The World Wide Web has suddenly put a potential global readership at everyone's fingertips. You don't have to impress an editor into giving you a job, or win the lottery and buy a printing press. There's relatively little censorship or control and lots of websites where you can publish your views, stories or articles free of charge. Some people just use bulletin boards while others submit items to the editors of niche sites which cover their particular interest or theme. You don't even need to own a computer. You can log on down at your local library or community centre and start sharing your ideas with the world. There are plenty of opportunities to build your own free website without needing special software or even any web design skills, so you can be an online publisher within minutes of having an idea for a website. But getting people to find your website is another matter.

2 Deadlines? You can forget them. Elaine Pritchard, project manager of Northcliffe Electronic Publishing, says:

> I remember working in Hull on a cracking story about an armed man holding a hostage in his flat. But it drove me mad as the hours went by, and the story developed, to be constrained by the fixed deadlines of the press. Even bringing out extra special editions didn't help much, because it seemed that every time an edition started rolling on the presses there would be another twist in the story. I remember envying the reporters on local radio who could at least provide hourly updates. Throughout my career in newspapers, the phrase I hated most was: 'As the *Mail/Telegraph/Times* went to press ...' No more of that. On the Internet you can update as often as you want, 24 hours a day, 7 days a week.[7]

3   You don't have to write to length any more. There are no big adverts which means your 400-word masterpiece has to be cut to 250 words. The Internet goes on forever – almost. Pritchard says:

> When it comes to writing 'news', I don't think there has to be any difference between writing for the web and for other disciplines. All the basic rules still apply … you want to grab people's interest at the start of the story and hold it until the end, you want to give them all the information they need – and personally I would still advise online journalists to imagine that a non-existent sub-editor may want to cut their story from the bottom. So make sure every par contains new information, which is less important than the previous par.

Statistics software packages can tell you how many people are visiting your website, which pages they are looking at, how long they are spending on each page, the route they took through your website, how they found it and where they went next. Pritchard says:

> To generalise, you find that most people use websites to find specific information quickly. Most people don't have the patience or desire to scroll down great long screens of the same story – unless it's something they are desperate to know. For this reason many news sites keep the headline stories very short and succinct, but offer a chance to click for more detailed information.

Another advantage of a news website is that it can pull lots of stories together and link them, making it easy to catch up on the background to a running story in one visit. Pritchard explains:

> For instance, many people no longer buy newspapers seven days a week, so you can easily miss out on instalments of a running court case. On a news website – like Northcliffe's 'this is' sites – you can index every story in a user-friendly fashion, so that someone who logs on to read today's events can be just a click away from the whole story to date.

WRITING STYLES

Newspaper websites tend to mirror newspaper styles. Pritchard says: 'In the case of the *"this is"* sites, we extract all the content directly from Northcliffe's individual newspaper production systems and post it to the sites.'

Some newspaper sites do sub-down newspaper copy or re-purpose it in some way to meet the style or production methods of their websites. But, by and large, most online operations are run on a bare minimum of staff resources. Pritchard comments:

> A lot of members of the public using older hardware still struggle to access audio and video but I guess that situation will improve a lot in the next couple of years. Video and audio on websites – for me – bridge the traditional divide between print and broadcast and create a combined media.

A couple of years ago at a Newspaper Society conference I heard a great speaker from an American newspaper. They ran a newspaper, a website, a TV station and a radio station. All the staff were multiskilled and were trained to work for all disciplines – so the same person could alternate between writing, filming, broadcasting, presenting, uploading to the website … the works.

WRITING FOR BBC.CO.UK

Nigel Bell, who joined the BBC in 1986, eventually moved into television journalism before helping set up the 'Nottingham Where I Live' website in 2000. He says people usually don't want more than 300 words. 'We've found that, even on what might appear the most interesting of subjects, there's at least a 50 per cent drop off if you try to take the user onto a second page. So clear, concise and no waffle has to be the watchword.'[8]

Web users are increasingly getting used to looking around the page. Bell says:

They won't necessarily read the article and then move on. They look for related web links and interesting facts. So don't feel every bit of information you've gleaned has to go in the body of the text. You can put facts and figures in easy-to-read boxes, either to the side or in the body of your work.

Ultimately the way you write for your particular website is determined by the audience you are trying to reach. Your style will be different if writing for a young audience. Older users might be more used to the newspaper style of writing. Bell adds:

The homepage is the key to attracting users to your site. It has to be simple yet attractive. Too cluttered and you'll scare people off, too bland and they'll think what's within is bland. Pictures attract users but beware of making your page too heavy. If people have to wait a long time for a page to download they'll give up and go elsewhere. This sometimes means you have to sacrifice picture quality in order for a speedy download.

From a BBC perspective, Bell says audio and video are key selling points to their websites since it allows the Corporation to draw on its TV and radio services, which is something most other sites cannot do (certainly to such a great and varied degree). He says: 'As the web moves from being a computer-based resource to being used on your TV set and telephone, the use of audio and video will become more important.'

CHECKLIST

✓   Keep it simple. Your intro, or first paragraph, should be a maximum of 20 words and concentrate on what the story is about rather than specifics like when and where it happened. Avoid abbreviations, long titles like the names of committees and big words that lots of people won't understand.

✓   Think human. In many cases it's a good idea to write your intro around the people it affects.

✓   Think drama. If you've got a particularly odd or unusual incident, then it should be mentioned in the intro. If you've got a number of newsworthy items, try to include them all in the first 2 to 3 paragraphs.

✓   Answer all the questions. You might not include the 'when' and 'where' in your first few paragraphs but they'll need to go somewhere in your story.

✓   Learn from others. Listen to the radio, surf the net, watch telly and read newspapers. If in doubt, see how the experts do it.

✓   Get your facts right! Make sure you check your work and, if in doubt, check again.

✓   Think balance. Getting the other side is vital.

✓   Speak to people, don't read to them. Broadcasters should try visualising the person they are talking to. They can then exploit this intimacy by using words like 'us' and 'we'. And they can make sure they write as they talk by reading the story out loud.

✓   Use contractions. Broadcasters (not newspaper reporters) can again make their stories sound like ordinary conversation if they use, for instance, *isn't* rather than *is not*.

✓   Avoid repetition. Show your audience that you've got an imagination and don't need to repeat the same words ad nauseam. And don't use foreign words. Capisce?

NOTES

1 All quotes from Simon Irwin taken from author interview, 2003.
2 All quotes from Richard Taylor taken from author interview, 2003.
3 All quotes from Martin Wells taken from author interview, 2003.
4 All quotes from Mark Tattersall taken from author interview, 2003.
5 All quotes from Barnie Choudhury taken from author interview, 2003.
6 All quotes from Jerome Quinn taken from author interview, 2003.
7 All quotes from Elaine Pritchard taken from author interview, 2003.
8 All quotes from Nigel Bell taken from author interview, 2003.

INTERVIEWING

Some years ago I was researching a news item on euthanasia where a brother and sister had injected their mother with a lethal dose of morphine. She was dying from breast cancer. Eventually they agreed to do an interview. It was shot in my home, simply lit using a two-man crew and myself …

On the strength of the interview, I secured a documentary commission. A producer and director were brought on board. They insisted on doing the interview again as mine was 'too rough and ready.' This time it was done in a studio with lots of lights, tracks and a crew of four excluding me, the interviewer, the producer, and director. The interview was stopped several times while cameras were placed on dollies or a small jib to get 'better shots'. The result looked amazing. The commissioners and executive producers viewed it, and hated it. I asked if I could show the original interview, which had been cut for a news item. The rushes were found and it became the backbone of a documentary that won several awards. The brother and sister were given a conditional discharge and walked free from court.

The moral of this tale is simple, and it goes for all interviews. Don't be taken in by technology, techniques and gizmos. What really matters are human beings telling powerful human stories.

Mike Blair[1]
editor
Central News East

Interviews are the life-blood of journalism. They have the power to change minds, governments and even history. They are the voice of the people involved directly in the stories that make up the news, and to try to get a true picture of what's happening, you need to hear from them. Interviews are also a minefield through which the journalist must walk with great care. Ask the wrong question, of the wrong person, or make the wrong interpretation, and the story can be grossly inaccurate. Careers or even lives can be shattered.

The interview is a complex and delicate process and is governed by a series of rules; rules that journalists have learned through years in the field, from taking chances and from making mistakes. These rules are not written down. They cannot be memorised or recited. But they form a code of professional and personal judgements that serve to elicit information and grant respect to those from whom that information is sought. They also make life easier for the journalist. They help you to get to a relevant person quickly, or coax a reluctant onlooker, or persuade those in the know to reveal that extra piece of information.

This chapter is a way into some of those rules. It will explore the complexity of the interview in its many different guises. It will describe and analyse some of the best practices and techniques adopted by experienced journalists over the years. It will provide a rough map with which the new journalist can track their way through the interviewing process, and ensure they're not only prepared for whatever interview they're asked to do, but that they know how to best conduct it, so that the relevant voices of the story are heard.

The chapter is divided into separate media areas. It will look at interviewing techniques for newspapers, radio, television and online broadcasting. There are a number of basic guidelines that can help you whatever your medium. These are outlined below.

IDENTIFYING THE STORY

The first and most basic rule to follow when tackling the unpredictable world of the interview is to 'know the story'. It sounds simple, but the significance or meaning of a story is often beguiling, even to the most experienced reporter. There may often be the chance to discuss a story idea with a producer or editor. If this is the case, make sure you do it. Now is not the time to pretend to know what you're being asked to do. If the wrong person is then tracked down, to give the wrong interview, for what may have been the wrong story in the first place, the consequences will be far more serious.

There is always more than one way to approach a news story and the producer may see it in a different light, having an already partly formed idea of how it will fit into a wider news agenda. You should find out what line he or she wants you to take on it, or what they see as the 'top line' of the story. Don't try to be clever at this stage and avoid discussion for fear of looking ignorant. A producer will most likely welcome your attempt to clarify the issue and acquaint yourself with the news agenda as he or she already sees it. It's also possible that the approaches or elements of the story can be discussed in more detail. Perhaps the producer hadn't thought of something you point out when drawing up a list of possible interviewees. Who knows, you may get them to see the story as you do, from a slightly better angle!

FINDING THE RIGHT INTERVIEWEE

On many stories, particularly human interest stories, you don't have a choice. There's obviously no substitute for the mother of the boy who suffers from a crippling disease and desperately needs an organ donor. Or for the elderly woman who gets beaten to the ground by a mugger for the contents of her handbag. Their first-hand testimony is essential to the story. But when it comes to experts on any given story, you can afford to be more choosy.

Chris Mills[2]
BBC reporter

Imagine you have been asked to cover the following story:

An elderly woman who lives in a flat on her own in an inner city estate has been recently burgled. In the burglary her two front windows were smashed. As the flat is council owned, they have boarded up the windows, but have not yet replaced them. This was two weeks ago. Since this time the woman, who is partially disabled, has been living without windows and has repeatedly asked the council to come and repair them. A council spokesperson has said the windows are an irregular size and have had to be ordered, hence the delay in fitting them. It is November and the weather is cold as well as very wet and windy.

You now need to find the right interviewees. The first thing to ask yourself is: 'What's the story? What's the top line?' Try to answer this in a sentence: 'Disabled elderly woman is left in the cold in her own burgled flat by council who've failed to repair her smashed windows.' It's fairly straightforward.

The next thing to do is to make sure you know who you want to talk to and how important they are to the story. Remember the story can only be told by the right people, i.e. those directly involved. The most important person is the elderly woman. You also need to talk to a spokesperson from the council, making sure that you pick the department directly responsible for the window repairs. These are the main interviewees. But there are others you may want to think about at this stage. What about neighbours who may be able to give you an idea how the elderly lady has been coping? After all, she may be unwilling to complain about it, thinking this would make her less likely to get the council's assistance. There may be family members who've also tried to repair the windows themselves, or who've been involved in caring for the elderly woman.

Remember that the council has said that the windows are an unusual fit – perhaps it would be worth talking to an independent window fitter who would be able to say whether the council is telling the truth, or simply making an excuse. These are all secondary interviewees. But at this stage of your research you should be thinking about every conceivable angle to the story. You don't want to be chasing interviewees up at the last minute while you're out filming. This may happen of course, but the more preparation you can do at this stage the better.

Once you've tracked down the elderly woman, the council spokesperson, a concerned relative, and an independent window fitter, you're ready to go out and get the interviews. It's always a good idea to try to get people to meet you at the scene of the story, in this case at the elderly woman's flat. This may not be crucial if you're doing a newspaper story, but if you're recording your interview for radio, or filming it for television, you will always be better off getting your interviews at the location. For instance, if you're doing a television interview, you would be best advised to film your council spokesperson looking at the windows, or for radio, recording him walking through the flat, rather than in an office that bears no relevance to the actual story. Although for print journalists this is not as important a consideration, it's still advisable to try to conduct interviews at the scene. The scene is a part of the story and may give you ideas about other questions that you want to ask but hadn't thought about before you got there. Just before you go out to get your interview, spend a few minutes thinking about what information you're trying to get, and what questions you want to ask in order to get it.

FORMULATING THE QUESTIONS

> Normally for national daily news, an interview will be reduced to a clip of around 15 seconds' length. Because camera crews are expensive, it's normal practice to talk to the interviewee on the phone to establish what they'll say, and to stress the importance of clarity, brevity, and simplicity.
>
> Geoff Byrne[3]
> BBC news producer

It's wise to chat through a range of questions with your interviewee beforehand to give them some idea of what you would like them to say. This means that you need to have a very clear idea in your own mind as to what part of the story they represent, and how you want them to communicate that. It's obviously not always that straightforward and can all change when you actually meet face to face, but it's good preparation and helps you to keep your mind focused on the story. Remember, you haven't even left the office yet.

When thinking about formulating your questions, refer to the five main questions raised in Chapter 3. The questions 'who?', 'what?', 'when?', 'where?', and 'why?' are an ideal starting point. But you will probably want to know more than this. These questions can start you off, but if you don't think outside these parameters, you may miss more subtle parts of the story and come back with something rather dull and predictable.

Think again about the top line of the story. Taking the original scenario, for instance, you'll want to get a 'feel' for what the elderly woman has had to go through, sitting in her flat in the cold. You'll also want to ask the council spokesperson how he or she could have caused this to happen. Try to identify with the feelings of the people involved in the story. You're not just trying to extract information, or get at the facts. You are also trying to identify what it would be like to experience a particular situation.

You may want to write down possible questions as they come to mind, but don't refer to them when you're actually doing the interview. They should act as notes to help you focus. When you're either taking notes, or recording or filming the interview, your attention should be on listening to your interviewee, not on trying to read the next question on your list.

Last but by no means least, make sure you have everything with you before you leave. It's essential that you have complete names and addresses of your interviewees to hand, as well as contact numbers in case you run into traffic problems, or get lost and are delayed. If you're doing the interview for radio, make sure all your equipment is in working order, and if you're using non-digital equipment, that you have the relevant tapes. If you are operating the camera, check your equipment fully first, or make sure that your camera operator is fully prepared. There's nothing worse than turning up without an essential piece of kit, and having to make excuses about forgetting batteries or microphones. It hardly creates the right impression and could very well lose you the interview, and the story.

FIRST IMPRESSIONS

> For me the most important part of any interview is the time you have with the person you're interviewing before it starts. This is crucial in 'emotional' scenarios. It gives you the chance to bond – to be seen to have a human face – and to care about the issues you're discussing. It also means you get the chance to have what amounts to a dry run for the interview, giving you an opportunity to gauge which questions will get the most powerful responses.
>
> Mike Blair
> editor
> Central News East

Meeting your interviewee is the most important part of the whole interviewing process. It sounds obvious, but make sure that you make eye contact in a confident and sympathetic manner and be polite at all times. You don't have to be overly formal, and you'll soon learn to gauge this by quickly judging the demeanour of the person you're meeting. It's said that most of us decide whether or not we like someone in the first two minutes. Therefore it's essential that you look smart, have a pleasant manner and are friendly and approachable. But try not to talk too much. Allow your interviewee to approach you and to communicate equally with you. It's often a good idea to chat about something more general before launching straight into the subject of the interview. You need to show that you're not just interested in what the person can offer you in terms of an interview, but that you're genuinely interested in who they are, and how they feel or think about things.

Obviously these guidelines are variable, depending on the type of interview you're doing, and who you're meeting. If you're chasing a politician across a busy street and you only have two or three minutes to get a question asked and answered, there isn't time for niceties. What you must always do is to say who you are and what news organisation you represent. After that it might just be straight into your question. But a politician is aware of the rules of the game and won't be expecting you to make small talk.

CONDUCTING THE INTERVIEW

There are no hard-and-fast rules about how to conduct an interview, but there are a number of guidelines that it's wise to follow. Here it's helpful to look at the particular media forms individually, as the way an interview is carried out varies considerably depending on whether it's for newspapers, radio or television.

NEWSPAPER INTERVIEWS

Conducting an interview for a newspaper does give you slightly more freedom, at least from technical considerations, than for radio or television. You can be more conversational, as you're not constrained by the recording equipment. It doesn't matter if you happen to slightly interrupt what somebody is saying; you're not broadcasting it. But you must still be very careful with direct quotes. It's a good idea therefore to record your interviews with a dictaphone, unless your shorthand is excellent and you can write down exactly what's being said. If you record your interviews, you can also listen to the atmosphere or mood of the interview, and get a more accurate feel for the state of mind of the interviewee. This will help you write up the story more accurately later, and if you're writing a feature piece, it can add atmosphere and texture to it.

Note taking is also extremely important when conducting newspaper interviews. Remember that with a radio or television interview, what is recorded acts as your defence in the event that an interview is called into question, or challenged at a later stage. With a newspaper interview, you don't have that kind of record. Your notes are your only evidence that what was said at the time was reported accurately by you. Therefore if you can't record your interview, make sure your note taking is spot on. Keep all your notebooks as a record of your research and your interviews. If you were ever asked to produce your notes in court, or give evidence in court regarding an interview you conducted, your notes are your only testimony to the fact that you accurately and fairly reported what was said in that interview.

Always make sure that both you and your interviewee know exactly what is being spoken about 'on' and 'off the record'. If you are asking your interviewee to tell you something 'off the record', this indicates a shared understanding that whatever information they reveal won't be used in the piece. The American press refers to this as 'background'. Knowing that the information won't be associated with them protects the interviewee. It helps journalists get closer to the truth of a story, while protecting the sources they use. This rule also applies to radio and television interviews, but it is not used as frequently.

If your interview is for radio or television, then as soon as you start recording ask your interviewee to tell you their full name, to spell it if necessary, and to tell you by what title they wish to be referred. This is usually only the case if they represent an organisation or company. By doing this first, you will make sure that you have got a record of their correct name and position to refer to later on when writing your script or ordering your graphics. If you're conducting the interview for a newspaper, make sure you've written their name down and check with them that it's spelled correctly.

The following sections look in more detail at the interview process for radio and television. However, they also include more general guidelines that are of use when conducting any interview, so even if you're not working for radio or television, they are still worth reading.

Radio and television interviews are conducted in a slightly different way from newspaper interviews and should be looked at separately. The main difference is that you need to be aware of the recording equipment you're using and how it can help or hinder you throughout the interview process.

RADIO INTERVIEWS

Radio journalism isn't brain surgery. Make sure you're well briefed, don't get bullied or put off asking a difficult question, and make sure you listen to the answers you're given.

Mike Young[4]
broadcast journalist
BBC Radio Nottingham

Getting the technical side of an interview right is vitally important for a good recording, and this is discussed in Chapter 5, but it is equally important to approach the interview in the correct way. As with all interviews, the key to success is preparation. Where time allows, reporters should get as much background information as possible from newspaper files, the Internet or press releases. You need to know as much as possible about the story so that you can ask the right questions. The strength of a radio interview is that it shows *how* the questions are answered – with hesitation or aggression, for example – and this conveys as much as the actual words being spoken.

First of all you need to establish how the interview is going to be used. Longer interviews are not generally used in news bulletins, but they are used in news magazine programmes. In most cases, reporters going on an interview will be expected to produce a sound-bite or 'clip' for news bulletins, and use other parts of the interview as part of a package for longer news programmes. But however the interview is being used, you must have a clear idea of the aim of the interview before you launch into it. Is this a fact-finding interview, for example with a local government officer over the closure of schools, where you need to know how many schools are being closed, how much saving this will make, where the pupils and teachers will go, and why these particular schools have been chosen? Or is it an interview to get opinion, for example with the headteacher of a threatened school about how they feel about the closure plans, or a parent talking about the impact of the closure on their child? Or is it a personality interview with an actor or musician that needs to give an impression of the person behind the celebrity? Establishing the aim of the interview will help you to plan your approach and make sure you get what you need from it. As Mike Young comments:

> When I prepare for a radio interview, I first of all have a good look through our archives and surf the web to get a sense of where we are with the story so far. It's important to have a sense of taking a story forward and not to go over old ground. The next step is to 'paper edit'. I like to have an idea of the questions I want to ask and what I want to see and record for an item. As a reporter, I see no point in doing an interview on location which a presenter could do just as well live on the telephone. If I'm going out and about, I want a sense of place, sound effects, movement and sparkle. Once with a guest, be it in the studio or on location, it's important not to let a 'paper edit' close your mind to an interview developing and leading you to ask questions you didn't expect to ask. Be informed in advance but *listen* to your guest and respond accordingly.

Being prepared for an interview does not mean having a list of questions that you intend to ask. It's a good idea to have worked out two or three key points that you need answers to, but if you arrive with a list of questions there is a tendency to follow the list, rather than listen to what is being said and respond accordingly. Listening is as important as asking the right questions. Reporters need to be able to pick up on any new information being given, and where need be, to challenge contentious statements.

Questions should be brief and direct. Long rambling questions can confuse interviewees, and asking about more than one point at a time usually means that one point will not be answered. Try to avoid questions that can be answered with a simple 'yes' or 'no'. For example, in an interview about a rise in council tax with the local council leader, it would be better to ask 'What do you think about the proposed rise?' rather than 'Do you think the proposed rise is justified?' As Tim John,[5] newsreader with 106 century FM explains:

> You need to be both patient and persistent – that may seem contradictory but if you want that interview, you have to be able to judge which skill to use and when. An excellent knowledge of current media law is also essential. Most commercial newsrooms don't have the luxury of a lawyer available to look over your work – so the chances are, you'll be largely responsible for covering your own back.

Where time allows, it's a good idea to make your first question quite general. This will help to put the interviewee at ease, and allow you to make sure your recording levels are correct. Probing questions about contentious issues should only be used towards the end of the interview, when you already have something recorded, should the interviewee refuse to answer. It's very important for reporters to remain calm and polite at all times, no matter what the provocation. That said, being polite is not the same as being compliant. It is a reporter's job to ask questions on behalf of the audience, and at times this will include awkward questions that the interviewee may not want to answer. The key is to be courteous but firm in your questioning. Some interviewees will ask for a list of questions in advance, and this should be avoided. Instead outline the general area you plan to discuss. This will give you more flexibility during the interview, and make the piece sound more spontaneous.

If the interview is being used as part of a package, you also need to think about sound effects that will give the package atmosphere and a sense of location. For example, for a package about increased violence at a hospital accident and emergency department, it would be useful to have the sound of ambulances arriving, the hubbub of the waiting room, and the sound of patients being called by the nurse. Even if the interview with the A&E consultant is not recorded, for one reason or another, you can use these sound effects to bring the package alive so that listeners can 'see' the situation. Recording 'wild track' on location allows you more freedom in editing to create an engaging package, but it's no good thinking of this once you are back at base.

Before you leave an interview, do a quick check to make sure that it has recorded. It may be embarrassing to have to redo the interview there and then, but that is better than getting back to base and finding you have nothing. In checking that the interview has recorded, however, do not be tempted to play the whole thing back to the interviewee. Inevitably they will want to change something, so avoid letting them hear more than a snippet.

Finally, no matter how dry the story may seem to be, keep an open mind about it and try to approach it with interest. Your interest, or lack of it, will come across to the interviewee, and colour their responses to questions.

Mike Young says:

Don't be put off by being given what you see as a rotten story. On a quiet news day I was sent to a pub which a regular had attended most of his life. Once I got there I found out that the barman was planning a spoof wedding so this fella could tie the knot with the pub itself! It all came about because his wife used the immortal line 'You may as well be married to the Railway Inn rather than me.' With lots of beer flowing, I got a lot of people talking to me and with the use of some suitable bridal music, we mocked up a ceremony with the landlord as the 'vicar'. This ended up playing out on BBC 5 Live. Lateral thinking often makes magical, fresh radio.

TELEVISION INTERVIEWS

If you're doing the interview for television, you may or may not be working with a camera operator. If you're working alone, you need to also check the level on your camera microphone before you begin the interview. Remember to also take a white balance and check that you've positioned your interviewee in the right place, so as to make the most of the available light.

If you're working with a camera operator, you'll need to tell the interviewee to look at you and not at the camera, and to try to forget about the camera during the interview. Easier said than done, I know. But if you do see the interviewee starting to look into the lens, you should interrupt the recording and politely remind them to look at you. You need to position yourself as close as you possibly can to the camera, so as to ensure that the eye line is correct.

These rules also apply if you're the camera operator, but it may be more difficult to check throughout the interview. If you're filming the interview yourself, the same rules apply, but you also need to try to forget about the camera during the interview. You'll not be giving the interviewee your full attention, or listening to what they're saying, if you've got half an eye on the camera, or if you're thinking about the way you've framed the shot. Take the time to set this up at the beginning, but once you're satisfied that you've got the shot well framed and well lit, and that the interviewee is in the right position, then your full attention should be on the interviewee and the content of the interview itself.

LINES OF QUESTIONING

The first question will be about how they feel, and when the reporter thinks that they're ready, the main question can be asked, and asked again in a number of different ways until the answer of appropriate resonance and length has been obtained. This doesn't apply to an official spokesperson – they understand the game. And as for politicians, well anything goes. They expect to be quizzed, and the audience expects the BBC to be tough on them.

Geoff Byrne
BBC news producer

As the quote suggests, the line of questioning will be different depending on who you're interviewing and what kind of interview you're conducting. But there are general rules that apply here for all four media: newspaper, radio, television or online. If you're interviewing someone who isn't used to the media, then go more slowly and allow the person time to settle into the experience. You need to be aware of what interview you're after. Are you doing an interview to get clips for a two-minute news package? Or are you conducting a three-minute as-live interview for radio? You may not know at this stage how the interview will be used. Therefore you need to conduct it so as to cover a number of options.

If you feel that your interviewee has said something interesting that you definitely want to use, but they've made a mistake, or been too ponderous in their reply, you should interrupt the recording and ask them to say it again more succinctly. This is only relevant for broadcast interviews. Here it is really important that your interviewee understands just how concise they must be in order to come across well, and it's always a good idea to explain this clearly at the outset. Remember that people will want to express themselves as well as they possibly can and you can assist them in this. It's not rude to ask people to repeat themselves, or to be more concise, if you point out that this will improve their overall performance in the finished piece. Of course, you do then run the risk of putting words into their mouths and proving true the old joke that television is nothing more than ordinary people saying what news producers want them to say! As BBC reporter Chris Mills recounts:

> A reporter, now working for network BBC, used to write down the response he sought so it could then be parroted by his interviewee. I was once sent on a mining story by a producer from the BBC regional programme, *Midlands Today*. 'Get him to say this', I was told. 'What if he won't?' I replied. 'He will,' was the response. And he did.

The purpose of any interview is to extract information. But it's also about giving the viewer, reader or listener an idea of how people feel in whatever situation they're in. Returning to the scenario of the elderly woman in her flat, you will want to get her to communicate what it was like being cold, feeling let down by the council, having to confront a large organisation, all on her own. These questions are factual, but they're also about emotional responses to situations and they create what is referred to as 'human interest'.

In any type of interview, it's a good idea to ask your factual questions first, before moving on to these more searching ones. You could start by asking the elderly woman to tell the story of how she was burgled and her windows were smashed. Then ask her what happened next, so that you're encouraging her to tell you the story in her own words.

In a television or radio news package, if a person is very articulate and sums up their story very well, it could be that you use their voice throughout the piece as a commentary, and you might not write any script at all. However, it's more usual that these first questions won't be used, as you can sum up the story much more concisely. In a television piece you'd use shots of the flat and the boarded-up windows to illustrate what you're talking about. The clip you're most likely to use in this story is of the elderly woman saying how she felt about the experience. This will come from one of the more emotional questions you ask after you've heard about the factual detail of the story. You ask the questions in this order so that your interviewee can get used to talking to you, can run through the facts of the story in their own mind, and by recalling them, is in a better position to describe exactly how they felt at the time.

When you come to interview the spokesperson from the council, remember not to antagonise him or her with a directly accusatory opening question. This is a very common mistake to make, but if you wade in with your controversial question first, you'll end up getting nowhere and you may not get an interview at all. You need to lead up to it more slowly. This is true of any media in which you're working.

This can be very well illustrated by using an example of a BBC television documentary team who were producing a film about the IRA. Having spent some weeks persuading a high-powered spokesman from the organisation to talk 'on camera' about an alleged Protestant mass grave that was believed to have been the work of the IRA, they were finally told that the interview could be filmed in a secret location in Southern Ireland. While the five-member team were travelling out to the location, the producer spent a great deal of time with the reporter, making sure they were well equipped to deal with what was an extremely volatile situation. The reporter assured the team that he had the matter firmly in hand. The equipment was set up, the team then waited for three days for their interviewee to stop changing his mind about doing the interview, and they finally got the go-ahead. The reporter introduced himself to the interviewee, waited for the camera operator to confirm he was recording, and asked his opening question. 'So, can you tell us how many Protestants the IRA has murdered and buried in secret over the past 20 years?' The interview was over. The IRA spokesperson left the room and the production team never got a second chance. It was true that this was the question they all wanted to ask and the response they wanted to record. But had the reporter asked this question at the end of the interview, or had he approached the issue in a more subtle way, they may have got some kind of interview around which to construct their story. The reporter didn't think about the way in which he could build up to this final moment. He was more interested in coming across as the intrepid journalist asking the hard questions. As a result the team came away with nothing.

THE IMPORTANCE OF LISTENING

> The story you may go out on may not be the one you come back with. I was once despatched to interview an archer who'd returned from the Olympics to his home village in Lincolnshire, proudly sporting a bronze medal. The story was supposed to be about all the enthusiastic locals holding a party to celebrate his

(Continued)

(Continued)

return. Only after we'd recorded his interview did I discover that he was on unemployment benefit, and officials had stopped his money while he was in Barcelona representing his country because he 'wasn't available to work'. He was furious. This made a much better story. We forgot the first interview and recorded a completely different one. The report made national television and under pressure, the unemployment benefit office reinstated the archer's dole.

Chris Mills
BBC reporter

One of the most important things to remember about any interview you conduct is to listen to what your interviewee is saying. It's only by listening that you'll understand the whole story, or spot something that doesn't quite add up. It's not good enough to have thought about what your questions are going to be without thinking about the responses that you're getting. There are many occasions where there is a better news story buried more deeply within the original one. You might find that someone isn't being exactly honest about his or her role in the story.

You can make judgements about how trustworthy someone is by listening to what they're saying. Listen to the words, but listen to the silences as well. These tell you more about the person than you realise. Are they nervous when talking about a particular aspect of the story? Do they not know what to say in response to certain questions? You also have to listen in order to decide what other questions you need to ask. The questions you thought about when you initially researched the story may not now be adequate, and other questions will come to mind as a result of being involved in the interview. This is especially true of political interviews. You need to listen very carefully in order to hear whether or not your interviewee is avoiding the question, and how best you can bring him or her round to the same issue again.

If you don't listen to the interview you're conducting, then you are not taking an active part within it, and it won't tell you what you want to know. Listening is the hardest thing to learn, but once you master it, you'll be getting that much closer to the heart of the story.

WHAT ELSE IS NEEDED?

It may be that an interviewee says two interesting things at opposite ends of an interview. In radio they can be edited together without too much trouble. They can in television, but only with the aid of a cut-away shot, to avoid a jump cut. Ideally, the interviewer would ask the interviewee to merge the two thoughts and answer the question again in one sentence.

Geoff Byrne
BBC news producer

This section is primarily concerned with television interviews. After you've finished your interview, and both you and the interviewee are satisfied with it, you'll need to think about how best to illustrate it in the wider context of a package or film. Whether you intend to use a 15-second clip in a short news package, or a 2- or 3-minute segment in a feature or documentary, you still need relevant pictures to indicate to the viewer who is being interviewed, and in what context. This is also the case if you've been asked to carry out the interview for someone else.

Every interview for television needs to have accompanying shots to give the reporter time to introduce the subject and to place the interview clip into the wider context of the story. These are known as set-up shots and cutaways. The set-up sequence is a series of three to five shots that can be easily edited together in order to allow time for the reporter to write into the interview and introduce the interviewee. A cutaway is a specific editing shot that allows the picture editor to edit the sequence together, by providing the viewer with a number of shots of the interviewee performing a task or walking past the camera, before coming to the interviewee's clip. This will have been filmed in a slightly different location and perhaps from a slightly different angle. Therefore the cutaway is necessary as an editing tool. It's a shot that cuts away from the subject, the interviewee, to allow the viewer a visual break from the set-up sequence, before being presented with the subject in this different location where the interview has been filmed.

If you're doing the interview for your own news package, you need to think about the length of the piece. This will determine how many different shots you might need. Your set-up sequence may be 20 seconds long, or it may need to be a minute and a half. If you are using the interview in a ten-minute feature, you will want to do a number of different set-up sequences that illustrate a wider story. In this case, try to be imaginative, but do keep things simple. Try to avoid the clichéd sequences such as getting the book from a shelf, making a cup of tea or walking awkwardly straight past the camera. Try to make sure too that your set-up sequence bears some relevance to the story, and to your interviewee. If you're interviewing a high-ranking police officer and your story is about rising gun crime in inner-city Birmingham, you don't want to film him weeding his cottage garden.

You can achieve a lot while driving back to base, especially after interviews for radio and television. If you're working for radio, play the interview back and start to make mental notes as to what clips you might use, or how you want to edit certain sections together. The same can be done for television if you've recorded the interview on a portable dictaphone while you filmed it. This saves you precious time once you get back to script and edit the package.

WHAT CAN GO WRONG?

There are so many possibilities it's almost impossible to list them. Your interviewee could be tongue-tied or possess a cleft palate. Your interviewee

(Continued)

(Continued)

could be blissfully unaware of the facts and consequently a useless source of information. Your interviewee could be unavoidably detained on a flight from Hong Kong while you're waiting for her/him in a biting wind in Worksop. Your interviewee could try to lay down the ground rules for the interview and refuse to answer any questions on the issue in which you're really interested.

Chris Mills
BBC reporter

This section looks at some of the difficulties that could face you, whatever your chosen medium.

One of the main problems that you're bound to come across from time to time is that you'll be faced with an interviewee who just won't answer your questions. This isn't an easy thing to deal with and, again, there are no hard-and-fast rules. It usually happens in political interviews, where the politician is very experienced with dealing with the media. In such cases, if you're rather inexperienced, he or she could end up making a fool of you.

In these circumstances it is absolutely imperative that you've done your research, and that you know what you're talking about. It's no good trying to do a political interview unless you're sure of all your facts, and equally sure you know what you want from your interviewee. If you find yourself being mocked or challenged, remain calm at all times. It is also very important that you're polite. There is nothing worse than losing your temper, and if you do, you've lost any chance of rescuing the interview. If your interviewee loses his or her temper, that's up to them. If it's for television and radio, this may well be the part of the interview you end up using. But never be seen to encourage it.

Another technique that's worth using if your interviewee won't answer your questions is to actually point this out as part of the interview. This way you're demonstrating that you're aware they're being evasive and if you're recording the interview, you're also pointing this out to the viewer or listener. Often the interviewee feels that they've been 'found out' in some way, and they can become more willing to address the issue.

In the recent past, Jeremy Paxman interviewed the then Home Secretary Michael Howard for *Newsnight*. He asked him the same question about 12 times, and this was praised later as one of the interviews of the year, and broadcasters all over the world wondered at his persistence. Well, of course, he is a good interviewer, and Mr Howard was being evasive, but when I asked Paxman later, he revealed that all was not quite what it seemed. The next programme item wasn't ready, and he was getting a lot of noise in his ear from the director asking him to keep talking, until it was ready. Because he had to keep talking, and because of the noise, all he could think of to do,

(Continued)

was to keep asking the question over and over again. Jeremy Paxman was being modest, but the story does show that lofty ideals and technical cock-ups sometimes go hand in hand.

Geoff Byrne
BBC news producer

RADIO AND TELEVISION PROBLEMS

There is a whole host of technical things that can go wrong with an interview, from the camera battery dying in the middle of the most poignant moment of the story, to the audio material being recorded at the wrong level, and the entire interview being unusable. Some of these things can be avoided through thorough checking before and after the interview, as well as by developing a clear knowledge of the equipment you're using. Others can not. All you can do if the equipment lets you down is to apologise and try to remain professional and calm. Again, it's a good idea to let your interviewee know what's going on so that they feel part of the process. This way they're more likely to sympathise with you, rather than get frustrated and blame any mistakes or delays on your ineptitude.

A different problem might be that when you meet your interviewee for the first time, you realise that, although they were coherent and confident over the phone, they're a gibbering wreck in front of a camera. This is best dealt with by turning the camera off and talking through the interview question by question in some detail. You may even rehearse some answers before turning the camera or tape back on. This may make the eventual recording rather stilted, but it does allow the interviewee to feel more in control of the whole process. You can also remind them before the recording that they can stop at any time and re-do their answers if they're not happy with them. But do bear in mind that for this approach, you may have to allow a good deal more time for the interview to be conducted. It's imperative that you never seem to be impatient, even if that's now you feel, as this can shatter the interviewee's confidence and they could very well end up refusing to do the interview at all.

DIFFICULT INTERVIEWS

This section looks at some challenging situations and how best to deal with them. These examples are relevant to any medium.

THE DEATH KNOCK

This can be one of the most difficult interviewees you ever have to do, but it can also be the most rewarding, resulting in some of the most powerful and memorable interviews. The 'death knock', as it's known in the newsroom, is when you interview a close relative of someone who has died in an accident or as a result of a serious crime.

It's worth remembering that this sort of interview is often chosen by a news producer or editor to give to a young journalist to see how they cope with both the request and the actual situation. Be ready to accept the invitation, even if you can't imagine doing anything worse.

The very first thing you need to do is to make sure you know the relationship of the interviewee to the person who's just died. It sounds obvious but there is nothing worse than asking someone how they feel about their nephew having been killed, only to find out it's their son. A mistake of this kind will almost certainly guarantee that you come back to the newsroom empty-handed.

When you have ascertained all the facts you can about the situation, and know exactly who it is you're going to interview, think carefully about first impressions. You may get the chance to speak to the person on the phone. This is when you need to be polite, but not overly detached. If the victim is a child, it is perfectly reasonable to use first names when referring to him/her. It also establishes a sense of your being on the same wavelength as that of the family. However, don't be patronising. If you're talking to a wife or husband about their spouse, I'd advise against using first names, at least in the first instance.

You need to quickly say who you are, and which organisation you represent, but then communicate your respect and sympathy for the family – and mean it. Try to imagine what you would feel like in their position. At this stage it is very important that you allow them to take the lead in the process. It is very common that when people have experienced a loss, they want to talk. If they start to tell you things on the phone, don't try to cut them short by saying, 'We would like to come round and record an interview with you.' You may well be pushed for time, or worried that if they tell you how they feel at this stage, they'll be unlikely to want to repeat it all again, but to interrupt would be incredibly insensitive and in terms of securing that second chance, wholly counter-productive. You need to listen. Don't ever assume that you know something you've not been told first-hand. To make assumptions in this situation, and to get those wrong, is unforgivable and can lead to some very unhappy scenes.

If you ascertain that they want to speak on camera or that they don't mind being recorded for radio, arrange a time as soon as possible for you to meet. It's crucial that you follow up this first contact quickly so that you don't end up being the fifth camera crew in line treading a path to the door hoping for some emotional outpouring. If this does happen, you need to reassess the situation whilst you are at the location and make a decision about whether or not you can intrude, and how best to approach the relative. In all of these situations you must not lose sight of what has happened to the person you're interviewing. Although you're doing a job, don't ever forget that you're human and that this is a terrible experience for the person into whose private grief you've been invited.

If you get to the location without having spoken to any family members on the phone beforehand, you must use exactly the same considered approach. If you're doing a radio or television interview, approach the family alone, leaving your camera man or any radio recording equipment in the car. You need to show that you can engage with the situation, and establish some kind of rapport and trust, before you even think about asking for an interview. Turn off your mobile phone. This should be the case when you're doing all interviews, but in this situation it's imperative that you don't have anything interrupting the delicate mood of the situation.

As soon as you are inside the house, start to ask the interviewee about the life of the person who has died. This provides an opportunity for the family to remember their loved one, and to celebrate his/her life. Be a part of this. You need to listen to everything that is being said. But this is also your opportunity to make mental notes of the layout of the house and where it would be best to conduct the interview. Do not show that you're doing this. Your first priority is to listen and engage in the conversation. It's also an opportunity for you to identify what might make a good clip for your interview and to remember how to get back to that when the interview is being conducted.

When it is appropriate, excuse yourself and go and get either your recording equipment or your camera operator. You need to make it clear that this is what you're doing, as introducing a third person into the situation may destabilise the trust that you've built up so far. Once you're out of ear shot, this is also the time when you can quickly brief your camera operator as to the layout of the house, the lighting conditions and whether or not it would be better to come outside to conduct the interview. If the situation is extremely volatile, I would suggest that you use a minimum of equipment and even do the interview hand held – without a tripod. The worst thing you can do is keep a distressed person waiting while you and the camera operator sort out technical problems.

Make sure your camera operator knows the names of everyone involved and allow time for her/him to also express their sympathies with the bereaved. Don't ever lose sight of the fact that you are all people, and this situation is real and shocking. You may be doing a job, but people's feelings must be respected first and foremost. If your camera operator merely comes in, sets up the equipment and waits for a sign from you to start recording, he/she will come across as terribly insensitive and this may shatter the fragile trust that you've been so carefully building up.

Before you start the interview, make sure you ask your interviewee if they're comfortable with the recording. It may seem obvious as they've already agreed to do an interview, but it is often the case that when they see the recording equipment, especially a camera, the enormity of the situation becomes clear, and they realise for the first time what they've agreed to do.

There are no hard-and-fast rules as to how to conduct an emotional interview. All I would advise is to go slowly, and not to try to make a distressing situation more so. Ask questions about the dead person's life: what did they enjoy doing?

What were they like? What made them special? This is the opportunity to paint a picture of a loved one, and to remember a life, not just mourn the loss of it. The answers may be longer than you want, or more ponderous. I would advise you not to ask people in this situation to repeat themselves, or to be more succinct as you might in other interviews. You can allow emotional interviews more breathing space, and if the answers are longer, it shouldn't matter. Make sure you remember what the relative is saying. If they mention that their son or daughter enjoyed horse riding, make a mental note of this during the interview.

After you've finished recording, you should ask whether they could show you some pictures of the victim doing the things they've talked about in the interview. You can either film the pictures while you're there, which is the best thing to do, or ask if you can borrow the pictures. In the latter case, you must make sure they are returned promptly and in the same condition as you borrowed them. Also, remember to write a note of thanks and sympathy to accompany them. Remember to be brief when you film your set-up shots and your cutaways. You need to judge the situation carefully. How far can you direct the interviewee and will they understand what you're asking them to do?

There are some producers who always want to see the tears and the obvious signs of distress in an emotional interview. I would urge you to be cautious here and to exercise your own judgement. How far do you intrude into someone's grief? How will that person feel when they see the interview later? Will you make the situation more painful for them? You must make sure that even though they're telling you how distressed they feel, that they retain their dignity. That becomes your responsibility. If someone breaks down, or shows obvious signs of distress, stop the interview. Show them you're empathetic and can exercise control. If your producer doesn't get the tears he or she expected, so be it. At the end of the day, they'll never know. But you will. You'll know you didn't deliberately cause a grieving person even more distress, or make a spectacle out of them for the sake of your film. And that's a far better prize than anything else.

DEATH AS A RESULT OF CRIMINAL BEHAVIOUR

If the death has occurred as a result of a crime, then you're on to a good news story. However you mustn't forget all of the issues outlined above. People who've lost loved ones as a result of crime are often much more distressed and they may experience heightened emotions of guilt or shame or anger, all of which they may want to express. The situation is highly volatile and you must approach it with extreme caution.

Remember that there are legal issues to think about. You may be sent out to a crime scene immediately and do your interviews with the bereaved family as soon as you arrive. But by the time you get back, the police may have arrested someone, and by the time your edited piece is broadcast, that person may well have been charged. Now the case is 'active' and reporting restrictions apply. You must make sure that any interview clips you use don't break those restrictions (see Chapters 7 and 8).

The family or relatives of the victim may well not want to talk to you if the crime has just happened or if they're too shocked by it. Do not pressurise them. You can, however, approach neighbours to ask for information, or to get their reaction to the news. But remember that they could have witnessed the crime and may be used by the police at a later stage, so care should be taken when you use their clips that what they say will not break any reporting restrictions by prejudicing a future trial. It's also important to bear in mind that it is insensitive and could be inflammatory to approach neighbours in full view of the family. Make sure you choose a house that isn't in sight of their own, and use your own judgement at all times. If the situation is becoming more volatile by you being there, withdraw and wait until things settle down. You need to make sure that you keep your producer fully informed of your movements, and of your reading of the scene.

INTERVIEWING THE ELDERLY

The most common mistake to make when talking to and interviewing the elderly is to assume that the person you're talking to is not as intelligent, or 'switched on', or as capable as yourself. It is excruciating to see some interviews conducted with older people where the interviewer treats the person as though they have only just learned to speak and insists on addressing them in a kind of over-sweet baby talk. Elderly people are often brighter, wiser and certainly more experienced than you – so never speak down to them.

You do need to take time though when interviewing the elderly. They may need to be coaxed into appearing on television, as they're unlikely to be as media aware as younger people. They may feel shy or embarrassed. You need to make sure they're not overwhelmed by the recording equipment. It might be a good idea for your camera operator to show them the camera, or if you're doing the interview yourself, let them handle the camera and tell them exactly what you're doing, as you do it. If you let them into the situation without being patronising, you'll soon build up a rapport that will make the interview go more smoothly.

As in any interview with people who may feel vulnerable, you need to build up trust. This means carefully phrasing your questions and not rushing your interviewee. Always chat with them beforehand and ask them what they'd like to talk about. Even if this isn't the clip you'll use, let them feel they have some control over the process and they're not just being directed by you. You could also find that they tell you something unexpected which makes the story a stronger one. This is why it's always important to listen hard to your interviewees. Although you need to come prepared to an interview, always remain flexible and be prepared to hear something unexpected that could alter the entire situation. Again it's about listening, and reacting to what you hear. When you conduct the interview, take your time. If you need to stop and start again to remind them to look at you and not at the camera, or while they're collecting a thought process, do so patiently. Never sound frustrated or impatient and allow them as much time as they need to tell their story. It's often a good idea to try to build in more time to conduct these interviews and to remind your producer that it may take longer than an ordinary news interview.

INTERVIEWING CHILDREN

Many of the same rules apply here, but there are also legal requirements that you need to take into consideration. You need to get parental permission to conduct an interview with anyone under the age of 16, and it's best to get this in writing. If you're doing interviews or filming at a school, permission must be sought from the headteacher, or in the absence of the head, from the classroom teacher. Again, it's a good idea to get this in a written form.

The best thing to do when interviewing children is to get down to their level, both metaphorically and literally. Sit on a chair, or kneel down so that you can talk to them face to face. The camera operator should do the same. You don't want to end up with an interview where the child is gazing up into the sky at you. By getting down to their level, you're also making it easier for the child to start to trust you, and this will encourage them to talk more openly.

Children will very often not talk in complete sentences, but will answer with one or two words. In this case do make sure that your questions are also recorded and are not 'off mike' (see Chapter 5) so that the clip will make sense. Another way round this is to interview more than one child and to edit the responses together as a vox pop, where it doesn't matter so much that the answers are not complete.

LIVE INTERVIEWS

The appeal of the live interview is the same as the appeal of motor racing, the viewer is hoping for a crash. A crucial element is suspense, or jeopardy.

Rob Pittam[6]
reporter
Working Lunch

The live interview serves a number of purposes. For a news programme, it brings a sense of immediacy. It also means the reporter can respond to events as they happen, and for breaking news the recorded interview may well be out of date by the time the programme is on air. The live interview adds an element of tension; for whereas the viewer knows a recorded interview has been edited and checked, with a live one almost anything could happen. It also means that once you go on air, you have the freedom to ask your interviewee almost anything you like, even other areas that they might have initially said they didn't want to discuss. In practical terms, a live interview can be used by a producer to keep the programme on time, by reducing or increasing the length of time made available to the live element. This means that the reporter has to be able to think quickly, and adapt to rapidly changing decisions.

Live interviewing is not easy. As the quote above suggests, there are many opportunities for the whole thing to fall apart, either as a result of technical problems, unpredictable interviewees, or just the inability to foresee what problems may arise. There are also many elements that are out of your control, from changes in the weather to the behavioural quirks of the technical team. But there are certain things you can do to make sure that you're as prepared as possible (see Chapter 5).

In a pre-recorded: or 'as-live' interview, there is much more time spent on the technical aspects: getting the shot nicely framed and making sure the sound is clear. These things can very easily be sacrificed for the sake of getting the live element. This puts more pressure on the reporter to hold the viewer's attention, and to guide the viewer through the interview.

The difficulties with live reporting are both technical and journalistic. Unlike the conventional radio or television interview, you are not just reliant on yourself or one other person. Here you're relying on every piece of equipment you're using, the most important of which is 'coms' – your talk-back to the studio. This can cut out halfway through an interview and leave you high and dry. If this happens, it's not advisable to try to bluff your way out of it by guessing what the studio might be asking. You need to touch your ear and actually say that you can't hear the question. This allows the producer to make the decision about whether or not to continue with the interview. In a live interview, it's difficult to concentrate on what the interviewee is saying as well as trying to listen to the studio or mentally preparing your hand back. Usually you are freewheeling without any notes, so you can forget important facts, figures or questions. As Rob Pittam comments:

> Every single live has the potential to go horribly wrong, so never relax too much, but always remember that your audience out there is praying for you to cock up, so if you do end up looking stupid you can relax in the knowledge that you're giving them what they want.

TELEPHONE INTERVIEWS

These are never ideal, but sometimes they may be necessary. They're usually used for both radio and television in one of two ways. They're either used for interviewing abroad, or for interviewing from the scene of a disaster when there is no other form of recording equipment available. In this case, they're usually conducted with those who are first at the scene and they do add immediacy to the story.

As with any interview, your first impression with an interviewee is usually by phone, so it's worth practising your telephone manner. As stressed earlier, you need to be clear-spoken and polite at all times. You also need to ascertain fairly quickly that it is a convenient time to talk to someone. Make sure you give your name and the organisation you're working for as early as possible so that the person is aware that it is a media enquiry.

When talking to someone on the phone, we all tend to make reassuring listening noises throughout the conversation, such as 'Uh uh' or 'Umm', so as to reassure the other person that we're still there. You will need to point out to your interviewee that once you start to record the interview, you will be quiet so as to hear what they have to say without interruptions. This way, when they no longer hear these noises from you, they'll still know that you're there.

BI-MEDIA CONSIDERATIONS

There are some interviews broadcast on both radio and television that have been conducted by one reporter. In most organisations this will involve a television reporter covering the story for both media. If you're asked to do this, there are certain implications that this throws up, and it's a good idea to be aware of them.

There are two ways to conduct a bi-media interview. The first way is simple – you conduct one interview, but you record it on the camera as well as on to the tape. There are, however, disadvantages to this. The main one is that you will often have to provide different types of interview for the two media. As we've discussed earlier in the chapter, you may be asked to get a short clip for a television package, but need to record an as-live two-minute interview for radio. Therefore it's usually better to do separate interviews, the television one first.

This way you can get your interviewee to relax and get used to the interviewing process, while conducting what is the shorter interview. After they've had what is effectively a run-through, they should feel more confident and able to handle the longer radio interview without becoming tongue-tied or stumbling through their answers. This is an ideal situation, but often you won't have the time to do this, or your interviewee won't want to spend this amount of time just to fulfil your brief. If this is the case, you'll have to conduct the one interview for both. In this event, make sure your questions are fluent and recorded properly, so that the interview can be used in its entirety if needs be.

CONCLUSION

The main points to remember when conducting any interview are to treat your interviewees with respect and care, to modify your behaviour to suit whatever circumstance you find yourself in, and to make sure that you have a firm grasp on what the news story is, and what you want from your interviews. If you're unsure about the story, or do not know where your particular interviewee fits in with it, it will be very clear to them that you're not in control of the situation.

The secret to good interviewing is research. The better informed you are, the more successful and worthwhile your interview will be. But be flexible. Be prepared to listen to the people you're talking to and adaptable enough to change a line of questioning, or even redo an interview, if the story starts to develop in another direction. Remember that you are in control of the interview process, and as long as you explain that process to your interviewee, they will be as eager as you are for the interview to be a success.

If you find that you are in a volatile or possibly confrontational situation with an interviewee, the best thing to do is to remain calm and not allow yourself to become emotionally involved with the situation. Remember that your job is to extract information from people, not to share any views or have a particular judgement of the story. If an interviewee looks as if they may become aggressive or even violent towards you, stop your interview and try to distance yourself from the situation, without passing any comment on their behaviour.

Interviewing is a talent that needs hard work, practice and experience. The best thing that you can do at this early stage in your career is to make sure that your research is as good as it can be, that you have sound grasp of the story you're covering, and that you treat the people you interview politely and fairly so that they feel they have not been compromised by the process, and you feel that you've got the information you need. A successful interview, whether it be a chat in a local pub or a hard-hitting political grilling, is one in which both parties feel they've been involved in a process that has enabled the right information to be communicated whilst not compromising any individual's personal position.

NOTES

1 All quotes from Mike Blair taken from author interview, September 2003.
2 All quotes from Chris Mills taken from author interview, September 2003.
3 All quotes from Geoff Byrne taken from author interview, September 2003.
4 All quotes from Mike Young taken from author interview, February 2004.
5 All quotes from Tim John taken from author interview, January 2005.
6 All quotes from Rob Pittam taken from author interview, September 2003.

BROADCAST SKILLS

Behind every news package broadcast on radio or television is a range of technical skills that the broadcast journalist needs to master. These include being able to record interviews, write and record links between interviews, add music and sound effects for radio, and edit the whole piece together. Technological advances have gone a long way to speed up and simplify these skills, but they have also increased the pressure on broadcast journalists to produce more than a simple package on a story for a news magazine programme. More often than not, radio and television journalists are expected to produce various versions of the same story in different formats to feed the different needs of radio and television stations throughout the day.

It is no good being the best interviewer or researcher in the world, and pulling off the most exclusive interview for the programme, if you don't know how to record the interview properly for radio, or how to film it correctly for TV. In this chapter the basic skills needed to be able to present material for broadcast on radio and television are outlined.

RADIO SKILLS

There are a number of skills needed to be a radio journalist. I think the most important skill in the world of radio – certainly commercial radio – is the ability to juggle many balls at the same time. You might be on-desk reading bulletins while putting together the evening programme, or recording pieces while editing a package. Having a hands-on approach is very much needed because of the commercial pressures and smaller news teams these days. The ability to change your plans at the last minute is imperative. Breaking news waits for no man and you will often have to include a story at the very

(Continued)

last minute to be ahead of the game. You may also have to drop or amend stories while you are live on air.

The ability to ad-lib from bullet points or brief notes is a skill that every broadcast journalist should have. I think persistence is a key quality, because you'll often have an idea of who you want to interview regarding a story, but they are subsequently not available, cancel at the last minute, or don't come back to you. I think a good radio journalist should be diplomatic, persuasive, an excellent listener and certainly a team player.

Ryan Martinez[1]
news editor
106 Century FM

As Ryan Martinez outlines above, radio journalism is hard work because, in effect, you are working to a deadline every hour. On any story covered by a radio reporter, the priority is to feed the next bulletin with up-to-date information, and if possible audio, while working towards creating a package that illustrates the whole story. A deadline every hour places reporters under a lot of pressure, but it is important not to cut corners in preparing to go out on a story because you could end up with poorly recorded audio, or at worst, no audio at all.

The first duty of a reporter is to check the facts of any story, then write a copy line based on those facts for the next bulletin. That done, the reporter needs to check with the news editor about what is required for future bulletins. On a breaking news story, for example, the news editor might want the reporter to get to the scene, assess the situation, then do a live voice piece, or a two-way, into the bulletin either from the radio car, or down the phone. On less urgent stories, the news editor might want a voice piece recorded, or at least written, before the reporter goes out on interviews, then an audio clip for use in bulletins until the package can be aired in the news magazine programme. It is important to know before you leave base exactly what is required by the news desk so that you can prioritise what you do.

Before leaving base to go on an interview, you need to check your equipment. Make sure recorders are fully charged, and if you think you might have several interviews to do, or you are planning to do a long interview, take some spare batteries as a safeguard. Next check the microphone and lead to make sure they're working. Most microphones are fitted with a foam 'sock' to cut out the noise of the wind in outdoor interviews. Even on a wind-free day the slightest breeze can sound like a gale if it's picked up by the mike, so it's advisable to make sure the microphone always has a sock on it. Socks are also useful for indoor interviews because they cut down the chances of 'popping' noises that can be picked up from interviewees, although, as we discuss later, the best way to avoid this is to make sure the mike is positioned properly.

Most places outside the studio are less than perfect for recording interviews. Wherever your interview takes place, you need to assess the situation and make sure you work around anything that might cause distortion on the recording. Modern offices, for example, tend to be full of computers and other electrical equipment that will cause a 'buzz' on the recording, although it will be barely audible to those in the office. If the computers can't be turned off while you conduct the interview, make sure you record well away from the source of the sound. Similarly, be aware of air conditioning vents, and record well away from them, and ask for telephones to be unplugged while you conduct the interview.

At the other extreme, large empty rooms – for example, a gymnasium or a warehouse – can cause problems because the sound bounces off the walls. While this can be quite atmospheric at times, it can also result in the final product sounding very hollow, as if it had been recorded in a cave, which might not be appropriate. To minimise the effect of a large open space, try to conduct the interview in the corner of the room, and position yourself and the interviewee in a 'V' shape to trap the sound as much as possible. If you are sitting down for the interview, make sure you position yourself at about 45 degrees to the interviewee, and sit as close as possible to each other, so that your bodies act as a shield for the sound.

> I've seen a reporter place a guest right by a kerb ensuring great levels of car noise only to nearly lose him as a bus passed by just inches away.
>
> Mike Young[2]
> broadcast journalist
> BBC Radio Nottingham

Particularly for outdoor interviews, it's vital to check that the location you select for the interview is safe for both you and the interviewee. As Mike Young comments above, getting traffic noise behind an interview on inner-city congestion gives the piece great atmosphere, but that should be secondary to the safety of the interviewee. It's also useful to assess weather conditions for outdoor interviews. High winds cause problems for recording, and most people don't want to stand in pouring rain to be interviewed, so be aware of the conditions and try to have a back-up location in mind.

In any event, wherever you do the interview, you need to think carefully about how you position yourself and the interviewee. Inevitably you will be much closer to the interviewee than you would normally be if you were simply having a conversation with them. This can be quite intimidating for the person you are talking to, who may feel their space is being invaded. It's worth putting them at ease by explaining that you need to be close to get a good recording. If you are standing to do the interview, position yourself to one side of the interviewee, so that you are close but not threatening. Standing directly in front of someone tends to make them step back, and you can end up literally backing someone into a corner while you are recording. If you're sitting down for the interview, arrange the chairs in an 'L' shape, so that you are side by side. Never interview anyone across a desk. Even the smallest desk will mean that the microphone is not close enough to get a crisp recording, and even if you manage to position it for the interviewee, your questions will be off-mike. There is also the danger that in trying to hold this awkward pose, or to get your voice on-mike, you will end up moving the mike and getting mike rattle on the interview.

Modern microphones are reasonably robust, but they are sensitive to movement, especially where the lead goes into the microphone and where it connects to the recorder. To avoid mike rattle, make sure that the lead into the recorder is not being pulled, and loosely wrap the other end of the lead around your hand so that where it connects to the microphone it will not be knocked. Spend a few moments making sure that you are comfortable in the position you take for the interview, then hold that position throughout.

The next stage is to take level for the interview. Although it is possible to manipulate sound after recording, interviews recorded at too low level that have to be boosted will end up with a lot of hiss on them, which is distracting, while those that are too high level will distort and be untransmissible. The aim is to have a crisp and clear recording, so it's worth spending a few moments chatting to the interviewee with the recorder on 'pause', to make sure you're getting balanced sound.

The microphone should be about a hand-span away from the interviewee's mouth, slightly below their chin. If you have positioned yourself properly, this will not be intrusive to the person being interviewed, or uncomfortable for you. Although the exact position will vary from one person to another, the microphone should be about the same distance between the person being interviewed and the interviewer, so that all that is required for questions to be on-mike is a slight tilt of the microphone. If the interviewee has either a loud or a quiet voice you'll need to make adjustments so that your voices are balanced. It's a good idea to start the recording by the interviewee giving their name and position. This not only helps you to identify the recording afterwards, but it can also be used later for them to introduce themselves within an edited package. Positioning the microphone properly should also avoid 'popping' on the interview. The microphone should never be positioned directly in front of the interviewee's mouth in the position usually adopted by singers. In that position it will pick up the hard 'p' and 'b' sounds in words and cause them to pop. Instead make sure the microphone is below chin level so that the interviewee is talking across the top of it.

Most recorders allow you to either set the levels manually or use automatic level control. While it may seem easier to use automatic level control, this needs to be used sparingly and only in certain conditions. Automatic level control works by keeping the signal below distortion point, and boosting it when it falls too low. The problem is that to keep the signal even, the automatic control boosts any background noise to keep the signal at the same level as speech and this causes a 'surging' effect on the finished recording. Manual level setting produces a better-quality recording and gives you more control. For example, if you are doing a report on traffic congestion, you might want to interview an official at the side of a busy road to give the piece a sense of location and atmosphere. With the recorder on manual, you can set your levels so that the traffic noise is registering at a low level, then move the microphone close to the interviewee until their voice registers at the correct level. This will give you a recording that has traffic in the background, but your interviewee will be heard quite clearly. If the interview were conducted on automatic, the result would be that the traffic noise was boosted every time there was a pause in the speech, which would not only sound unnatural, but might also lead to parts of the interview being lost by the background noise. Generally, automatic control should only be used in near perfect recording conditions.

Every location has a unique background ambience created by its environment. For example, a swimming pool will sound echoey and hollow, while a furnished room will have a more muted background sound. Where the background noise is noticeable – inside a pub, at the scene of a fire, a school playground, and so on – it's advisable to record a few minutes of the environment on its own to be used in editing. For example, in doing a package about a school breakfast club being started at an inner-city school, you might want to record the noise of children having breakfast, with the sound of cutlery on plates and the general hubbub of children talking and moving around. This could then be used at the start of a package to provide atmosphere and set the scene of the story, then faded under links recorded in the studio to maintain aural interest and bring the package to life.

> In addition to the usual journalistic skills required for any media, radio journalists need to know how to distinguish between what makes compelling, compulsive listening and what is run-of-the-mill, ordinary or mundane radio listening. In other words, how can they make their story into a 'must listen' piece of radio journalism.
>
> Phil Dixon[3]
> managing director
> Saga 106.6FM

LIVE REPORTS FOR RADIO

Increasingly, radio journalists are required to deliver live reports from the scene of a story. In part this is because ISDN lines are now routinely installed in key locations like shopping centres, council buildings and football grounds so that broadcast-quality audio is available easily, and also because the quality of telephone lines has improved. But live reports also stress one of radio's strengths – its immediacy. A live report from the scene of any story can bring a bulletin to life by emphasising that this is happening *now*.

For most on-the-hour bulletins, radio reporters covering a breaking story would be expected to do a voice piece. This is a 'cue', or introduction to the story, that is read by the news reader, who then links to the reporter by saying something like 'Our reporter at the scene, Jan Smith, has more details …' The reporter would then give the latest developments of the story in about 25 seconds. In reality, many live reports are pre-recorded a few minutes before the bulletin and played out 'as-live' so that bulletin timings can be accurate, and to avoid any technical glitches happening on air. But whether it is pre-recorded or live into the bulletin, the reporter has to be able to deliver the story in one take and make it sound professional.

As with all stories, the secret is to prepare. If you know you're expected to do a voice piece from the scene into the next bulletin, then you need to gather as much information as quickly as possible as soon as you get to the story. The next priority is to send a cue back to the studio that has the latest development in the top line. After that you need to spend a few minutes writing your script, making sure you tell the story in a logical manner, but also that you describe the scene in front of you. You are the eyes of your listeners – tell them what you see. You also need to think about where to position yourself to send the report. If the story you're covering is a demonstration, you'll want to have the noise of the demonstrators in the background, loud enough for listeners to hear, but not so loud that it drowns out your report. Standing next to someone blowing a hunting horn while you do your report is not a good idea for obvious reasons, but neither is standing inside a building overlooking the demo because none of the atmosphere will be conveyed.

Usually the station will contact you a few minutes before the bulletin to make sure that you are ready and take level from you. By then you should have your script ready, and be able to give its duration. If it is pre-recorded, the normal procedure is to count in – 'three, two, one …' – to make it easy for those at the other end to get a clear start to your report. If the voice piece is live, the bulletin will be fed through your telephone, or headphones where you are reporting from an ISDN line or radio car, and you take your cue from the newsreader introducing you. Most live reports end with an SOC (standard out cue) that gives the name of the reporter and the location, often with a station name check as well: 'This is Jan Smith, reporting for Metro News, live from Newcastle Quayside'.

Voice pieces are usually always scripted, even when they are live. They need to tell the story clearly and concisely, avoiding repetition, and to a set duration. The best way to achieve this is to read from a script. The same is not true for the other form of live reporting used more often into news magazine pro-grammes, or longer bulletins – the reporter two-way. This is when the reporter on the scene is interviewed by the news presenter in the studio. A good two-way should sound like an informed conversation between the reporter and presenter. It's much less formal than a voice piece because it's a dialogue, so it needs to sound spontaneous.

As with the voice piece, the reporter needs to consider the location for doing the two-way, and send a cue over to the studio as early as possible. The reporter also needs to consider what questions the presenter should ask so that the story can be told in an interesting but logical fashion. Scripted two-ways are rarely as effective as those done with the reporter responding spontaneously. The secret is to make a note of key facts that you need to include in your report, then treat the two-way as a conversation. Before going live, talk to the presenter and outline what questions should be asked. The standard format is for the story to be told in three questions. For example, in covering a pro-hunting demonstration, the presenter might start by asking what is happening now, then move on to ask if there has been any trouble, and round off by asking if the demonstration has achieved its aims. This would allow the reporter to describe the scene and how many people were there, give some background to the story, and end the report by giving the views of the demonstration organisers and the police controlling the event. That way the two-way tells the story logically, with each question developing it by providing more information.

Ideally, the presenter should do more than ask stark questions. For example, the opening question might be something like: 'It sounds quite noisy there – so what's going on?' This sounds more conversational and draws the listener in. The reporter also has to be careful not to pack too much into each response: the story needs to unfold over the three questions without information being repeated, so do not be tempted to tell the whole story in the first response. You should also try to make each response about the same duration so that the two-way sounds balanced and flows well.

A variation on this sort of report is an illustrated two-way. This is where the presenter interviews the reporter at the scene who gives a first response, then links into either a live interview, or a pre-recorded audio clip, before rounding the report off with a final response from the reporter. Where the two-way is illustrated with pre-recorded audio – for example, a vox pop of the demonstrators – this will have been sent down the line earlier and will be played out from the studio. In this event it is important that the reporter tells the studio when and how the audio should be played into the report. This is also important when the two-way is to be illustrated with a live interview, but on top of that it's vital to fully brief the interviewee so that they know what to expect. Normally, the interviewee will be on hand before the start of two-way so that the studio can take their level. The reporter must then make sure that the positions used in taking level are kept until the end of the piece. Live interviews can involve the interviewee hanging around for quite a long time before they are 'on', so it's important that you explain the whole procedure in advance to reassure the interviewee and keep them as relaxed as possible. You also need to explain that even after the interview is over, you may still be live, and they should not say anything until the report is completely over and you are no longer linked to the studio.

Live reporting can be nerve-racking but it's radio at its best, bringing events as they are happening to the audience. Where once going live into the news was reserved for big stories, technological advances now mean live reports, or at the very least 'as-live' reports, are a standard part of radio news, and a skill that radio journalists need to develop. For all the stress they can cause, live reports are also the most exhilarating part of a radio journalist's job. The key is to know the story – and trust your ability to tell it.

VOX POPS FOR RADIO

A vox pop is a series of edited responses to a question. They are used on their own or as part of a package to give a flavour of public opinion on a particular issue, whether it is light-hearted or serious. The most important part of a vox pop is the part that is never heard by listeners – the question. This needs to be reasonably direct and straightforward so that the people being questioned will have an instant response. It's also important to frame your question so that it can't be answered with a simple yes or no. The question needs to be open, so that instead of asking 'Do you think hunting should be banned?' you might ask 'How do you feel about hunting?' which allows for a better answer. Once you have decided on the question, you should not change it halfway through doing the vox pop or you will misrepresent the respondents when you edit it all together.

A vox pop is not a survey but in most cases you need to try to get a variety of voices covering both men and women, different ages, and different ethnic backgrounds. The exception is when you are asking a particular question of a particular group. For example, if you wanted to ask schoolchildren whether or not AS levels should be scrapped, you would only vox pop school-age children. In any event, the finished vox pop should feature between three and seven voices edited together. As with all audio, you need to start with the best response to your question, and end with the second best one. Any responses that are poorly recorded, or difficult to understand, should not be used, no matter how witty or pertinent they are. The responses should all be around the same duration so that the vox pop sounds balanced and is not dominated by one voice. In most cases the responses will be between three and seven seconds long. It is also important to make sure that the background noise is the same behind all your respondents. It sounds very odd to have three responses recorded in the street alongside one that was recorded in a quiet room.

Although it might seem to be a good idea to approach a group of people when you are doing a vox pop, you need to make sure that only one person talks at a time. People talking over each other sounds confusing and will not come across as well as one voice after another. The idea is to have a series of clear, short responses that will engage the listener whether they are played out on their own in a bulletin, or as part of a news package. The key is a well-formed question and skilful editing.

AUDIO EDITING

Digital audio editing is now standard in radio newsrooms across the country, although several different systems are used. Nonetheless, all digital editing systems work on the same principles: the audio is transferred to a computer screen and appears as a 'waveform', which can then be manipulated in a variety of ways. Digital audio editing is often compared to word processing because it uses the same cut and paste principles. The main advantage that digital editing has over analogue editing is that no matter how often you manipulate the original recording, the sound quality does not diminish. It is also much faster to edit digitally, and any mistakes can be rectified at the touch of a button.

Most systems used in newsrooms, like Adobe Auditions and DAVE in commercial radio, and Radioman at the BBC, have at least two sound channels; usually they have four. This allows reporters to add sound effects or music to packages, by recording them on different channels and mixing them together at the appropriate levels. It is possible to do this on a single channel, but it's much easier if each sound source has a separate channel that can be individually adjusted before being brought together in the final item.

With so many different digital editing systems in operation, it would be difficult to give a detailed account of editing a package here. The best advice is to get to know whatever digital editing system is available, so that the general principles can be transferred to any system. One of the pitfalls of digital editing is the tendency for reporters to look at the waveform, rather than to listen to how it sounds. This can mean that every gap in the waveform is edited out, and the result sounds very unnatural and stilted because there are no pauses or breaths. Another drawback is that because it is so easy to put music behind a package, every package ends up with bland music behind it which does nothing to enhance the piece. When using music in a package, try to make it relevant, and do not overuse it. Also try to avoid using music that has lyrics behind interviews, because this can distract from what is being said. Sometimes what is being said is strong enough to stand on its own. Being able to manipulate sound makes editing much easier, but it is not a substitute for having a poorly recorded interview in the first place. Recording audio at the correct level in the first place not only saves time in editing, it also provides much crisper audio.

Once a reporter has all the interviews and actuality they need to make a package, they need to get back to base as soon as possible. On the way back it is a good idea to listen back to the interviews and work out what parts you will use, and roughly in what order. Back at base the reporter will usually be asked to provide a cue and clip for the next bulletin. The cue will explain the story and set it up for listeners, and the clip, or sound-bite, should then illustrate the story.

The cue for a news package will normally always be shorter than the cue for a news clip because the package tells the whole story, while the clip is just one aspect of that story and the rest needs to be provided in the cue. Nonetheless, the cue for a package is important: it is the cue that tempts listeners to listen to the package, and a boring cue will put listeners off. The cue should be written before you start editing. It provides the angle of the story and so directs the way the package should be edited.

Once the clips for the package have been selected, the reporter then needs to write a script that will link them together. The best news packages allow the listener to understand the story through effective clips, and also to have some sense of experiencing the event through actuality taken at the scene. On the pro-hunt demonstration, for example, the package might start with the sound of the demonstrators for a few seconds, before it is faded under the reporter explaining what was happening and linking into the first interview clip. Having the sound of the demonstration brings the package alive, and allows listeners to 'picture' the scene, but it is important to fade it down under any voices so that they can be clearly heard and are not drowned out by the actuality. Links need to be direct and concise: the story should be told by those taking part in it, not the reporter, so get to the clips as quickly as possible and keep the reporter's voice to a minimum.

The package should start with your strongest audio to hook the audience into the story. This might not always be the most logical start to the story, but it will be the most effective. The second strongest clip should be used at the end of the package, so that the last thing the audience hears about the story is memorable. In between, the story is told using other clips linked by the reporter, with actuality, sound effects and music used to enliven and enhance the final piece.

What makes a good radio news programme is, in short, good team work and organisation. Whether it's locally or as part of a wider network, a programme takes a great deal of planning. If you're presenting or producing one, you rely on your colleagues to provide stimulating and emotive content to keep the listener hooked. If you're reporting, you'll need to be creative and organised enough to deliver what the programme requires.

In many commercial stations the programme itself is ultimately the responsibility of one person, so you'll need to have a good technical knowledge plus the ability to know what to do (and say) if something goes wrong. Communication with newsroom colleagues is also essential – because the very nature of news means that things are constantly changing, stories develop, running orders change while on air and programme items like packages are often late. On air – the programme needs to be compelling and immediate, giving just the right amount of time to each story. It also needs to have 'pace' as well as allowing enough time for the programme to 'breathe' 'If you spend too much time on one issue, the listener will get bored and turn off. Similarly, not giving a story enough coverage could mean listeners going elsewhere to get their information.

(Continued)

(Continued)

Personally I believe that a programme should sound like a programme – not just an extended news bulletin. A producer/presenter/reporter should think about the options open to them. Does a package require music? Should it be presented from location? Should it be done live/as live? Is a report appropriate or should we use a guest or reporter two-way instead? These sound like major decisions – and indeed they are – but when producing/presenting, you usually know the answer before you've entered the story into the running order!

Tim John[4]
newsreader/reporter
106 Century FM

TELEVISION SKILLS

A TV journalist needs the same skills as those in radio and newspapers – a good eye for a story, a concise writing style, and the ability to meet the pressure of deadlines. In addition it's important to be able to use pictures to best advantage. Often the pictures will dictate how the story is written and produced. For example, a television news item will usually begin with the most exciting visual images rather than simply following the chronological sequence of events. This can sometimes be a tricky technique but it's vital to master.

Nick Kehoe[5]
journalist
Central News East

Television is all about moving pictures. The viewer has to be engaged visually right from the start of a news package, with action shots and case studies of people. Too many clips of people being interviewed behind a desk or standing in the street will not do this. This means that reporters, either working as video journalists or with a camera crew, need to be constantly thinking, as far back as the planning process, about how to get interesting shots that will tell the story and engage the viewer. The art of shooting and editing a news package is too complex to go into detail here, but the following outlines the basic ingredients needed to make any package for television.

A package for television, as for radio, combines different elements to tell the whole story. The most important element in a television package is the pictures that tell the story. On the pro-hunt demonstration story, for example, it would be vital to have pictures of the demonstration, but you would also want to have interviews with key people, perhaps a vox pop with demonstrators or by-standers, and maybe even a 'piece to camera' (PTC), where the reporter addresses the audience directly from the scene. Other elements might include music, where it is appropriate, or graphics to help explain facts more easily. There are so many elements to a television package that it's important to have a clear idea of what you'll need before you go out to film, so that you have all the shots you will need to help in the editing process. It's no good waiting until you get back to base to find that you need a PTC or some cutaway shots to bridge between one interview and another. Thinking through the range of shots you'll need, and how they will fit together in the finished product will help clarify what needs to be done at the scene of the story. However, you also need to be open to change your plans if the story changes while you are at the scene, or if something unexpected happens.

Kehoe highlights the importance of filming skills for television journalists:

> Increasingly, TV journalists have to be able to use cameras and do their own editing. This will become even more commonplace in the future and give broadcast journalism students a considerable advantage over journalists of a similar age who've spent a year or two in newspapers.

Generally, you should always use a tripod to film. This gives steady and professional pictures. Although there is a trend towards 'Personal Digital Production' packages, where the whole package is personalised by the reporter/camera person using small hand-held cameras, traditional news packages still feature steady pictures. In any event, before you start filming at any scene, you must 'white balance' the camera to get the correct colour on your pictures. White balance is a function which gives the camera a reference to 'true white'. In effect you're telling the camera what the colour white looks like, so the camera will record it correctly. Since white light is the sum of all other colours, the camera will then display all colours correctly. If you fail to do this the pictures will appear blue. A white balance is done by focusing the camera on a white sheet, for example, the page of a notebook, and pressing the white balance control. You need to perform this procedure at the beginning of every shoot, and every time the lighting conditions change. They can change outside as often as the sun comes in and out. It is especially important to re-white balance when moving between indoors and outdoors, and between rooms lit by different kinds of lights.

CAMERA SHOTS

In order to keep your package visually interesting, it's important to use a range of different kinds of shots that show what is happening from different perspectives. The names of these shots can vary from one newsroom to another, but the following shots are all used in package making.

- **GV OR VLS.** The shot used to identify the location of the story and establish the scene is known as a General View (GV) or a Very Long Shot (VLS).

This, as its name suggests, is a panorama of the entire scene that allows the audience to establish the setting. In the demonstration story, for example, this would be a shot taken from a vantage point that showed the demonstrators making their way through the streets.

- A **'medium shot'** reveals more detail about the scene, perhaps showing a particular group as they march along.
- A **'pan'** is a shot taken from left to right, or from right to left. This sort of shot might be used to emphasise the number of people taking part in the demonstration, where the camera would pan down the length of the street as the demonstrators march by. Pans need to be used sparingly or they can make the viewer feel quite dizzy. They also need to start and end with a steady shot to make editing easier.
- A **'tilt'** moves the camera up and down. This might be used if you want to show a tall building but you can't get it all in your shot, you might start at the bottom of the building and go up to the top, or vice versa.
- A **'zoom in'** moves you closer to the subject. For example, in the demonstration you might want to draw attention to a particular demonstrator holding a placard, or wearing fancy dress.
- A **'zoom out'** or reverse zoom, moves you further away from the action. For example, you might choose to focus on a particular demonstrator before zooming out to show the whole scene. Like pans, zooms should be used sparingly – too many can leave the viewer feeling as if they've been on a fairground ride. Avoid using too many moving shots. They can be visually tiring. Instead intersperse them with static shots.
- A **'point of view shot'** shows the view from the subject's perspective, usually with the camera behind the person. This can be useful in editing if the interviewee is talking about the scene in front of them.
- A **'cutaway'** is a shot of something other than the current action, but of relevance to it. This could be general views of the demonstration to illustrate what an interviewee is talking about, or it could be a close-up of the interviewee wringing their hands while talking. Cutaways are used as a 'buffer' between shots, to help the editing process, to lengthen shots, and to cover joins in interviews.
- **LS and MS.** When it comes to interviewing people, different kinds of shots are used. A 'long shot' (LS) shows the whole person, from head to foot, in the frame, while a 'mid-shot' (MS) shows the person from the waist up.
- A **'close-up'** focuses on a particular image and can be quite striking. In interview terms, a close-up would show only the head, but it is also useful to use close-ups to enhance expression, mood or atmosphere. Close-ups of hands can demonstrate in very subtle fashions the moment of a caress with an open, gentle curving hand, or the passion of anger through an image of a clenched fist. 'Extreme close-ups' are used to focus in on particular details, for example the lapel badge being worn by an interviewee, or a particularly angry demonstrator whose shouting face could fill the whole screen to show the passion of the event.

Just by reading through the list of shots, you can begin to envisage how they can be put together to create a visually engaging package. A typical television package will cut from one shot to another as often as every five seconds, but in order to be able to edit properly, a much longer duration has to be shot. Each camera shot needs to have a 'roll-up' time before you start the shot. You point the camera at the action you want to film, let tape roll for three seconds, and then do your camera shot. After you've made the shot, leave the tape running for another three seconds before stopping. This way, you'll have a clear beginning and end to the shot, which is vital for the editing process. You need to do this at the beginning and the end of a piece to camera as well. Each shot can be anything between three and seven seconds long, depending on its type, and it's best not to keep the camera rolling while moving from one shot to another.

INTERVIEWING FOR TELEVISION

The location for a television interview is vitally important and should reflect the story, or the position of the interviewee. For example, an interview with the police officer in charge of controlling a demonstration would be better at the scene of the demonstration than in the police station away from the action. Wherever possible it's a good idea to get 'set-up shots' of the interviewee. These are pictures that can be used to introduce the interviewee before they start talking. A typical example is when politicians are interviewed. Often pictures of the politician leaving a building and walking out of shot are used to lead into the interview outside the same building. In the example of the demonstration, a typical set-up shot would be a medium shot of the organiser marching with other demonstrators to lead into an interview with the marchers going past behind. Set-up shots should feature the interviewee doing something – working on a computer, making a cup of tea, flicking through a photograph album. These pictures can then be used to cover the script you need to get to the interview.

Interviews for television are generally of a shorter duration than those for radio. It is better to have two clips of around 15–20 seconds each rather than one long one. It is also quite common for interviews to be 'overlaid' with pictures. For example, sometimes before an interviewee is seen in vision, we hear their voice over pictures that illustrate what they are talking about, or halfway through an interview shots that refer to what is being said are used under the voice of the interviewee.

Once you have established the location for the interview, you need to set up the camera so that the interviewee is in three-quarters profile, looking to one side and slightly towards the camera but not directly at it. Each interviewee you use in a package should be shot so that they face in different directions. The police officer, for example, might be shot looking to the left, while the demonstration organiser would be shot facing right. This alters the pattern of shots and provides some variety in the package.

While filming the interview, you also need to think about any cutaways you might need to cover edits. These might include close-ups of the interviewee's hands (but only if they are expressing something), or extreme close-ups of their lapel badge. Cutaways of the reporter are known as 'reverses', and typically they show the reporter listening to the interviewee and nodding. These 'noddies' are useful ways to edit an interview, but need to be used carefully or they could imply that the reporter agrees with whatever is being said.

Care also needs to be taken in positioning the camera to film reverses. If the interviewee is positioned looking towards the right, then the reporter needs to be shown looking to the left, as if at the interviewee, otherwise in the edited version it will appear that both the reporter and interviewee are talking to a third person and not to each other. This is known as 'crossing the line' and it applies to all filming, not just interviews. 'The line' is an imaginary boundary that separates two people, and if it is crossed, it's visually confusing because there is a sudden change of viewpoint. For example, in an interview at the demonstration, the camera person might set up with the marchers in the background. As long as that position is maintained, the camera can film the interviewee, then move to film the reporter doing noddies. But if the shot of the reporter were taken so that the marchers were behind the camera, it would look very odd because the change of viewpoint would break the illusion of a conversation between the interviewee and the reporter.

PIECES TO CAMERA

A piece to camera is where the reporter talks directly into the camera. They are used in different ways and to different effect. Sometimes a reporter will do a PTC because there are no pictures. This is most common when reporting a court case because cameras are not allowed into court. In that event, the reporter might stand outside the court to report the verdict before linking in to library shots of the defendant, or shots that show the location of the crime. PTCs are also used to explain facts in a direct and concise way. This can be most effective if the reporter is framed to one side of the shot, leaving the other side of the frame free to have a graphic that illustrates statistics. But most generally, PTCs are used to show the background action. For example, in the demonstration story it would be unthinkable to do a PTC that did not show the marchers in the background. In any event, a PTC should never be shot against an anonymous background, as this adds nothing to the story.

There are various ways to shoot a PTC. The most common is a 'stand-upper' where the reporter stands in a relevant location and makes the report. But it is also effective to have movement in a PTC. For example, walking alongside marchers at a demonstration, where the camera starts on the reporter as they are moving and stops as they come to an end. Similarly, the camera might start with a medium shot of the marchers, and pan to the reporter standing still, or else start with the reporter stationary, and pan to the action of the march.

In any event, you need to think about where you are going to use the piece to camera in advance. Sometimes it will be appropriate to use the PTC at the start of a report, for example in covering a court case. Other times it can be used as a bridge between two strands of a story. And it can also be used as an end to the package where the reporter can sum up the story and give a standard out-cue (SOC).

Generally, PTCs should be short, not only because they tend to slow the action in the package, but also because the reporter sometimes needs to memorise what they say and deliver it convincingly to the camera. The best advice is to keep PTCs short and simple. Rather than work from a script, it's best to work from an outline that includes any vital facts, but will allow you to deliver the information in different ways. Repeating the information in different ways, and using familiar language that will not trip you up, will help you to appear more relaxed and natural, and avoid the glazed look of someone desperately trying to remember a script. You need to converse with the viewer and engage them in what you're saying. Although PTCs should appear to be relaxed, it's important that they are rehearsed repeatedly until you are satisfied with the result. It is also a good idea to do more than one version – perhaps using different shots, or doing one with an SOC – to give you a choice when it comes to editing.

TELEVISION VOX POP

The approach to a television vox pop is similar to that of a radio one. You need to first of all establish a question that is open, and cannot be answered with one word, and that is clear, to avoid vague responses. When filming vox pops, you need to get the interviewees to look at you, not the camera. Also you need to change the side that you film from, so that in the edited version the first respondent is looking to the right, and the second to the left, and so on. You also need to take care in framing the respondents to make sure that the background is suitable, and they do not appear to have trees growing out of their head. Ideally you should try to get a good range of men and women of different ages and ethnic backgrounds.

GRAPHICS

Facts are the life-blood of journalism, but too many in a short space of time in a television package can be confusing for the viewer. This is where the use of a graphic comes in. A graphic is either a still or moving illustration of facts. These can range from a still of a map showing the location of a particular event, to a moving bar chart that shows which way people voted over the past three general elections and how this relates to the composition of the House of Commons. Computer technology means that creating effective graphics for television is relatively easy these days, and although graphics can slow the pace of a package by moving away from action shots, they are a valuable tool to help explain complex ideas or a series of important facts.

CAPTIONS

Captions are used in television to identify interviewees without the reporter having to do so in the script. Generally the information they contain should be as brief as possible – usually just the name of the person and a few words to explain their position, for example 'Peter Walker, March Organiser'. Most digital editing systems have a function that allows you to create captions, but you need to make sure that they can be easily read, and positioned so that they do not cover an important part of the picture. The caption for an interviewee should appear on screen as they start to talk, and be held for another five seconds before disappearing. This allows the viewer to take in the image of the interviewee, then read their name, before cutaways or overlays to other shots are edited into the interview.

TELEVISION LIVES

> Lives are becoming so commonplace now that it's unlikely that people will be able to work as television reporters in future unless they can do them.
>
> Nick Kehoe
> journalist
> Central News East

As the analysis of television news in Chapter 1 showed, and as Nick Kehoe, confirms in the quote above, there is an increasing tendency for live links into pre-recorded packages. As with PTCs, the best advice is to keep these links simple and short, but it is also a good idea to refer to the location as a way of explaining why the report is coming from that location, and also to draw attention to the fact that it is live. For example, a live link into a package about the pro-hunt demonstration might show the reporter standing where the march had been with the debris of placards and fliers lying around. The reporter might then say 'Here in Market Square the last of the demonstrators are making their way home and the clean up of the streets is just beginning. It looks quite peaceful now, but the scene was very different earlier on …' then go to the start of the pre-recorded package that shows the demonstration at its height.

Another live situation that is increasingly used is a reporter two-way. As with radio, this involves the reporter being questioned from the studio by the presenter. As with radio, the two-way should be relaxed and informative. Unless there are a lot of facts and figures involved, reporters should avoid using notes so that they come across as authoritative and in control. The exception to this is court reporting, where it is acceptable for the reporter to look down to check comments made in court. While having some notes can be comforting, there is always the temptation to continually refer to them rather than trust that you know the story, and this can break your concentration and cause you to stumble. The story needs to unfold in a natural way, with the first response providing the latest or most important information, followed by either background information, or more detail, before rounding off in the final response. The presenter and the reporter need to work together before going live to establish the general questions and make sure the story will come across clearly.

Generally the reporter will be framed in either a mid-shot or a close-up, and the framing of the reporter is particularly important when the two-way is illustrated with a live interview. For example, the report might begin with a close-up of the reporter for the first response, then the camera would pull back to reveal a two-shot of the reporter standing with the interviewee while the reporter introduces them and asks the first question. The camera could then move to a close-up of the interviewee, pulling back to a two-shot for the final question and response, and ending with a close-up of the reporter. This allows the pictures to focus on the main person at each stage of the report, and avoids having the interviewee standing in shot like a spare part as the reporter rounds up.

This might sound very complicated but the secret is to fully brief both the interviewee, and more importantly, the camera person. It is vital that the camera person knows at what point they should pull back or zoom in or the end result will be muddled visually. This means that the whole event has to be carefully choreographed, and wherever possible it should be rehearsed, at least once, before going live.

TELEVISION EDITING

Most television newsrooms now use non-linear digital editing, which makes the process of creating a package much simpler because it's possible to add or remove sections out of sequence. Although there are many different programmes for digital video editing, the process is similar in all of them. The first step is to load the footage onto the computer where it is digitised into a series of clips. The clips to be used are then selected, using a drag and drop technique, and entered into a 'timeline' that puts them together and builds them into a package. The technique is similar to that of digital audio editing, in that any mistakes can be instantly rectified because cuts are made to a copy of the digitised footage, not the original. An exhaustive account of the editing process is more suitable for a technical manual, but what follows is some general advice to bear in mind when creating packages.

Before you start to edit, you need to write a cue for the package. As with radio, the cue provides the direction of the package, and should hook the viewer into it. You need to write the cue before you begin editing so that the start of the package leads on from the cue and does not repeat what you might say in your first link. Having viewed your footage, it's a good idea to do a rough story board of the item as a guide for you to get from one strand of the story to another.

The package should start with your best pictures, and in most cases these will be action shots that will immediately engage the viewer. Starting a package with a shot of the outside of a building – unless it is in flames – is a complete turn off. As a general rule, you should establish the pictures for a second or two before bringing in your voice. This allows the viewer to take in the scene, and also means that if the top of the package is missed in play-out, the story will still be complete. The natural sound that goes with the shots should always be left in. Ambient sound adds atmosphere to the package. It should be lowered under any voice-over to help the package to sound more natural and cohesive, rather than muted. Even where music is used in a package, shots should not be muted, although the ambient sound might be barely audible.

Once you have established your opening and closing shots, tell the story as logically as possible. It is impossible to say how long every shot should be, and each one should be judged on its merit. How visually interesting is it? How much information does it contain? Interview clips should be broken up with cutaways to relevant pictures. It is at this stage that you find out whether or not you have a wide enough range of shots to link the various elements of the package together and keep the pictures moving.

Scripting a television package requires careful thought because you are writing to visual images and the viewer needs to be able to take in the pictures as well as understand what you are saying. Avoid being too literal – you do not need to describe what the viewer is seeing, they can see this for themselves.

The best writing enhances the images. It can do this by providing information that is not in the pictures. For example, over shots of a pro-hunt demonstration the reporter might say how many people were taking part, and where they had come from. Or the script can act as an audible pathway leading the viewer through the images. The words should be clear and simple, but they should always be related to the pictures in some way. It's no good rushing ahead of your pictures, or lagging behind so you need to pace the script to the images that you have on the screen.

Remember that pictures and words should always be partners, never rivals. Your script should be talking about either what is on the screen or what is about to come up on the screen. For instance the script should not be saying 'At this time Prime Minister Blair is addressing the Labour Party Conference' over shots of him leaving Number Ten to attend the conference. Sound and pictures must always work in harmony. Because the words need time to be understood, it is often necessary for them to slightly precede the pictures, which can be understood at once, if we know what we are supposed to see. When the visual interest of one picture has been exhausted, the viewer can then pay attention to words preparing the way to the next picture, but again try not to be too literal.

Particular care needs to be taken when you are scripting over graphics or maps. Whenever you have a graphic on the screen, the words must reiterate whatever words are shown on the screen. Remember that the viewer cannot take in too much – they cannot read the screen and listen to words separately, so you have to use the same words that are on the screen to avoid confusion.

It's a good idea to vary the way you link into interviewees. As with radio packages, the best way is to make a statement that is then illustrated, or expanded upon, by the interviewee. However, you need to be careful not to repeat what the interviewee says. Although that sounds like common sense, it is a common mistake for reporters to say 'the demonstrators say they'll not give up without a fight' followed by a clip from a demonstrator saying 'we won't give up without a fight'. Finally, wherever possible, watch the finished item through carefully to make sure it makes sense. In the intensity of creating a package it's very easy to get too close to a story and miss out a vital piece of information that because you know it, you assume everyone else does.

ONLINE SKILLS

Online journalists need to have the skills of a print journalist and master complicated software programs. In many, but not all, cases an online journalist will not gather the material themselves, but work from material provided by radio and television journalists. That said, they are also expected to initiate their own stories, and have the ability to operate digital cameras to illustrate them, as well as manipulate those visual images through the use of software programs like Photoshop. Online journalism covers many areas, but to get a flavour of the skills needed and the kind of work they do, BBC interactive producer Terri Sweeney[6] outlines her job below.

To work in any field of journalism I believe you have to be someone who can feel passionate about the piece you're writing – whether that's writing a review of the latest gig by Kasabian or the Government's new White Paper on tackling obesity.

As an online journalist, your job is to put your audience in the picture on the issue, news story or feature that you're covering. Like print, TV news or radio, the same rules of journalism apply. This means writing the information clearly and with balance and impartiality. However, the advantage of online journalism is that you're given some creative scope to put the information to people differently and to have some fun with it – depending on your budget!

For example, a Radio 1 campaign, both online and on-air, to give young people information on sexually transmitted infections and safer sex was produced online in the form of a Flash game. As an online journalist I worked with designers and technical staff to make this, and had the editorial control over the content in the game. The information was still there, but not in the form of a 1000-word article.

Online journalism is no longer 'online'; it's 'interactive'. It's finding out who your audience is, and getting them involved in what you're writing – through message boards, chat rooms, their comments on a news story, to soliciting their images from an event as it unfolds and publishing them on your website.

The emergence of new platforms including Digital Satellite, Freeview and Digital Cable TV have also changed the face of online journalism. As an online journalist you often re-format your content to make it more available to these platforms so TV viewers can press their red button on the remote control and get your content on their TV screen.

Digital radios are also having an impact on the role of an online journalist. Writing the DAB text (which you can see on digital radios, scrolling across the LED box) and Live Text (for example, live comments from the audience on your screens during *I'm a Celebrity* ...) are part of the role of most producers in large broadcasting networks.

Online journalism is changing, so you have to be ready to work across a number of platforms. The core skills you need are listed below.

- **The ability and the desire to write.** This includes spelling, grammar and punctuation. If writing is all you want to do, then online journalism is probably not for you. Your time can sometimes be spent rewriting or editing from TV or radio news, rather than getting out there and creating the piece yourself.
- **Interest in people.** Most news stories and events affect people in some way. If you're not a people person, then you won't get the best out of your interviewees when you do get time to go out and research your piece or call up a source.
- **Attention to detail.** Accuracy is really important – from the spelling of someone's name, to giving the facts of a story. Your audience has to trust that you have got it right because if they're reading your piece, you're their main source of information.
- **Creativity and lots of ideas.** For example, on how to tackle dry subjects or how to put information or news to people differently – whether in a graph, an interactive drag and drop game, or a quiz.
- **Awareness of the Internet** and the desire to use it to its potential and reach as many people as you can.

People are fascinated to read and hear about other people. They like to see images of who they're reading about too. It's important that it's easy to navigate through any content, and that it's not repetitive. Online writers can make use of bullet points, diagrams, charts, shorter sentences, more subheadings and anything that makes it easier to digest information. People don't necessarily want to read copious amounts of text online as it gets tiring for the eyes, but digestible chunks of information can still give them the facts of the story. A graph can convey all the statistics you want to get across at one fell swoop.

Journalism is constantly changing, from smaller broadsheets and WAP phones to news bulletins and football scores by SMS text. Online journalism is still quite young. 'Streaming' audio and video of news events on the web is still an arduous task and if you've ever tried to listen to Pete Tong's *Essential Selection* or the *Today* programme online, you'll know that the quality is not as good as a DAB digital radio broadcast. But broadband technology is here, so with greater space and faster downloads, who knows what the future of online journalism will be.

Most pre-school children now have access to a PC at home. Those who don't will certainly have access at school. Adults who don't have a PC can log on at no cost at their local library or use drop-in centres, WAP phones, and Internet cafés. Arguably, the demand for websites and online content will only increase.

As the events of September 11th unfolded, the BBC's News Online website was the first port of call for most of the people trying to find out more, in both the UK and the USA. The number of people logging on to read the news was so excessive that the news site, which has several servers across Docklands and in New York, ground to a halt for a short while. The story was online before reporters even had a chance to get their cameras out.

The immediacy of updating the web with a news story, and the ability to refresh the page as and when developments unfold, means that a number of news sites on the Internet (CNN, BBC News, Sky News) have become trusted sources of news and often the first place people check when a story breaks. Often the big news stories break when people are at work, so they can surf the net if they have Internet access.

Similarly with sporting news – Euro 2004 saw unprecedented numbers of people logging on to read about football. So it's not just hard news that gives online journalism its credentials.

Online journalism is definitely a multimedia discipline because you will inevitably have access to audio and video footage in a news environment. You will often edit audio and video for the web once you've received it from TV or radio journalists on a big network, so an interest in these fields as well as the web is an advantage. It makes the job more interesting too.

The BBC is investing in new areas with the growth of interactive TV, new and emerging platforms (WAP phones, iPods, Podcasting, MP3 players, video phones, MMS and SMS messaging) and other ways that people can get access to the news, features, sport and other information. The BBC is also opening the arena to the audience, publishing comments on breaking news, enabling message boards and live chat rooms while you watch TV, listen to the news, or surf on the Internet. Online journalists will find themselves facilitating chat rooms, overseeing radio and TV production teams' use of their websites, and basically doing a bit of everything.

As an online journalist, you're no longer online, but working across many areas of broadcast technology. Technology behind the creation of websites has been streamlined, with the use of templates, and content management systems. As an online journalist, you concentrate on the content you make, the ease of interactivity for your audience, and providing the story in a fair and balanced way.

For the future, I think the key is to be prepared to work across a number of disciplines, but one of the advantages of this is if you want to move on from online journalism at any point you'll have a good grounding in most areas of broadcast.

CONCLUSION

The skills of a broadcast journalist have changed in line with the introduction of new technology in the industry. These changes mean that journalists in radio and television are now more responsible for the entire process of producing news items: long gone are the days when a radio reporter handed over their material to an editor to edit, and increasingly television reporters are expected to edit their own material. On top of this, advances in technology mean that broadcast news programmes can go live more easily, so the skill of performing in a seemingly spontaneous but professional way is increasingly in demand. From its inception online journalism has always demanded a high level of technical skill, and as Terri Sweeney explains, the job of an online journalist now requires the ability to work across a number of disciplines to make stories accessible to a broad audience.

But while technical skills are now a necessity for any broadcast journalist, they are not enough on their own. Journalism is about communication, and being able to relate to a wide range of different people on a variety of levels is equally vital. A good journalist is able to persuade reluctant interviewees to tell their story, to stop politicians in their tracks with pertinent questions, and to help jargon-ridden boffins explain their ideas in easily understood language. They also understand their medium and can use sound, pictures and interactivity to their best effect. And finally, they know their audience and how best to present their work in a way that will interest and inform them.

So while the skills of a broadcast journalist now include more technical ability than ever before, the technology should never be allowed to dominate the process or get in the way of telling the story. Ultimately the job of a journalist is to ask the right questions of the right people and to relay that in an engaging and balanced way to the audience.

NOTES

1 All quotes from Ryan Martinez taken from author interview, December 2004.
2 All quotes from Mike Young taken from author interview, February 2004.
3 All quotes from Phil Dixon taken from author interview, January 2005.
4 All quotes from Tim John taken from author interview, January 2005.
5 All quotes from Nick Kehoe taken from author interview, November 2004.
6 All quotes from Terri Sweeney taken from author interview, November 2004.

AN INTRODUCTION TO THE ENGLISH LEGAL SYSTEM

> It is necessary to understand the English legal system. I think it's very important to know how it got to where it is today …. Even if its origins have long since disappeared, it's important to know how it started … because then … students will understand the context of why it is how it is now.
>
> John Boileau[1]
> editorial manager
> Carlton Television

Pick up any newspaper, turn on your television or radio, or access a news website and it is a certainty that the first news story that you come across will in some way touch upon a legal issue of relevance to the changing social landscape in which we live. In addition, the coverage will probably have been framed by the complex plethora of rules and regulations that affect the day-to-day activities of working journalists and the nature and extent to which they are able to report the story.

Students of journalism and those in the profession need to have a sound and up-to-date understanding of the legal system within which they operate. A familiarity with the legal institutions and processes that regulate social activity and inform current political, economic and sociological debates is crucial to the intelligent reporting of news events and in fulfilling the media's role as a vital source of information and defender of public interests. This chapter seeks to identify key legal systems and principles and in particular to raise an awareness of the day-to-day significance of law to the world of journalism. An overview of the substantive legal provisions which affect the work of journalists is considered in the following chapter.

In this chapter the various sources and divisions of English law are described. The reader is introduced to the composition and jurisdiction of the current system of courts and tribunals and a quick reference guide is given to key legal personnel. A 'Glossary of Legal Terms' is also provided at the end of the book.

The English legal system includes the law as applicable to England and Wales. A different legal system applies in Scotland and journalists working in an international dimension should be aware of the need to check local rules and regulations.

DIVISIONS OF LAW

There are a number of ways in which the law can be categorised. This mechanism enables the user to compare, contrast, distinguish and comment upon aspects of the English legal system. These divisions of law do overlap and their meaning is dependent upon the context in which they are used.

COMMON LAW AND CIVIL LAW

In this context, the term 'common law' is used to define the development of legal principles through the judicial interpretation of statutes and judge-made case law as a contrast to the Continental system of civil law.

COMMON LAW AND STATUTE LAW

Common law is the body of law derived from custom or judicial precedents where no statutory provisions are to be found. Statute law is the body of law created by Parliament. A legal rule may exist in common law and then be changed through the introduction of a statute that the courts must then take to be the source of that law.

PUBLIC LAW AND PRIVATE LAW

Public law is concerned with the legal relationship between the state and the individual and the exercise of power by the state. Criminal law is an example of public law, although some areas of civil law also fall into this category. Private law, in contrast, covers the legal relationship between individuals.

CIVIL LAW AND CRIMINAL LAW

Civil law is concerned with the rights and duties of individuals towards each other. The state provides the machinery for dealing with any disputes, but otherwise plays little part.

CIVIL LAW

Object	To resolve disputes.
Parties	A claimant sues a defendant.
	The case is referred to as <u>Smith v. Jones</u>. Smith, the claimant, brings a civil case against Jones, the defendant. Orally this is expressed as 'Smith *and* Jones'.
Appeals	Should the case go to appeal, then the person bringing the appeal is the appellant and is named first, with the respondent named second.
Court	Civil courts include tribunals, county, High, Court of Appeal, House of Lords.
Evidence	A case is decided on the balance of probabilities: that the claimant's case is more probably right than not.
Outcome	If the claimant is successful, the defendant is found liable and there is a judgement for the claimant. The defendant may be ordered to pay damages, do or not to do something by an injunction or be required to fulfil a contractual obligation by specific performance.
Examples	Breach of contract, property disagreements, defamation.[2]

In criminal law, the state is concerned to enforce law and order in the community. Crime affects the whole community and is seen as a serious threat to the good order of society. Criminal law makes such behaviour an offence and is designed to protect the public and in certain circumstances ensure that the rights of individuals or groups are protected. The state is responsible for the detection, prosecution and punishment of offenders. It is possible, though unusual, for individuals to bring private prosecutions.

CRIMINAL LAW

Object	To maintain order, to punish and deter.
Parties	The state (Crown Prosecution Service) prosecutes a defendant. The case is referred to as <u>R v. Jones</u>. The R stands for Regina (Queen) or Rex (King).
	Orally this is expressed as 'The Crown *against* Jones'.
	On occasion the Government's law officers may bring prosecutions, for example:
	<u>AG v. Jones</u>. The Attorney General against Jones.
	<u>DPP v. Jones</u>. The Director of Public Prosecutions against Jones.
	<u>Smith v. Jones</u>. A private prosecution by Smith against Jones.
	A person is charged, tried, acquitted, convicted, or sentenced on an indictment or count or charge.
	A person is indicted or tried for theft (for example).
	A person pleads guilty or not guilty to a count or charge or indictment of theft or to theft.
	A person is acquitted or convicted or found guilty of theft.
Court	Criminal courts: youth courts, magistrates' court, Crown Court, Court of Appeal, House of Lords.
Evidence	Beyond reasonable doubt.
Outcome	The defendant may be convicted or acquitted. If convicted, the defendant may be punished or sentenced, given probation or a fine.
Examples	Murder, theft, rape, contempt.[3]

NATIONAL LAW AND INTERNATIONAL LAW

The term 'national law' is a means of classifying the set of internal legal rules that apply to a particular nation state. International law includes agreements created through custom and treaty that seek to define a range of relationships between states.

SOURCES OF LAW

Sources of law can be divided between the historical and the legal. Historical sources are those that have influenced the development of the law and to which the content of the law can be traced, examples being common law, equity and custom. Legal sources are those that create new rules of law, and these consist of legislation and judicial precedent.

HISTORICAL SOURCES: COMMON LAW

The expression 'common law' consists of a number of different meanings depending on the context. First, it refers to the Law of England that emerged after the Norman Conquest, establishing the authority of the central state. Second, the expression 'common law' can be used to describe the principles of law developed by the courts of common law. Third, the 'common law' can mean the substantive law that has developed over the years by the courts through decisions made in individual cases as opposed to those rules of law developed by Parliament.

EQUITY

Whilst the common law was in many ways an improvement on the systems it replaced, by the 14th century it had become increasingly rigid. Many individuals who were unable to seek redress for wrongdoings at common law began to petition the king as the 'fountain of justice'. Over the years these petitions increased and the king passed them to his principal minister, the chancellor. By the end of the 15th century the Chancellor was sitting in his own court, the Court of Chancery, issuing decrees in his own name rather than in that of the king. A significant aspect of this system of law known as equity was that many of the principles upon which equity operated had a moral basis and served as a 'gloss' on the common law to provide redress where the common law was defective.

By the 19th century, however, the Judicature Acts 1873–75 abolished the old courts of common law and the Court of Chancery, establishing in their place one Supreme Court of Judicature, each branch of which had power to administer both rules of common law and equity. It was also provided that in those instances where common law and equity were in conflict the rule in equity was to prevail.

LEGAL SOURCES: LEGISLATION

Since the 19th century, Parliament (the Monarch, the House of Lords and the House of Commons) has developed to become the originator of one of the most important sources of law; statute law or Acts of Parliament. The ideas for new legislation or amendments to existing rules reflect party political policies and changes in society's values. More specifically, these ideas may originate from a range of sources including Government departments, Royal Commission reports, law reform bodies, interest groups, professional organisations, public opinion and pressure from the media. The department concerned with introducing a particular piece of legislation will draw up proposals and give instructions for the drafting of the Bill to the Parliamentary Counsel. Drafting is a skilled and difficult task. The draftsmen are seeking to satisfy a number of conflicting aims, which include comprehensibility, brevity, certainty, procedural legitimacy, legal effectiveness and legal compatibility (Bennion, 1978).

During the consultation stage for proposed legislation, the Government will often issue documents for discussion in the form of a Green Paper. If the Government determines to proceed with the proposals, the draft legislation, known as a Bill, is then presented to Parliament. Before the Bill becomes an Act of Parliament, it must undergo approval stages in both the House of Commons and the House of Lords. Once any amendments are agreed, the Bill receives Royal Assent. It is now an Act of Parliament and, unless otherwise stated, comes into force. It is not uncommon, however, for all or parts of the new legislation to have different commencement dates.

Parliament is also able to delegate its general law-making power. Parliamentary time is limited and delegated legislation such as by-laws, Orders in Council and Statutory Instruments allow for flexible and responsive lawmaking, often in areas where local expertise and technical knowledge are required. Concerns regarding the accountability and scrutiny of delegated legislation exist and in themselves may be the subject of a potential political news story.

Once a statute is in force, the judiciary is bound by and must apply the legislation. However, words are an imperfect means of communication and the judiciary performs a vital function in interpreting statutory provisions where the words used are unclear, or where the provisions are particularly complex.

To facilitate the interpretation of statutes, certain guidelines have developed which are known as rules of statutory interpretation. You may wish to visit the website www.hmso.gov.uk/acts, which provides access to statutory provisions.

JUDICIAL PRECEDENT

The function of the judiciary is to interpret and apply the legislative provisions or the established common law principles to the facts in the case before them at that particular time. Judgments made in previous similar cases, detailed in published law reports, are used by judges to enable them to determine the dispute before them and to develop a consistent and settled understanding of the law. This concept, known as the *doctrine of precedent*, plays a part in all legal systems, for one of the main characteristics of law is that a court, where the facts are similar, should follow a decision in a previous case. In English law the rules demand that in certain circumstances a past decision must be followed whether the court agrees with the precedent or not. This is known as the doctrine of binding precedent or *stare decisis*. When a case comes before the court, the judge(s) will consider the evidence, determine the facts and then apply the existing legal principles to those facts. Judgment is then given on the case that will determine a winner and a loser. The judgment also details the legal reasoning behind the decision. The *ratio decidendi* is that part of the judicial decision which is necessary in order to determine the law on the issue before the court, and it is this aspect that is said to be binding in subsequent cases involving similar facts.

OVERRULING AND REVERSING

The power of a court to overrule a previous decision is often said to be a means of allowing the doctrine of precedent to be flexible. Overruling takes place when an earlier case is considered in a later case and held to be wrongly decided. Reversal is where the same case is overturned on appeal. The court hierarchy will determine whether a court is able to overrule or reverse a previous decision.

DISTINGUISHING

Distinguishing is a means of avoiding an otherwise binding precedent. Cases are distinguished on their facts and a court can refuse to follow a previous decision if it can find some material difference of fact between the present case and the previous one.

It is argued that the doctrine of binding precedent provides certainty, ensures the impartiality of the judiciary, and controls the number of cases coming before the courts whilst allowing for the gradual development of legal principles. In contrast, it has also been suggested that it is too rigid, allows for illogical distinctions, is backward looking, limits judge-made law and is not responsive enough to changes in society.

THE EUROPEAN INFLUENCE

It is important for journalists to have an understanding of the English legal system in its European context. Membership of the European Community (Union) has had a significant impact upon issues of Parliamentary sovereignty whilst incorporation of the European Convention on Human Rights into English law is changing the relationship between Parliament and the courts and bringing about an increased awareness of human rights throughout society.

It is worthwhile spending the time reading around the subject of European law. An awareness and appreciation of the systems and processes is invaluable. On a more pragmatic level, a journalist can look very stupid if they get the various European institutions mixed up.

THE EUROPEAN UNION: COMMUNITY INSTITUTIONS

THE COUNCIL OF THE EUROPEAN UNION

Based in Brussels, this is a political body with the final say on nearly all legislative matters and the Community budget. Each Member State sends a delegate to represent them. The delegates will vary depending on the subject matter being considered. The representative from the UK will normally be the relevant minister. For example, if the issue relates to economic matters, the UK will be represented by the Chancellor. When the Heads of State meet, the session is referred to as a European Council or Summit.

The Presidency of the Council is held by each Member State in turn for a period of six months. The voting arrangements vary depending on the type of Council decision.

THE COMMISSION

Based in Brussels, the Commission's members are drawn from Member States, but act independently. Committed to the interests of the Community, they formulate proposals for new Community policies and act as the Executive of the European Union.

THE EUROPEAN PARLIAMENT

Based in Strasbourg (with committees in Brussels), the European Parliament is a debating forum made up of directly elected Members of the European Parliament (MEPs). The members sit according to their political persuasion rather than by country. The Parliament is in the main advisory and supervisory, raising issues with both the Council and the Commission. It has the final say in some budgetary matters and its powers have increased in recent years.

THE EUROPEAN COURT OF JUSTICE (ECJ)

Based in Luxembourg, the court consists of judges and advocates general chosen by agreement among the governments of the Member States. The advocates general assist the court, providing independent opinion on the case in hand, which the judges can consider. Attached to the ECJ is the Court of First Instance.

The ECJ undertakes direct action against Member States and Community institutions and provides authoritative rulings on the interpretation of Community law. Applications for such rulings come from national courts, not the individuals in a case. It should be noted that the ECJ is not bound by the doctrine of precedent to the same extent as the courts within the English legal system.

SOURCES OF EUROPEAN LAW

THE EEC TREATY AND PROTOCOLS, AS AMENDED BY FURTHER TREATIES

The primary treaty is the Treaty of Rome, which was incorporated into UK law by the European Communities Act 1972. The Treaty has been amended by subsequent legislation such as the Maastricht Treaty and the Amsterdam Treaty. Some of the Treaties are immediately applicable law in the UK, this is usually determined by the ECJ. The ECJ will consider whether the Article is clear and concise, whether it envisages further action by the Community or Member States for its implementation, and the degree of discretion given to Member States in deciding how to implement it.

EUROPEAN SECONDARY LEGISLATION: REGULATIONS, DIRECTIVES AND DECISIONS

- **Regulations** are binding in their entirety and directly applicable in all Member States. No national legislation is necessary to implement them. As a result they give rise to rights (and obligations) for states and individuals.
- **Directives** are binding on all Member States. The directive will generally set out an objective to be achieved by all the Members, but it is up to the individual Member State as to how it will implement the particular directive; they therefore normally require implementation by national legislation. If a directive is not implemented by a Member State within the required time period, then the ECJ is able to make the directive directly applicable. A directive can be relied upon by individuals against a defaulting Member State. For a directive to be effective in this way it must be precise, clear and unconditional.
- **Decisions** are normally individual acts, or binding orders addressed to a specified person, state or institution of the Community.

JUDGEMENTS BY THE EUROPEAN COURT OF JUSTICE

Decisions of the ECJ have direct effect in the UK. National courts (not the individual parties) are able to refer cases to the ECJ under Art. 234 of the Treaty of Rome on the interpretation of points of community law of relevance to the decision being made by the national court. It is not appropriate to refer to this process as an appeal.

THE EUROPEAN CONVENTION FOR THE PROTECTION OF HUMAN RIGHTS AND FUNDAMENTAL FREEDOMS (ECHR)

The ECHR is concerned with the protection of civil rights and freedoms. It should not be confused with the European Union, despite there being an obvious overlap in membership.

Article 1:	States that the parties to the agreement shall secure to everyone within their jurisdiction the rights and freedoms defined in Articles 2 to 18. The main Articles are as follows:
Article 2:	Protection of Life.
Article 3:	Freedom from Inhuman Treatment.
Article 4:	Freedom from Slavery, Servitude and Forced or Compulsory Labour.
Article 5:	Right to Liberty and Security of the Person.
Article 6:	The Right to a Fair and Public Hearing.
Article 7:	Freedom from Retrospective Effect of Penal Legislation.
Article 8:	The Right to Respect for Privacy.
Article 9:	Freedom of Thought, Conscience and Religion.
Article 10:	Freedom of Expression.
Article 11:	Freedom of Association and Assembly.
Article 12:	The Right to Marry and Found a Family.

The European Court of Human Rights, which sits in Strasbourg, hears applications from individuals or Contracting States alleging breaches of the Convention rights.

In October 2000 the Convention was incorporated into English law by the Human Rights Act 1998 (HRA). Prior to this, whilst the United Kingdom was a signatory to the Convention, it could not be directly enforced in English courts. As a result, alleged breaches of the Convention had to be pursued in Strasbourg, which was a time-consuming process. The Human Rights Act now allows individuals direct redress for human rights violations by public authorities and requires Ministers and officials to pay regard to the Convention rights when devising policy and framing legislation in the future. Advocates who support this development argue that it marks a shift to a more fundamental and positive approach to human rights in the UK. It is also suggested that it will change the relationship between Parliament and the courts and reinforce the notion of identifiable rights which States are bound to respect and further.

Incorporation of the Convention has important implications for the media. Given the significance of the informational and mediating role of the journalist within the public sphere, Western values dictate that it is imperative that such individuals remain 'free and independent'. This reinforces the strong ideological component of 'serious journalism' that serves to bolster the core tenets of democratic states: justice, freedom and truth. As a means to achieve these normative objectives, most societies promote the concept of freedom of expression. The core principles of Article 10 provide protection for freedom of expression, which lies at the heart of the day-to-day activities of the working journalist. It is acknowledged that this fundamental right should not be lightly interfered with, but it requires responsible and accountable usage.

By their very nature, the working practices of journalists and the issues raised in news coverage create clashes with other fundamental freedoms. Examples to illustrate this tension are easy to find, the most obvious being the conflict between a journalist's 'right' to report a story and an individual's right to privacy. All rights, but in particular freedom of expression, are vulnerable to systematic abuse in one form or another. Ultimately it is up to the courts to maintain the appropriate balance between these conflicting interests. It is worth taking time to reflect on individual news stories and events and consider whether or not the English legal system strikes the right balance between freedom of expression and other competing rights and interests.

THE COURTS

I want them to have some practical experience of how the court system works. It's an amazing system and I expect people to have been out to see it at first hand. I want people to know about contempt of court, for the self-evident reason that they can get themselves into trouble if they don't know about it. I want people to know about prejudice in reporting cases.

John Boileau
editorial manager
Carlton Television

How did I learn the law? I worked for a freelance news agency and I learned the law by having to cover Penryth Magistrates' Court on my own six months into my training as a journalist.

Mike Blair[4]
editor
Central News East

(Continued)

My first visit to the courts was very intimidating. I didn't know what to do when the judge entered the court. Should I nod every time the judge went in or out, or was one nod at the start of the day sufficient?

Lisa Teanby[5]
editor
Saga 106.6

Every individual who was interviewed in the process of researching this chapter stated that it is essential for the student journalist to take the time and effort to become familiar with all aspects of the court system. While law classes and mock newsdays are valuable for teaching and learning, there is quite simply no replacement for taking the time to visit the courts on a regular basis. As a student journalist, you will not have full access rights to all courts but time spent, for example, at your local magistrates' court will not be time wasted. Such visits will enable you to build up contacts both within the court, the legal profession and amongst your colleagues in the industry. Your first visit will be daunting, but the confidence gained is essential to enable you to report court cases accurately and effectively. Knowing your way around the building, the staff and the system means that you'll be brave enough to ask the questions which will not only make your coverage better, but will ensure you don't make silly mistakes which might result in libel or contempt proceedings. Combine this with your developing knowledge of media law, and you'll also be in a better position to challenge the courts when there are attempts to impose inappropriate restrictions on your coverage. If you're still not convinced, don't forget that 'court reporting can be quite fun!' (Will Green, recently qualified radio journalist).

Chapter 8 provides guidance on visiting the courts whilst this chapter introduces the student of journalism to their structure and composition.

THE STRUCTURE AND PERSONNEL OF THE COURTS

It is necessary to draw a distinction between:

- courts with civil or criminal jurisdiction;
- 'courts of first instance' or 'trial courts', in which proceedings may be begun; and
- 'appellate courts' which hear appeals from the decisions of courts lower in the court hierarchy.

THE CIVIL COURTS

There are a number of possible routes through the courts exercising civil jurisdiction; the route depends on the court in which the proceedings are begun. There are three courts of first instance: the magistrates' court, county court and High Court. Whether or not proceedings can be commenced in any particular court depends on the subject matter, the money value of the claim, and the complexity of the case. Most civil trials do not involve a jury, except in defamation, malicious falsehood, fraud and false imprisonment cases. Journalists can access certain details about the case directly from the courts.

COURTS OF FIRST INSTANCE

THE MAGISTRATES' COURTS (CIVIL JURISDICTION)
- **Jurisdiction**   Certain family law, administrative law and minor civil functions.
- **Composition**   The courts are staffed by magistrates who are also known as Justices of the Peace. These are generally non-lawyers and unpaid. They sit in panels of three and are assisted by a legally qualified magistrates' clerk known as a legal adviser. When they are dealing with family matters there must be at least one female and one male justice sitting on the bench.
- **Appeals**   In family matters an appeal is heard by the Family Division of the High Court. Other appeals are heard by the Queen's Bench Division of the High Court.

THE COUNTY COURT
- **Jurisdiction**   The county court jurisdiction is quite extensive in civil matters. Generally this includes family law-related matters and disputes between individuals or companies seeking compensation for an alleged harm that they believe they have suffered. There is some overlap with the High Court, which generally deals with high-value civil claims or more specialised cases.
- **Composition**   Circuit judges and district judges.
- **Appeals**   Appeals lie direct to the Court of Appeal (Civil Division), although appeals against a decision of a district judge go before the circuit judge.

Small Claims   Disputes involving smaller sums can be allocated to the small claims track to be resolved by arbitration. The arbitrator may be a district judge or an 'outside arbitrator'. The important feature is that no solicitors' costs are allowed. This coupled with the informal nature of the hearing, encourages the litigants to represent themselves and thus reduce the cost and delay involved.

THE HIGH COURT

- **Jurisdiction**   The High Court has a wide general civil jurisdiction with no financial limits. It also hears appeals from inferior courts and tribunals. The High Court is divided into three divisions.

  - The Chancery Division, which hears cases concerning land, wills, trusts, estates of deceased persons, bankruptcy, company law, tax and property. The nominal head of the Chancery Division is the Vice-Chancellor.
  - The Family Division, which hears cases dealing with child welfare matters and divorce. The President is the head of the Family Division.
  - The Queen's Bench Division (QBD), hears common law cases, in particular claims in contract and tort. The head of the QBD is the Lord Chief Justice.

- **Appeals**   Appeals from a decision of the High Court generally go to the Court of Appeal (Civil Division) and then to the House of Lords. An appeal may be made direct to the House of Lords by what is known as a 'leap-frog' procedure.

THE COURT OF APPEAL (CIVIL DIVISION)

- **Jurisdiction**   The Court of Appeal hears appeals from the High Court and county court and certain other courts and tribunals.
- **Composition**   Senior judges called Lord Justices of Appeal serve the court; the most senior judge is the Master of the Rolls. Most cases will be heard by three judges whose decision is by majority.
- **Appeals**   May be allowed to the House of Lords.

THE HOUSE OF LORDS

- **Jurisdiction**   The House of Lords hears appeals from the Court of Appeal and sometimes direct from the High Court.
- **Composition**   Appeals are heard by Lords of Appeal in Ordinary, although the media often shorten this to 'Law Lords' in their coverage of appeal cases. Normally five judges sit together, although seven can sit in important cases. The decision will be by majority, although separate opinions are often given and are crucial to the doctrine of precedent.

TRIBUNALS

In addition to the civil and criminal courts, there also exist a vast number of tribunals set up by Acts of Parliament to hear and decide disputes on a court-like basis. The composition of a tribunal varies, although as in the example of an employment tribunal, they are usually made up of three members comprising a chair (often a lawyer) and two lay representatives.

THE CRIMINAL COURTS

There are basically two routes through the courts exercising criminal jurisdiction. The route depends on whether the criminal case is tried *on indictment* (in the Crown Court) or *summarily* (in a magistrates' court). This largely depends on the 'category' of the offence.

There are three categories of offences:

- offences triable only summarily;
- offences triable either-way;
- offences triable only on indictment.

Summary trials are held in a magistrates' court. An appeal may be taken as of right to the Crown Court against conviction and/or sentence.

Individuals aged over 18 who are charged with an either-way offence are required to indicate their plea. Should the accused plead guilty, the magistrates proceed as in a summary trial. If the accused pleads not guilty, then the magistrates are required to determine whether the case should be tried summarily or be tried by jury at the Crown Court. If it is decided that the case will be heard in the Crown Court, a formal committal for trial will normally follow. At a committal for trial, the magistrates acting as examining justices will generally check that the prosecution's evidence discloses the elements of the offence charged.

Serious indictable-only offences are sent for trial in the Crown Court. If the defendant pleads not guilty, the trial will be heard by a jury, presided over by a judge. If the defendant pleads guilty, no jury will be needed.

THE CRIMINAL CASES REVIEW COMMISSION (CCRC)

- **Jurisdiction** The CCRC operates independently of the executive and the judiciary. It considers any allegation of a miscarriage of justice resulting from either a conviction or sentence in either the Crown Court or magistrates' court, either after a referral of leave to appeal or after the dismissal of an appeal. The CCRC does not overturn convictions or sentences, but it may refer the case back to a relevant court for reconsideration.
- **Composition** There are 16 commissioners, around 25 case workers and a full-time staff of over 65.

CORONERS' COURTS

- **Jurisdiction** Unnatural or violent deaths must be reported to the coroner, who will order a post-mortem examination to be carried out. If it appears that the death was not as a result of natural causes, or if the cause is unknown or falls into other specified categories such as the death of an individual whilst in police custody, the coroner will hold an inquest. There are a number of possible verdicts including 'suicide', 'accidental death', 'unlawful killing' and 'open verdict'. Verdicts are said to be *returned* by a jury or the coroner *records* a verdict if sitting alone. Coroners' courts also deal with treasure trove cases.

- **Composition**   An inquest may involve a jury, but most are heard by a coroner alone. Coroners are doctors or lawyers of five years' standing.
- **Appeals**   Whilst there is no legal appeal against the verdict of a coroner's court, the decision can be quashed and a new inquest ordered by the High Court following a judicial review.

LEGAL PERSONNEL

Journalists may be required to know and make use of the formal titles of key personnel within the English legal system in a range of contexts. Details of a number of significant positions are provided below and information on the names of current post holders can be located from a variety of sources, including www.hmcourts-service.gov.uk.

Lord Chancellor	Head of the judiciary. This is a political appointment. Written as 'Lord Bloggs L.C.' Orally referred to as 'Lord Bloggs, Lord Chancellor'.
Lord Chief Justice	President of the Court of Appeal (Criminal Division).
Master of the Rolls	Member and President of the Court of Appeal.
(M.R.)	(Civil Division). Orally referred to as 'Lord Brown, Master of the Rolls'.
President of the Family Division	The most senior judge in the Family Division of the High Court.
Vice-Chancellor	Effectively heads the Chancery Division of the High Court.
Lords of Appeal in Ordinary	Also known as the Law Lords, they sit in the House of Lords and the Privy Council. They are referred to by their specific titles.
Lord Justices of Appeal	Member of Court of Appeal. Lord Justice or Lady Justice. Plural: Lords Justices, Ladies Justices. Orally referred to as Lord Justice Bloggs, or Lords Justices Bloggs and Jones.
High Court Judges	Known as puisne judges (pronounced puny), they sit in the High Court and also hear serious criminal law cases. In law

	reports they are referred to as Bloggs J. In news reports they should be referred to as Mr Justice Bloggs or Mrs Justice Bloggs.
Circuit Judges	These judges sit in the Crown or county court. In court they are addressed as 'Your Honour'. In reports they should be referred to as Judge Adam Bloggs or Judge Eve Bloggs.
District Judges	Full and part-time appointments hearing civil cases.
Recorders	A legally qualified part-time judge sitting in the Crown Court. In reports they should be referred to as recorder Mr Adam Bloggs or Mrs Eve Bloggs.
Magistrates	Unpaid part-time lay magistrates hearing certain civil and criminal cases. When sitting magistrates are addressed as Sir or Madam.
The Attorney General	The Government's main legal adviser and a political appointee.
The Solicitor General	Deputy to the Attorney General.
The Director of Public Prosecutions	Head of the Crown Prosecution Service.
The Crown Prosecution Service	The national prosecution service which is separate from the detection and investigation of crimes.
Barristers	Legally qualified, barristers act as advocates for clients in civil and criminal cases. In addition they give opinions on legal problems and draft legal documents. Governed by the Bar Council.
Solicitors	Legally qualified, solicitors undertake some advocacy work, but the majority of their time is spent on work such as conveyancing, wills, minor crime and giving legal advice.
Legal Executives	Legally trained, legal executives work with and support the work of solicitors.

CONCLUSION

This brief introduction to the English legal system might appear to be rather dry and students of journalism might initially question its relevance. Knowledge and comprehension of the legal system is, however, one of the foundation stones for much of the work that journalists do. An understanding of the systems and processes will enable the novice journalist to have a better appreciation of the specific laws that affect their activities, and assist them in performing their role more effectively. One last word of caution: the law is a dynamic subject, so while it appears to be stating the obvious, do ensure that you refer to up-to-date textbooks at all times.

NOTES

1 All quotes from John Boileau taken from author interview, 2003.
2 See Chapter 7.
3 See Chapter 7.
4 All quotes from Mike Blair taken from author interview, 2003.
5 All quotes from Lisa Teanby taken from author interview, 2003.

THE JOURNALIST AND THE LAW

It is essential that working journalists are aware of the specific rules that regulate, control and influence their activities. This knowledge will help journalists to avoid expensive legal pitfalls, challenge attempts to suppress stories, and identify when it is necessary if not essential to seek senior management advice or make that telephone call to the lawyers. This single chapter cannot provide comprehensive coverage of a notoriously complex discipline. It does, however, seek to provide simple introductory summaries of substantive areas of law including, amongst others, privacy, copyright, the protection of sources and reporting elections. The law of defamation and contempt are referred to in slightly more detail, reflecting the consensus amongst working journalists that they are of particular significance for students of journalism and practitioners alike. The aim is to heighten the awareness, recognition and appreciation of the law as a mechanism of social control with specific reference to its impact upon journalism practices.

DEFAMATION

Libel is bloody expensive and hugely embarrassing.

Mike Blair[1]
editor
Central News East

The law relating to defamation is of key importance to all journalists. Some suggest that it is an instrument of censorship whilst others argue that it serves as a spur to accuracy and professionalism. All students of NCTJ or BJTC accredited courses will spend time exploring this complex area of law and applying that knowledge in practical newsday activities. Students who attend placements in busy newsrooms may find that they are tested on their knowledge of defamation law, and will soon discover that the editor will be far from impressed if they are unable to identify potentially libellous material. Working journalists confirm that it is vital for them to keep up to date with changes and developments that may have come about as a result of new legislation or new precedents[2] created in libel cases brought before the courts. Put simply, if you want to get a job as a journalist, and keep it, you need to know your way around the basics of libel law.

Defamation, also referred to as libel, is generally a civil action. This means that the wronged party has a choice whether or not to sue the alleged wrong-doer. A number of factors will influence this decision. The potential claimant must consider the stress involved in bringing a case before the courts. An action can take a long time to resolve. Despite the increase in 'no-win-no-fee' arrange-ments (also known as conditional fee agreements), most cases are very expen-sive and the claimant will not be entitled to legal aid. Most defamation actions are heard before a jury, and whilst the jury will be guided by an experienced judge, the outcome can remain unpredictable. The high level of damages in many cases may appear to be an attractive proposition, but awards are deter-mined by the jury and can vary considerably. One final consideration for the aggrieved individual to take into account is that in normal circumstances the media are able to report every juicy detail of any subsequent defamation court case, which will mean an inevitable referral to the original offending statement in all its glory. But the trainee journalist who believes that the combined effect of these pressures make it unlikely that a potential claimant will proceed with legal action should take heed. The same considerations of expense, potentially high damages and the unpredictable nature of the outcome are just as relevant to journalists and the organisations that employ them. So in sum, the claimant would need to be rich, insured or mad to bring a libel action, whilst the jour-nalist must be wealthy, insured or have a solid defence to treat this notorious area of law with anything but the utmost caution, care and respect.

If they can afford it, all individuals and organisations have the legal capacity to sue, although it should be noted that in English law the dead cannot sue or be sued for libel. In addition, local authorities, though not their officers or offi-cials, are unable to bring an action for damages for defamation as it is deemed contrary to the public interest and in particular freedom of expression for the organs of government, whether central or local, to have that right. Most editors when asked about complaints made to them concerning allegedly libellous material also indicate that some organisations or individuals are more litigious than others. Rightly or wrongly they acknowledge that this does impact upon editorial decision making. It is also worth noting that the growth of 'forum shopping' allows those aggrieved by the spread of defamatory statements across the globe to commence their legal action in the country of their choice. With its highly repressive libel laws it is no surprise that the 'libel tourists' will often opt to bring their actions in the English courts.

Examples of individuals who are most likely to sue:

- people linked to terrorism
- barristers or solicitors
- international or domestic companies
- film stars/TV personalities/pop singers
- MPs (not members of the Cabinet)
- other professionals
- police officers and trade union leaders.

Examples of people who are least likely to sue:

- judges
- vicars.

Alastair Brett[3]
legal manager
Times Newspapers

CRITERIA FOR PROVING DEFAMATION

In bringing a defamation action the claimant must prove that:

1   the statement is defamatory;
2   the words refer to the claimant; and
3   the words have been published.

Note that the claimant does *not* have to prove that:

1   the statement is false;
2   any damage has been suffered; or
3   any intent on the part of the defendant.

1   THE STATEMENT IS DEFAMATORY

Providing a working definition for what is or is not a defamatory statement is difficult. In a great many cases it is actually fairly obvious, and the main concern is how the journalist will defend any potential action by an aggrieved individual or organisation.

The standard definition that most students studying media law will become familiar with is:

the publication of a statement which reflects on a person's reputation and which *tends* to lower him in the estimation of right-thinking members of society generally; or make them shun or avoid him; or exposes him to hatred, ridicule or contempt, or disparages him in his business, trade, office or profession.

This definition is not exhaustive and the exact borderline in any situation can be difficult to define or predict, particularly as the test is a subjective one as seen through the eyes of the 'right-thinking member of society'. From the media's perspective this is the ordinary reader, listener or viewer who can be expected to reflect on a news story and ask: 'What is the journalist trying to say to me?' Journalists need to be very careful about their use of language as words can be ambiguous and create a variety of meanings. They should also consider the juxtaposition, tone and context of their story as the innocuous and unintended may become misleading and potentially defamatory. Work should be proofread carefully to avoid typographical errors and library materials should always be checked for accuracy. Journalists should also stick to reliable double-sourced facts, consider alternative potentially innocent explanations and avoid jumping to conclusions, allowing the audience to make up its mind on the matter.

2   THE WORDS REFER TO THE CLAIMANT

The claimant must prove that the defamatory words published refer to them. This may be directly, or if the individual or organisation is not actually named, that a reasonable person would understand that the words refer to the claimant.

3   THE WORDS HAVE BEEN PUBLISHED
TO A THIRD PARTY

This is unlikely to be in dispute, given the nature of journalistic activity, but in legal terms the requirement is that the statement must be published to a person other than the claimant. If a complaint is made about a publication and there are concerns about the content, then websites should also be checked. Organisations should have an effective system in place for removing the offending item (if appropriate) as each visit to a website provides a potential new actionable publication.

WHO CAN BE SUED?

The claimant can decide whom they wish to sue, and it is important for the trainee journalist to appreciate that this does not mean just the originator of a potentially libellous statement. Anyone involved in the publication of the libel and worth suing could find that they are subject to an expensive legal claim. This is an important principle to understand and many students on journalism courses initially struggle to appreciate that they cannot simply report that Mr Bloggs says that Mr Jones is a cheat and a liar and assume that they are safe because the allegation came from another person.

DEFENDING YOUR POSITION

A good journalist can go a long way in avoiding expensive libel claims through the professional and ethical reporting of events. If journalists check the facts, produce an accurate and balanced account of events and avoid embellishing the story, they will reduce the likelihood of possible legal actions and will also be in a better position to defend fictitious or vexatious claims.

The main issue, however, for working journalists is to be well versed in the defences that the law provides to defamation actions. This is not a consideration that the journalist should turn to *after* they receive a letter of complaint, but should be at the forefront of their thinking as they research and construct their story. The aim is to avoid litigation.

The main defences available to a journalist turn on the following issues. If the damaging allegation is:

1   a statement of fact (can the journalist prove that the statement is *true*?)
2   an expression of opinion (can the journalist show it to be a *fair comment*?)
3   contained within a report that is entitled to the protection of *privilege* (can the journalist show that the coverage is *fair and accurate*?)
4   a matter of serious public interest (then the journalist may be able to rely upon the developing defence of *common law qualified privilege*).

To the trainee journalist, the list of defences might appear to provide a warm and protective security blanket. However, the reality is that each defence raises a number of complex considerations and the novice should always refer up to the editor if in any doubt before risking a potentially libellous story being published. In defending a story that an allegation is, for example, true the journalist is required to have cross-checked all their facts, have reliable and believable sources and witnesses, supporting evidence and accurate contemporaneous personal notes.

If there is no realistic defence available, then the journalist must be aware that in repeating the damaging allegation in a news story, they are leaving themselves and their organisation vulnerable to legal action. In such circumstances they might consider rewriting the story and omitting damaging assertions that cannot be defended, or they may have to spike the story until they are able to find sufficient evidence to support the allegations made.

Journalists are only human, and errors are occasionally made, although this should never excuse sloppy journalism. In certain situations it is possible to respond by making a suitable correction and apology. This should be undertaken by an experienced editor who would also be well advised to seek legal advice.

Journalism students will spend considerable time absorbing the rules covering libel during their course of study. As practising journalists, they will hone the application of this knowledge through experience gained on the job, careful writing, checking and by keeping up to date with the continuing developments in this dynamic area of law through professional training opportunities.

> You must keep notes of off-screen interviews, backgrounds and briefings. Keep rushes of contentious stories so that contacts can't be challenged.
>
> Mike Blair
> editor
> Central News East

Below are some 'top tips' from newsrooms in how to reduce the risk of an expensive libel action.

CHECKLIST TO AVOID LIBEL

✓ If you are at all unsure, discuss the situation with colleagues on your news team.

✓ If you're still unsure, refer up to the editor. Don't think that this will make you appear stupid. You'll feel more than stupid if you get it wrong and the editor is tearing you off a strip before putting you on a 'final warning' under the organisation's disciplinary procedure.

✓ Stick to the facts.

✓ Can you prove that the statement is true?

✓ Check all your names and facts are correct. Then check again.

✓ Someone else told you the allegation ... Sorry you are simply repeating the libel and potentially you and the organisation you work for can be sued.

✓ 'But I didn't mean you!' Tough, unless you have evidence that you took all reasonable care, you may be liable.

✓ Use your words carefully. 'A taxi ran into a van' implies fault on the part of the taxi driver, so rewrite as: 'A taxi and a van were involved in a collision.'

✓ 'I know, I won't mention the person's name!' Sorry, if it is possible to work out who your statement refers to, you'll leave yourself open to a potential legal action, and sometimes from more than one party.

✓ Avoid misleading headlines and teasers.

✓ Keep notes. These should be accurate and contemporaneous.

✓ Keep recordings.

✓ Get 'informers' to sign statements.

✓ On radio, television or webcasts watch for the intonation and tone of your voice. A defamatory inference may be drawn from this.

✓ Consider background music. Can an inference be construed?

✓ Be especially careful with those more likely to be litigious.

✓ Attribute statements and obtain a balance.

✓ Make use of the various privilege defence provisions. If it is appropriate, for example, get an MP to raise a question in the House that you want answering. If you then publish the statement appropriately, it attracts the defence of statutory qualified privilege.

✓ Watch for 'tunnel vision' – keep an open mind and don't jump to conclusions. Stick to the facts.

✓ Seek comments from the subject matter whenever possible, but note that simply allowing a person the 'right of reply' does not safeguard against the person suing for libel.

✓ Be careful with cuttings/footage library or database material, as they may be inaccurate and may even have been the subject of a correction or apology. A fresh publication could lead to a fresh threat of libel proceedings. This is particularly relevant for website/Internet sources of information. The Internet is a marvellous facility but needs careful checking as content is often out of date or simply inaccurate.

✓ Make use of your skill with words.

✓ Can you save some parts of the item, rewriting to alter elements to limit exposure?

✓ Remove parts in the story that are not legally supportable.

✓ Avoid misleading 'headlines'.

✓ Use *allegedly*, but understand that this word does not have some magical quality. It will not protect you, but in a good balanced item it will help.

✓ Avoid generalisations.

✓ If in doubt scrap it, keep your job and live to fight another day!

CONTEMPT

> There is no doubt that recent controversy over contempt has centred on publications made at or shortly after the arrest of a crime suspect. These publications often form only part of massive media coverage, from the date of the crime itself ... But how close to the wind are the media sailing? Is too much prejudicial material being published?
>
> Justin Walford[4]
> legal adviser
> Express Newspapers

The law of contempt addresses the competing interests of the principles of open justice and ensuring an individual's right to a fair trial. Along with the threat of libel action, the fear of being held in contempt of court will always be a key legal consideration for working journalists. The student of journalism can expect to spend a considerable amount of their study time on both the law of contempt and related court-reporting restrictions. Journalists and editors all confirm the importance of knowing and working within the boundaries of the relevant legal provisions. Editors have a particular interest in ensuring appropriate standards are met, as it is they who will be brought before the court to answer contempt charges and, if found guilty, face a possible term of imprisonment. Journalists actively involved in any contemptuous new coverage, however, should be assured that whilst they might themselves avoid the direct wrath of the court, they will find that the wrath of their employer is equally swingeing.

The media have had a long love affair with crime, with crime news remaining a staple of much local, regional and national news across the world. This trend, evidenced in journalism and reportage, is arguably a reflection of the wider public interest and fascination with crime. Media interest in crime serves not only a voyeuristic function, but also provides an opportunity to inform, educate, highlight faults in the system, and act as a check on the legal process. The seemingly insatiable appetite for crime news remains as significant today as it has ever been and, given this fact, it is clear that journalists must be familiar with the law of contempt and have a working knowledge of how it influences and structures news coverage. Whilst the news agenda in this area is in the main focused upon the reporting of crime and related court cases, the student of journalism should note that the contempt provisions and additional numerous reporting restrictions are also applicable to particular civil actions.

The basis for much legislation that curtails the journalists' freedom of expression in the interest of protecting the right to a fair trial is based upon the belief that 'in the hurly-burly of today, yesterday's paper may be dead, but not the influence which it exerted' (Wiseheart, 1922: 523). Fears concerning prejudicial media coverage of specific cases underpin the legitimate debate concerning the point at which the nature and style of news coverage of a particular case begin to affect the accused's right to a fair trial.

Whilst there is little conclusive evidence that the more sensational examples of media coverage of crime are indeed prejudicial, the approach adopted in the English legal system is based upon a strong belief in the importance of maintaining public confidence in the criminal justice system, ensuring fair individual hearings, and a strong judicial abhorrence of 'trial by media'.

Examples of criminal trials that have raised very public concerns about perceived prejudicial media coverage litter the records. In the UK, for example, the trials of Rosemary West, Colin Stagg, Lisa and Michelle Taylor, Peter Sutcliffe and Ian Huntley epitomise concerns regarding salacious, sensational, inaccurate and prejudicial media reports. West was imprisoned in November 1995 for the murder of ten young women and girls. The nature of the offences, which involved sexual violence and the disposal of the bodies beneath the killers' home created a predictable media frenzy. Stagg was accused of killing a young mother in front of her two-year-old son on Wimbledon Common. In 1994 his trial collapsed when the judge threw out the police evidence, yet the media coverage both before, during and after the trial meant that Stagg has remained a virtual prisoner in his own home since the 1990s. Forensic evidence uncovered in 2004, some ten years after the initial trial, suggests that the murderer was indeed someone other than Stagg.

It is interesting to note that the nature of the media reports of the arrest of Sutcliffe, the so-called Yorkshire Ripper who killed 13 women and left 7 others for dead between 1975 and 1980, was an important factor in persuading Parliament to approve the more draconian sections of the Contempt of Court Act 1981. In 2003 Ian Huntley was found guilty of murdering two schoolgirls in the village of Soham. The events provoked such potentially prejudicial comments in newspapers and on the radio that the judge in the case threatened to postpone all reporting in the case. Rosemary West, and the Taylor sisters' trials both resulted in legal appeals founded upon the suggestion that their trials had not been fair as a result of pre-trial publicity.

The number of criminal cases that have been halted or quashed on judicial acceptance that pre-trial publicity did, or would have rendered a fair trial impossible appears to be on the increase. This disturbing development raises a number of concerns. Whilst it is crucial that individuals have the right to a fair trial, it is equally important for individuals to be brought before the courts and for justice to be given the opportunity to be done.

Technological developments and in particular the impact of the Internet upon the rapid transfer of information around the world presents particular problems in relation to pre-trial prejudice and fundamental difficulties for the viability of national provisions restricting media reports of crime. During the Rosemary West committal procedure, for example, accounts of evidence appeared on the Internet and were leaked back into the UK, directly breaching statutory reporting restrictions applicable under Section 8 of the Magistrates' Courts Act 1981. In the 1993 trial of two boys accused of killing two-year-old James Bulger, the names of the boys and prejudicial discussion on German, French, and Italian satellite, in French newspapers and on many Internet bulletin boards were accessible within the trial area. In October 2003, the Attorney General warned newspapers that fevered coverage of rape allegations against eight Premiership footballers could prejudice any future trial, and concerns were raised about the websites that carried the names of players rumoured to be involved.

The decision to bring a contempt action against the media rests with the Attorney General, which is a political appointment. Of particular concern is the fact that the Attorney General does not make the criteria used to determine whether or not to prosecute very clear. On a number of occasions publications which have appeared to be in breach of Section 2(1) have not been prosecuted. For example, in November 1999 a disc-jockey and travel presenter at the Preston radio station *Rock Fm* commented on air about the then ongoing Harold Shipman murder trial:[5]

Innocent until proven guilty of course, because that's the way it works in this land. It's innocent until proven guilty as sin . . . Put us taxpayers out of our misery, because we're paying for this. Admit to it, it's a fair cop, you're caught red-handed, be done with it. (*Media Lawyer*, 2000 26: 22)

The Attorney General did not instigate proceedings. This lack of clarity sends out confusing messages to the media in terms of what is and is not permissible.

In October 2000 the Human Rights Act 1998 came into force and incorporated much of the European Convention on Human Rights into English law. The Act provides the UK with a modern charter of fundamental human rights, enforceable in national courts. This radical shift enables the media, relying directly upon Article 10 of the Convention, to challenge the validity of the English approach to contempt actions.

Students of BJTC and NCTJ accredited courses will study the law of contempt and an array of civil and criminal reporting restrictions in extensive detail. Such coverage is beyond the remit of this single introductory chapter on media law. This section, therefore, will provide an outline of how these complex aspects of law overlap, so that the student is able to set the detail of their studies within a more accessible framework.

Contempt can be an issue in a whole raft of ways:

1   contempt in the face of the court
2   scandalising the court
3   criminal proceedings
4   civil proceedings
5   the common law
6   deliberations of the jury
7   reporting restrictions
8   challenging the courts.

These are each discussed in more detail below.

CONTEMPT IN THE FACE OF THE COURT

This covers the actual events in court. The presiding judge can hold an individual in contempt for inappropriate behaviour. In one case, for example, an individual in the public gallery was held to be in contempt when he wolf-whistled a female member of the jury. Incidents such as the wolf-whistling incident are not part of the formal court proceedings and as such do not attract the protection of privilege. It is legitimate to report the event but care should be taken in relation to the law of defamation. Specific comments that may have been shouted out by an individual might be of a defamatory nature, and journalists are advised to make use of such phrases as 'a disturbance took place' rather than any direct quotations. It is anticipated that all journalists will appreciate the serious nature of court proceedings and it is unlikely that this area of contempt will cause them many personal difficulties. Reflecting upon this area of the law does serve to reinforce the importance and benefits to be gained from visiting the range of courts in your area whilst studying or training to be a journalist. Courts can be very intimidating places, and when your news editor tells you he wants you to cover a court case, you certainly don't want it to be the first time that you've ever set foot in one.

SCANDALISING THE COURT

A journalist can be held in contempt for 'scandalising the court'. This form of contempt attempts to control and limit publications that are calculated to undermine and challenge the authority of the courts and the judiciary. Very few cases have been brought in recent years. It is, after all, arguably the role of the journalist to question the performance and behaviour of the judiciary, so long as such scrutiny is in the public interest and undertaken in a fair, accurate and balanced manner.

CRIMINAL PROCEEDINGS

Section 2(1) of the Contempt of Court Act defines contempt as any publication which 'creates a substantial risk that the course of justice in particular proceedings will be seriously impeded or prejudiced.' This rather ambiguous phrase is left to the courts to interpret. Judges are only able to take action over material deemed to have created a risk that was published after a case becomes active. They have very limited common-law options to deal with material published before this period and can only advise jurors during the trial to ignore pre-trial publicity and to focus upon the evidence presented in such circumstances.

It remains the case that judges in the UK are particularly concerned about the effect of media publicity upon *laymen* in the process. Whilst some cases indicate a suggestion that judges do believe that jurors are able and have the will to ignore the effects of publicity, a prevailing undercurrent reinforces concerns for jurors, witnesses and even lay magistrates, despite any evidence that they are in fact adversely affected.

Reports that refer to the character of the accused, confessions, photographs, details concerning past criminal records, predictions concerning the verdict, or material which creates an 'atmosphere' of prejudice are seen as increasing the risk of being held in contempt. However, the provisions are insufficiently defined and it remains the case that the student of journalism and novice journalist would be well advised to stick to the letter of the law in the early stages of their studies and careers. It is also the case, however, that editors will expect their experienced journalists to push their coverage to the boundaries of what is legal to avoid missing out on a good story in a competitive marketplace.

In summary, it is a contempt of court to publish information which *creates a substantial risk of serious prejudice or impediment to proceedings*. This involves two stages: (a) will the publication affect the case? and (b) if so, would the risk itself be serious?

A number of factors will be taken into account in determining this issue.

- Is a judge, magistrate(s) or a jury hearing the case? The judiciary argues that judges are not susceptible to prejudicial reporting. But if a case involves a jury, the risk increases. Magistrates fall somewhere between the two extremes.
- The defendant's record. Steer clear of any references to the criminal record of the accused.
- Proximity of time. If the trial hearing is not imminent, then the risk of contempt may be reduced.
- The location of the trial. A case in one area reported in a local area elsewhere, in an inappropriate way, may not necessarily create a substantial risk of prejudicing the trial.
- The issue of identity. If the identity of the accused is an issue, then nothing must be published which identifies that person. Checks should be made with the police, the solicitor of the accused, and for any orders of the court placing restrictions on the media coverage.
- During the trial be careful if the jury are sent out. Statements made in court whilst the jury are out or those which are deemed inadmissible cannot be used in any reports.
- Comments by the defendant outside court proceedings. It is acceptable for the defendant to assert his innocence. Avoid details that may be used as evidence in court. Avoid defamatory comments made by the defendant.
- Comments made by witnesses outside court proceedings. Once the case is active, the journalist must be very careful when interviewing witnesses. These individuals may be required to give evidence in court and publication might be seen to contaminate their evidence.
- The verdict. Do not second-guess the verdict during the trial or while the jury is considering its verdict.
- Watch out for specific statutory restrictions imposed by a judge in the case. Under the Contempt of Court Act a judge may impose restrictions on reports produced by the media. Under Section 4(2) of the Contempt of Court Act a judge can postpone publication if it is felt that there is a substantial risk that the case will be prejudiced. Under Section 11 the court can prohibit the mentioning of names of individuals involved in the case. The media are able to state that such restrictions apply. Don't forget that other statutory restrictions may also apply.

Another important thing to remember is that contempt is a strict liability offence. This means that intention is not relevant and the prosecution does not have to prove that the act was intended, reckless or negligent.

Furthermore, the proceedings must be *active* for the contempt law to apply. A case is active if any of the following apply.

- A warrant for arrest has been issued.
- An arrest has been made.
- An individual has been charged.
- A summons has been issued (civil cases).
- A civil case is set down for trial.
- An inquest is opened.
- The court case is continuing.
- Awaiting sentencing.
- When an appeal is lodged (civil or criminal).

A case ceases to be active at the end of a court case, on acquittal or conviction. The student journalist should note that a statutory defence is available.

1 **Section 3:** The innocent intent defence. The journalist is able to argue that, having taken all reasonable care, he/she did not know, and had no reason to suspect that proceedings were active. This isn't quite as helpful as it might appear. Always double-check whether a case is active.
2 **Section 4:** A journalist can legitimately cover a court case as long as the report is fair and accurate, contemporaneous and in good faith. Such coverage will also provide a full defence to any potential defamation action.
3 **Section 5:** The public interest defence. This allows for public debate on the general issues that might be raised by an incident or on-going court case. The key is to avoid specific references to the case in hand.

It is vital to remember that a breach can result in a fine or imprisonment. Moreover it is contempt of court to use, or take into court for use, any tape recorder to make any recordings, unless prior permission has been given by the court.

Editors argue that of all the areas of law, contempt and related reporting restrictions are one of the most important legal considerations for students on journalism courses to understand and apply. Given the overlapping legal constraints and the vagueness of aspects of the contempt provisions, it can be a difficult area for the novice to master.

CIVIL PROCEEDINGS

It is a contempt of court to publish information that creates a substantial risk of serious prejudice or impediment to civil proceedings. The Contempt of Court Act 1981 also applies to civil proceedings, although given that most civil cases do not involve a jury, it is less likely to cause difficulties to journalists. (Note, however, that defamation actions are civil cases and are generally heard before a jury.)

THE COMMON LAW

Most journalists will be concerned to familiarise themselves with the provisions of the Contempt of Court Act 1981. Somewhat confusingly, the 1981 Act did not do away with all the old common law rules in relation to contempt. As such a journalist may feel secure that as a case is not active, he cannot be found guilty of the statutory offence under the 1981 legislation, but he may be guilty at common law. Common law contempt requires the prosecution to prove that the publisher published material that was calculated to prejudice the proceedings. The prosecution must show that the publisher *intended* to cause the prejudice. The journalist must, therefore, still take great care in how a potentially pre-active breaking story is covered.

DELIBERATIONS OF THE JURY

Under the Contempt of Court Act, it is an offence to seek or disclose information about a jury's deliberations or voting in the jury room.

REPORTING RESTRICTIONS

A number of restrictions apply automatically or may be applied by order of the court to the reporting of certain types of court cases and incidents. For example, restrictions apply to the reporting of certain cases involving children, incidents and cases involving a range of sexual offences, committal hearings and bail applications. Concerns also exist in relation to extensive media coverage which, whilst individual elements may be within the law, collectively create a 'jigsaw effect', enabling people to identify suspects as well as wrongly implicating others who are innocent.

There is a vast array of specific statutory provision, which can be invoked by the courts to restrain the activities of journalists. This is a crucial area of knowledge for the student of journalism to absorb. Coverage of the detail of these provisions is beyond the remit of this chapter. Students should use this introduction to the subject to affirm that alarms bells should ring when a news story that they are covering involves children, reporting the courts or incidents involving allegations of sexual assault. It is then imperative for the student journalist to check when and how relevant provisions apply to the story and equally importantly when they don't.

CHALLENGING THE COURTS

The myriad and complex set of reporting restrictions that exist in English law present a challenge for the student and working journalist to absorb. It is quite common to see the most experienced of journalists referring to their trusty legal textbooks to double-check just what detail can be included in a particular news item. Interestingly, it would appear that the courts also struggle at times with this issue and it is not unknown for restrictions to be applied inappropriately or excessively by the courts. Journalists do have the right and indeed the responsibility to make an application to the courts to challenge such decisions. This is an intimidating process, but should not be shied away from, given the importance attached to the free reporting of matters that should be in the public domain.

PRIVACY

I always believed the press would kill her [Princess Diana] in the end. But not even I could imagine that they would take such a direct hand in her death as seems to be the case ... She talked endlessly of getting away from England, mainly because of the treatment she received at the hands of the newspapers.

Princess Diana's brother, Earl Spencer, September 6 1997

In these understandably emotional times, those who wish to take it out on the British media should be reminded that Diana died in France, which has the strictest privacy laws in the democratic world, being followed by relentless French photographers looking for pictures with a global sales potential. France's privacy laws did not save her; but over the years they have emasculated genuine investigative reporting by French newspapers. Nevertheless, British editors badly need to mend their ways if they are not to play into the enemy's hands ... The public could also do with examining its own conscience: though quick to condemn such journalism, they continue to buy the papers which practise it in their millions.

Andrew Neil, September 1 1997

It is ... imperative that journalists act at all times in accordance with the standards of responsible journalism if they are to protect themselves from privacy claims.

Iain Christie
barrister, 2002

The desire for a private life is deeply rooted and privacy is not simply a legal problem, but an ethical issue for journalists to grapple with.[6] Much of the concern about invasions of privacy in the UK has arisen as a direct result of perceived inappropriate interferences by the media and the press in particular. Take a look at any of the tabloids and you'll find a story that appears to be treading a less than fine line between what is in the public interest and what is simply a prurient piece of gossip used to increase sales or an audience. In 2001, for example, the supermodel Naomi Campbell was distraught by the coverage in the *Daily Mirror* of her then drug addiction and the invasive photographs taken of her leaving a meeting of Narcotics Anonymous.

In defending such stories, journalists claim that they are serving the public interest and upholding the important concepts of freedom of information and expression. The nature of their work means that journalists as well as the authorities may legitimately investigate allegations of malpractice in public affairs or other legitimate areas of concern. It is also inevitable that this may involve issues that individuals or organisations, for legitimate reasons or otherwise, wish to keep out of the public domain. The Press Complaints Commission's Code of Practice also asserts that apparent invasions of privacy may be necessary to prevent 'the public from being misled by an action or statement of an individual or organisation'. Critics argue, however, that some journalists are duplicitous, hypocritical, dishonest, insensitive and abuse the public interest defence to justify particular publications. The difficulty for the law and indeed the journalist, therefore, is in drawing the boundaries between what is in the public interest and what is merely interesting to the public; in differentiating between what the public wants to know, needs to know and has a right to know.

There is no general right to privacy in English law. Privacy rights are only protected so far as they are compatible with the public interest. The main difficulty in English law is that it has been more attuned to property rights than human rights. Unless victims were able to demonstrate damage to physical property, their prospects of recovery were slim. Aspects of privacy are protected, however, by common law, equitable and statutory provisions. While protecting privacy interests may not have been the driving force behind these provisions, it remains the case that they are used by claimants to this effect. Samples of the various legal provisions which can be used to provide a means of protecting privacy are outlined below.

DEFAMATION

The law of defamation can be used in certain circumstances to protect privacy. Generally, injunctions that serve to prevent publication of allegedly defamatory information are resisted by the courts in preference to the interest in freedom of expression. It remains the case, however, that the threat of legal action in such circumstances can cause an editor to pull a story. This so-called chilling-effect means that the individual's reputation remains intact and in addition, aspects of the story touching on the individual's private life may also remain protected.

TRESPASS

The law of trespass is also relevant to the privacy debate. Property or land owners can choose to take legal action to protect their interests. This can take the form of an action to prevent a person re-entering their land (an injunction) or a request for compensation for any damage done to the land. In terms of privacy, this means that a property owner can use the law to remove journalists from his premises and if the journalist is deemed to be harassing, the individual can use the law to stop this unwelcome behaviour. The law of trespass, however, does have its limitations in terms of protecting privacy interests. Trespass cannot be used to prevent publication of information discovered during the 'trespass'. It also does not cover intrusion that originates from outside the area of land or premises ownership. So the law of trespass, for example, couldn't be used to prevent long-distance lens photography or someone using binoculars to see into your property.

So as a journalist, if you go on to someone's private property, you are a trespasser, and they can ask you to leave. What options are then available for getting the story? If there is a significant public interest aspect to the story, it may be legitimate to set up a 'scam' elsewhere to cover the same story. This is a technique used by investigative journalists such as Roger Cook and Donal MacIntyre. It can be expensive, but often makes compelling viewing. Approval from senior management is required.

Alternatively, if the story doesn't involve any covert activity, the problems of trespass can be avoided by simply seeking permission of the owner. For larger projects a *location agreement* can be obtained from the owner of the property. This agreement will normally cover such issues as:

- what parts of the property/land you have access to
- how long access is required
- what you'll be doing there
- the fee
- insurance issues
- rights of exploitation and publicity
- the right to rename the property if required.

NUISANCE

Nuisance is another civil action which can be used by individuals in an effort to protect their privacy. As with the law of trespass, it has only a limited use in directly protecting an individual's privacy. The law of nuisance seeks to protect all citizens' rights to 'the quiet enjoyment of their land'. In terms of being used to protect privacy interests, the law of nuisance might be used, for example, to prevent constant harassment by surveillance. It is of little use in the protection of *unknown* surveillance. Similarly it cannot be used in any way to prevent publication of material obtained through that surveillance.

COPYRIGHT

Copyright law can be used to protect against some disclosure of commercially or personally confidential information. The owner of a copyright interest can use the law in an attempt to prevent journalists (and others) publishing certain material, although the defence of 'fair dealing' may allow some flexibility.

DATA PROTECTION

Research indicates that only a small percentage of the population worries about personal information being known by others. The main concern centres upon inaccurate information being held, the inappropriate disclosure of information to others, and the risk of unjust inference. Journalists hold lots of information about individuals. This may well form the basis of genuine quality investigative work. Equally, it may simply be information held on a famous person, with no real justifiable public interest defence. The Data Protection Act and other legislation concerning personal records regulates the use to which these can be put and the circumstances in which they can be communicated to others. The problems for the journalist are that the data protection provisions:

- can be used to hinder/assist journalistic activities, and
- can be used as a way of protecting privacy rights.

BREACH OF CONFIDENCE

This is a developing action which has been used to protect privacy interests. The law acknowledges that there will be certain situations when a duty can be imposed on the recipient of information to keep it secret. The most obvious examples are expressed or implied confidentiality terms contained within contracts of employment. The courts have been willing to use the law in this area to provide injunctions and compensation for individuals and organisations.

The information must have 'the necessary quality of confidence about it'. The information must have been imparted in circumstances imposing an obligation of confidence. An unauthorised use of the information by the party who was under the obligation will give rise to an action. The journalist may be able to argue that the public interest in publishing outweighs the public interest in preventing disclosure.

A number of other statutory and common law provisions exist which can be used by individuals in an attempt to protect their privacy, or suppress a story, depending on your perspective.[7]

ARTICLE 8 OF THE EUROPEAN CONVENTION ON HUMAN RIGHTS

Incorporation of the ECHR into English law has led to a number of high-profile cases in which it has been argued that Article 8 has created a tangible right to privacy. Article 8 of the Convention covers distinct aspects of privacy: private life, respect for the home, and respect for correspondence. While the English courts increasingly look to the decisions of the European Court of Human Rights for guidance, it remains the case that, at present, there is no freestanding right to privacy in English law. Calls for the Government to enforce a statutory right to privacy to protect individuals against intrusion by the media and others have also been rejected in favour of self-regulation. For the student of journalism, the law relating to privacy can appear to be a very complex and confusing issue. That's because it is. The student will need to be familiar with the range of English legal provisions, the potential influence of Article 8, but equally importantly, the relevant sections of industry codes of practice.[8]

REPORTING ELECTIONS

In the run-up to an election, we do monitor how much time each party is given and that information is submitted to the regulators. We have a book with a running total of minutes per party, this enables us to say – 'Look they've not had much time, go and find a Liberal Democrat ...'

Mike Blair
editor
Central News East

All elections are good for news, features, exposés and documentaries. They generate profiles of candidates, constituencies or wards, provide an opportunity to analyse individual and party manifestos, and explore local and national issues. Media coverage of elections is constrained by a variety of legal provisions and regulatory guidelines. These constraints seek to reinforce and uphold the significance of freedom of speech during an election period whilst providing some protection from falsehoods and other abuses intended to interfere with the democratic process.

It is likely that a local media outlet will find itself covering an election of one form or another on a fairly regular basis. European elections are held every five years. UK general elections have to be held at any time within five years of the last election. Most local government elections are held for the whole council every four years, or for one-third of the council every three years. In addition, a range of circumstances can give rise to a by-election at virtually any time. For the student journalist, elections provide an excellent opportunity to gain valuable work experience. Local media outlets, keen to be the first with election results, may be willing to use trainee journalists to telephone through constituency poll details. Getting involved in this way provides a useful insight into the democratic process and the nature of political coverage amongst different media organisations. A sound and up-to-date awareness of the differing rules and regulations applicable during an election period is vital.

The election period runs as follows.

- **In a parliamentary general election** – from the date of the dissolution of Parliament or any earlier time at which Her Majesty's intention to dissolve Parliament is announced.
- **In a parliamentary by-election** – from the date of the issue of the writ for the election or any earlier date on which a certificate of the vacancy is notified in the *London Gazette* in accordance with the Recess Elections Act 1975.
- **In a local government election** – from the last date for publication of the election.

Print journalists and publishers may take sides and express prejudicial opinions in an election run-up, whereas broadcasters have to exercise 'due impartiality'; maintaining balance, fairness and accuracy at all times on matters of political controversy.

The main legal and regulatory provisions of relevance to election reporting are contained within:

- the Representation of the People Act 1983 and the Political Parties, Elections and Referendums Act 2000;
- specific broadcasting Regulatory Guidelines on reporting elections;
- general provisions contained within regulatory codes and producer's guidelines;
- law of defamation;
- Public Order Act 1986 (and related provisions); and
- Copyright, Designs and Patents Act 1988 (and related provisions).

A detailed consideration of these regulations and legal provisions is beyond the remit of this chapter, but selected issues referred to below reinforce the requirement for a heightened state of legal awareness amongst journalists when reporting upon elections.

SPECIFIC REGULATORY GUIDELINES: BROADCASTING DURING AN 'ELECTION PERIOD'

During the 'election period', broadcasters must maintain the highest standards of fairness, balance and accuracy. The Political Parties, Elections and Referendums Act 2000 (s.144) requires the relevant broadcasting authority to adopt a code of practice with respect to the participation of candidates at a parliamentary or local government election. At the time of writing, Ofcom's Broadcasting Code is due for publication in 2005 and will include a section on election and referendum reporting. It should be noted that this section of Ofcom's Code will not apply to the BBC, which is regulated on matters of due impartiality and accuracy in news by the BBC Board of Governors.

THE LAW OF DEFAMATION

The law of defamation, as noted earlier in this chapter, is a serious consideration for journalists. Whilst the working journalist should, of course, maintain the highest professional standards at all times, it remains the case that once an election has been called, candidates are arguably more sensitive about the content of media coverage. The law itself acknowledges the impact that the publication of false statements about the personal character or conduct of a candidate may have by creating a specific offence, if it can be shown that the publication was calculated to affect the election result.

The defence of statutory qualified privilege can be very helpful to the journalist when reporting during an election period, but your report must be fair, accurate, published without malice and the matter must be of public concern. The report is also subject to explanation or contradiction. It is essential that the journalist is aware, however, that the defence only applies in certain circumstances. If in doubt check, but here are some pointers for an election period.

- Election materials, for example manifestos, do not attract the protection of statutory qualified privilege, so don't quote from such documents blindly.
- Public meetings held during an election period do attract statutory qualified privilege.
- Statements made by candidates at press conferences are covered by statutory qualified privilege.
- Statements made by candidates during general interviews do not attract statutory qualified privilege.

THE PUBLIC ORDER ACT 1986

It is an offence to display, publish or distribute material that is threatening, abusive or insulting if the likely outcome is that racial hatred will be stirred up. Racial hatred is defined as 'hatred against a group ... by reference to colour, race, nationality or ethnic or national origins'. Just as a media organisation or journalist can be sued for repeating a libellous statement made by another party, so the journalist can also be prosecuted under the Public Order Act for reporting an inflammatory speech. This can become a serious editorial issue when reporting elections.

COPYRIGHT LAW

The main point of interest here is in relation to the recording of speeches at meetings during an election period. Technically, the speaker has copyright in what he or she says and could limit the use that is made of any recording of the meeting. In the main though, candidates welcome the publicity and this is unlikely to be an issue, but it might be the case that things were said that the candidate wishes he hadn't, and this might make an excellent news story. In such a situation the speaker might claim copyright over the material in attempt to stop the journalist using the material. The law states that the journalist is allowed to use the record of the words for the reporting of current events, but only in the following circumstances.

- If it is a direct record.
- If the speaker did not place restrictions on the manner in which the recording can be used or prohibit the recording *before* the speech is made.
- If the speaker did not limit or prohibit any use that can be made of the recording before it was made.

Should a speaker place restrictions on how a recording is subsequently used, an alternative is for the journalists to produce a fair and accurate summary of what was said, as limited extracts of the speech may be used without infringing copyright.

As an election draws closer, news organisations will do the following.

- Consider how they are going to cover the election.
- Collate statistical information on the current political balance and voting patterns within constituencies or across particular regions. Lists of electors are public documents and are free for journalists to inspect. Copies should be available at libraries and relevant local government offices.
- Collate accurate candidate profile information.
- Confirm and cultivate contact details for the main parties and candidates, including addresses, telephone numbers and websites.
- Obtain up-to-date details on the local authority electoral registration manager.
- Confirm the arrangements and location of election counts. Admission to the count is at the discretion of the returning officer.
- Remind staff of the dangers of defamatory statements.

- Remember that the law prohibits the publication of exit polls before the official poll closes, where the information is reasonably taken to be based on information given by voters after they have voted.
- Broadcasters have to take into account particular considerations.

  - The organisation must develop and manage an effective system for keeping records of political coverage to provide evidence of balanced coverage. This balance has to be achieved in terms of the coverage across a day, a week and the whole of the election period.
  - Checks must be made when broadcasters intend making use of members of the public, for example in phone-ins to local radio stations. Is the caller standing as a candidate or related to a candidate? Is the caller part of some elaborate scam to get publicity for a candidate?
  - Guests need to be booked well in advance, as every other media outlet will also be chasing them.
  - Take particular care during live discussion programmes because of the risk of defamation. If disaster strikes, mitigate. Disassociate yourself and your employers from the remarks. Your organisation may still be sued, but it may help reduce any damages awarded.

- Print journalists need to do the following.

  - Check the rules on election print advertisements.
  - Check editorials carefully for potential defamatory content.
  - Be aware that, unlike broadcasters, the law allows news media support through editorial comment.

COPYRIGHT LAW

The law of copyright (also referred to as an intellectual property right) is complex. For most students studying journalism, the first important concept to get clear is the nature of this legal interest and the ways in which it affects the work of journalists. As in most other substantive legal subjects introduced in this chapter, the student is advised to undertake additional reading to inform their understanding.

Copyright directly protects an owner's interest across a range of works generated through their skill and creativity. It also serves to protect the general public interest that exists in developing commercial and cultural activity and encouraging innovation. The law does not aim to provide a monopoly for a potential claimant but seeks to prevent others from copying an original work without the authority of the owner. This in turns ensures the exclusive right of the owner to profit from the reproduction and dissemination of his work.

The law does not protect ideas, but rather the expression of those ideas and recognises three broad classes of work:

1   original literary, dramatic, musical or artistic works
2   sound recordings, films, broadcasts or cable programmes
3   the typographical arrangement of published editions.

Copyright belongs to the author or creator of the work. It can be individually or jointly owned and if the work is created in the course of employment, then copyright will normally belong to the employer.

Copyright has a limited duration and in the majority of cases extends 70 years from the author's death. An infringement can result in damages being awarded to the injured party as well as the handing over or destruction of infringing copies if demanded. There are a number of defences available, including that of fair dealing, which is particularly useful in the reporting of current events and in criticism and review.

This aspect of law is relevant to the working journalist in a number of different contexts. Journalists need to consider if there are any copyright issues related to the story that they wish to cover. This does not necessarily mean that they will not be able to cover the story in the preferred manner, but it does mean that they may need to seek the copyright owner's permission, or check that their use of the material is covered by one of the defences, such as fair dealing. The broadcast journalist, by way of example, needs to reflect upon the potential copyright implications when recording an interview. There may be background music which raises copyright considerations and a copyright interest may exist in the spoken word itself in certain circumstances. Having produced a news story, the journalist should be aware that whilst there is no copyright in the news itself, the article or broadcast involved skill, creativity and production costs. This in turn, therefore, is copyrighted and the news organisation can control future distribution and use.

PROTECTING SOURCES

Every journalist knows that sources are the life-blood of a good story. On many occasions sources are quite willing to be named. It may also be crucial to produce such an individual to defend a legal action. There are circumstances, however, when sources will only come forward and provide information on the understanding that their identity will not be disclosed. Journalists need to cultivate contacts and confidential relationships to ensure that informants are willing to come forward with information of public concern and for journalists to perform their perceived role as public watchdog. The PCC and the NUJ make it quite clear that journalists should protect confidential sources of information.[9] For journalists therefore, the issue is ethical rather than legal.

The Contempt of Court Act 1981, which does not provide any special status or immunity for journalists, does state that no court may require a person to disclose the source of information contained in a publication unless it is established to the satisfaction of the court that disclosure 'is necessary in the interests of justice or national security or for the prevention of crime and disorder.'[10] While the law appears to provide support for the journalist who refuses to disclose a source, the reality has been that on the occasions when the courts have had to weigh one public interest against another, the decision has been to order those journalists to reveal their source. Should the journalist choose to follow his conscience and professional code of conduct, any refusal to comply with such an order may constitute contempt, leading to a term of imprisonment or a hefty fine.

Steve Panter, a reporter for the *Manchester Evening News*, ran a story in which he identified a prime suspect in the 1996 IRA Manchester bombing in which around 200 people were injured. A police officer was charged with leaking the information to the press and Panter was brought before the court and required to reveal his source. Panter refused to do so and having defied the judge's order, faced a potential prosecution for contempt and a possible prison sentence. In the end the Attorney General announced that it would not be in the public interest to bring contempt charges.

The student of journalism should also note that several other legal provisions, such as anti-terrorism and official secrets legislation, along with specific powers granted to the police, provide relevant bodies with the authority in certain circumstances to obtain information or documentation.

CONCLUSION

This chapter has provided a brief introduction to a number of legal provisions which affect the work of journalists in a variety of ways. The subjects covered are selective, serving to illustrate that an awareness and understanding of the law is vital to those working in the industry. Students of journalism should note that many other aspects of law from official secrets legislation to race relations provisions, from health and safety regulations to obscenity laws, will at differing times impinge upon their activities. Journalists are not lawyers, but they need to understand the nature and influence of the law, they also need to ensure that they remain up to date with recent legal developments. For the student of journalism, this means referring to the most current textbooks available. Legal journals, such as the bi-monthly *Media Lawyer*, are also useful for keeping up-to date with the latest developments (www.Medialawyer-subs@pa.press.net). For the working journalist, this should be supported through regular legal refresher training provision.

NOTES

1 All quotes from Mike Blair taken from author interview 2003.

2 For a definition of precedent see Chapter 6.

3 All quotes from Alastair Brett taken from 'Law for Journalists' conference, London, December 2002.

4 All quotes from Justin Walford taken from 'Law for Journalists' conference, London, December 2002.

5 Shipman was jailed for life in January 2000 for murdering 15 patients while working in Hyde, Greater Manchester.

6 See Chapter 10.

7 For example, harrassment, child protection and interception of communications legislation.

8 See, for example, the Press Complaints Commission, section 3 at http://www.ppc.org.uk. See also Chapter 10.

9 See section 14 of the PCC code of conduct at www.pcc.org.uk and section 7 of the NUJ's Code of Conduct at www.nuj.org.uk.

10 Section 10.

REPORTING THE COURTS

Court reporting is far more than sitting in court with a pen and paper. It is about examining the human angle, developing a story to its full potential and giving the reader a clear, balanced picture. If an individual is cleared by a jury or on a legal technicality, try to interview them. Their story is often better than anything anyone has heard in court.

Rebecca Sherdley[1]
Nottingham Evening Post

Imagine if Dominic Downey, our dear departed drowning victim from Chapter 3, had instead been arrested for drink-driving. The first problem you might encounter would be that, as a 15 year old, he would be heading for the youth courts and that we wouldn't be able to name him (for more on reporting restrictions, see Chapter 7).

So let's assume that a few years have passed and that Dominic is due to appear at Mickleover Magistrates' Courts (and don't forget that's where the apostrophe goes – more than one magistrate – a common error). Your first problem now would be finding out exactly *when* he is going to appear. That problem may be solved with the help of a friendly police officer. Alternatively, try ringing the court itself. If Dominic had committed a more serious offence and was eventually due to appear at Crown Court, the court may send lists of cases planned for the week ahead, or you can try the website www.courtserve2.net, which gives daily court lists for every Crown Court in the country. But beware – cases can be moved.

The rest of this chapter will focus on the basics of what you must have in your story and the different ways courts are covered by newspaper, radio, TV and online journalists.

GOING TO COURT FOR THE FIRST TIME

This can be fairly nerve-racking. You're faced with a new experience, or one that you've only seen in courtroom dramas. And knowing what you should do by now about the Contempt of Court Act, you may feel as though you're on trial yourself. You should, however, remind yourself that you are simply doing what you've (hopefully) been trained to do – report the news.

> No fundamental difference exists between court reporting and any other reporting. The requirements are the same: to understand what has happened and to report it fairly, accurately, clearly and in a manner to catch the attention of the reader. (Harris and Spark, 1997: 92)

Despite that, it's probably a good idea to try to go for the first time with an experienced reporter or track one down when you get there. If there are a number of courts, and there probably will be, it's worth getting there early to find which one you should be in. Ideally, you will also collar one of the most important contacts at court – the clerk. He or she will be able to give you key information like:

- the name of the presiding magistrate or judge (who is likely to provide key quotes for your stories)
- the name of the prosecuting lawyer (who will possibly be the same throughout the course of a court session and will feature prominently in your articles)
- details of cases worth looking out for.

Many courts now allow journalists to tape proceedings on the proviso that they will not use the recording for broadcast, and will surrender it to the court at the end of the day. But in some cases you may not be able to take tape recorders into court, which may put newspaper reporters with their impeccable 100 words-a-minute shorthand at an advantage. Most newspaper journalists need to have this useful skill if they are to become senior reporters – or even get a job in the first place.

One thing that you could do before you actually go to court is to acquaint yourself with the layout and personnel you will find there. Try visiting a website called www.juror.cjsonline.org, which shows interior views of courts and gives descriptions of some of the key players (judge, clerk, prosecution, defence) and also outlines the duties of other key court staff (ushers, probation officers, etc.).

One last thing about going to court: always dress to impress. As Keeble says, 'You won't be thrown out for wearing scruffy clothes but you may find judge, counsel and court officials less helpful' (2000: 207).

THE CASE ITSELF

Cases usually start with the prosecuting lawyer outlining what happened. This is a key element of the case which will contribute a large part of your story, so you should be ready to take a full note. Obviously, if a defendant denies the charge, this will be what the prosecution *alleges* happened. If the defendant admits his guilt, either he or the defence lawyer will offer mitigating circumstances – something which they hope will make the punishment less severe. Before the magistrate or judge passes sentence, they will ask if there are any other offences to be taken into consideration or if the accused has any previous convictions. But if the defendant has pleaded not guilty, the prosecution will call witnesses to establish the alleged facts. These witnesses may be questioned (or cross-examined) by the defending lawyer, who may then call his own witnesses. Finally, the accused may take the stand to be questioned by both sides before both prosecution and defence lawyers make their closing statements and the magistrates (or jurors) retire to consider their verdict.

CONTINUING COURT CASES

A reporter's life is made considerably easier if the accused admits his or her guilt, but some of the juiciest cases occur when the opposite happens. In the event of a defendant pleading not guilty, the reporter should take great care to make sure that his or her story does not imply that anything heard in court is fact (until, of course, the verdict has been given). The article, or broadcast, will thus be sprinkled with liberal doses of words and phrases like *alleged, the court heard*, and *Ronnie Rumpole, prosecuting, told Mickleover magistrates* (not upper case for magistrates this time because we're not referring to the court, in case you were wondering). Nothing is *fact* in a continuing trial (and you should say somewhere in your piece that it is continuing) but remember that if someone has admitted manslaughter rather than murder, you can still call them a killer. One other thing to remember – it is the style for most of the media that the accused (whether admitting or denying guilt) does not receive a courtesy title. So it's Dominic Downey at first mention, then Downey.

Here is a list of essentials to find out and put in your story.

- The name of the court (this should be fairly straightforward).
- The charge (sometimes these can be abbreviated, therefore *assault causing actual bodily harm* becomes *assault*; occasionally they may be a bit more complicated, such as *causing harm through furious driving on a pedal cycle*, in which case you might want to spell out that it's a little-known charge).
- The plea (whether they have admitted or denied the charge).

- The sentence (try to spell out what this is in full. If someone has faced two charges, got four years for one and two years for the other to run concurrently, say so).
- The full name and address of the defendant (you cannot be selective here and in some instances may even need to consider putting someone's street number in if they have a common surname and live on a long road: you must not risk the chance of libelling someone else with the same surname on the same road).

Other things you need to remember.

- Ideally you should have colour and drama high up in your story. What this means (for starters) is that you should never begin with words like 'A Derby man ...' or 'A court has heard ...'. Try the first two paragraphs of this story from the *Sun* (name changed, as you will see).

> A DRUNKEN cyclist who left a nurse brain damaged after he smashed into her at 20mph was jailed for nine months yesterday.
>   Dominic Downey sent the woman flying as she window-shopped in a pedestrian zone. (*Sun*, August 23 2000)

- Use the language of the layman, so 'jailed for nine months' (or if it's a youth who has been sent to a detention centre, say they've been locked up), not 'sentenced to nine months' imprisonment'. Similarly, say nearly two pints, not a litre.
- Use the right tense, so an intro like the *Sun*'s which started 'A drunken man has crashed his bike' would be wrong.
- Avoid using dashes in intros when they're not justified, as in: 'Disgraced Dominic Downey has been jailed for nine months after running over a student nurse – with his bicycle.' This makes it sound like it's almost amusing and also applies to other stories, not just court ones.
- Put names and addresses in capitals or clear handwriting when you're making your notes in court.
- Use quotes. Just like any other story, you should be seeking balance in your court reporting. However, you may find that when someone has admitted his guilt or been found guilty, the amount of mitigation may reduce or disappear altogether. But as a budding reporter, you should leave this decision to 'chop' quotes to your news editor or a sub-editor.

Remember that courts are serious places and contempt in the face of the court is a real issue. If the judge is unhappy with your behaviour, you can be fined or imprisoned on the spot. Courts can be intimidating, distressing, alarming and sometimes downright amusing. There follows a checklist of tips from students, lawyers and journalists to help you prepare for your first and subsequent court visits.

CHECKLIST

✓   Visit the whole range of courts.

✓   Go as often as you can.

✓   Find out what time the court opens and cases start.

✓   When planning to visit employment tribunals or coroners' courts, always telephone in advance as there will not necessarily be a case running every day. You should also check on the day you plan to visit these courts to avoid a wasted journey, as cases are often adjourned at the last minute.

✓   A visit to the courts can involve a lot of hanging around. Take a law book with you to read.

✓   Find out where the prison van accesses the court. If you're taking film footage, this may be one of the few shots that you can get.

✓   Establish the local interpretation of what constitutes the 'precincts of the court' because the law prohibits the taking of any photographs in this area.

✓   Get to know the usher(s). If they are not busy, they are often willing to answer questions.

✓   Get there early.

✓   If you are in doubt about what to do or where to go, check with the usher.

✓   As a student, avoid the seats saved for the press at this stage, but don't be a shrinking violet. Sit where you can hear and see what's going on, but not at the back.

✓   Do not get a fit of the giggles.

✓   Do not talk during the case.

✓   No chewing gum.

✓   Remove headwear as appropriate.

✓   Stand when the judge enters or leaves the court.

✓   Do not take recording equipment or cameras in to the court.

✓   The right to attend court includes the right to take notes of what is said there. This applies to the public as well as to journalists. Court officials will sometimes try to stop those in the public gallery from taking notes. It is worth checking politely with the usher if you have permission to take notes. If permission is ever refused, do not enter into a debate, but report it to your law tutor on returning to your college.

✓   When taking notes do so quietly. Shorthand helps. Be accurate and check the spelling of all names. Don't get this wrong or you could end up being sued for defamation.

✓   If there are journalists present, have a chat to them about the case and how they would approach reporting it.

✓   You can leave the court at any time, but choose your moment with care, and leave quietly. On your way in, check which way the door opens – inwards or outwards? There is nothing worse than moving quietly to the door to make your way out during a case only to find yourself scrabbling with the door for five minutes.

MAGISTRATES' COURTS

We owe it to all defendants to be accurate – however long their criminal record. First-time offenders may be stunned and ashamed that neighbours are likely to read all about them. Spell everyone's names correctly. If there is a dispute over a report, people will also list spelling errors and make the copy appear to be littered with mistakes. Assume that offenders – or their families – will be reading and re-reading your copy looking for something to complain about. One mother phoned to complain about a story covering her son's burglary of the family home. She objected to the description that he 'raided' the house. She also said the report should not have been placed on the page next to an indecency case.

Rod Malcolm[2]
freelance journalist

Magistrates sentence more than 90 per cent of all criminal cases. The remainder start out in front of magistrates on their way to higher courts. Rod Malcolm, who has been an East Midlands-based journalist since 1968, says that, because of the weight of the work, reporters may quickly gain the feeling that cases are similar. But he adds: 'They rarely are and it's the detail that makes the story.'

DRINK-DRIVING

Drink-driving is a good example. This leads to an automatic ban except in rare instances. Motorists may avoid a disqualification if they can show they were driving in an emergency. Another explanation is that their drinks were laced. Both arguments can be relied on to create copy.

Even when the drink-driver admits the offence, there is often a good angle. Malcolm says, 'One case involved a man who was hurrying home from the takeaway because he didn't want his curry to get cold. The police pulled him over for speeding then smelt alcohol on his breath.'

TRAFFIC COURTS

Traffic courts may seem routine but motorway speeders often have an interesting explanation. Malcolm describes how at one hearing, a businessman admitted driving at 110 mph. He was rushing to the airport with samples for a textile order. The samples were unsatisfactory, the £500,000 deal was lost and 6 people were made redundant. And he was banned for speeding.

In the same court session, a driver admitted doing 106 mph on the road. He was not banned because magistrates accepted his explanation that his speedometer was jammed at 65 mph – and he was amazed to be pulled over.

COVERING MORE THAN ONE COURT

Trying to cover several courts is a major worry and something that journalists usually try to avoid. It is very risky trying to get prosecution and defence to repeat what they've said in court. They may well refuse. But, if you're under pressure to cover other courts, you should be able to pick up the magistrate's decision from the court clerk. It's important to check the charge, just in case it was changed at the last minute. People pleading not guilty to a common assault may agree to be bound over to keep the peace. In that case, the charge is usually withdrawn.

MORE HELP AT HAND

As well as striking up a working relationship with clerks, ushers are very helpful. These are busy people but may well help if cases are being switched from one court-room to another. Prosecuting solicitors may well be prepared to confirm the defendant's name, age, address and charge. Defence solicitors may clarify details arising from their comments to court. They cannot be expected to add anything which harms their client. Police may offer guidance about imminent court appearances.

PRACTICALITIES

It is possible to avoid sitting through adjournments. Some courts sell results lists to the media. However, there is an advantage to listening to adjournments because you may get an outline of the case. This could be worth following up. Rod Malcolm offers the following advice:

> If you are attending an adjournment court, take other work with you. If you have stories to write, you may well find time for that. I also take council minutes, company annual reports – stuff that needs reading in the search for stories. When sent to court for a specific case, don't ignore all the other cases going on before it. Newsdesks don't know everything, though they sometimes like to think they do. It's quite possible that other matters may produce better copy.

WALKING A TIGHTROPE

There is evidence to show that local papers get into trouble for abusing report-ing restrictions while the national media get away with it. But defence solicitors are pushing at these rules, sometimes giving interviews outside court. What they do very rarely, however, is exercise their right in court to lift press restrictions. Care is needed in this field, even in reporting fulsome tributes to alleged murder victims.

Malcolm tells how in one case, a death notice in a regional newspaper described a man as a 'gentle giant who wouldn't hurt anyone'. This was used by the press but could be challenged by a man charged with murdering the 'gentle giant' who was allegedly involved in trouble shortly before his death.

HOW TO WRITE YOUR STORIES

For all but major stories, most media outlets prefer completed cases. Magistrates often hear cases, then adjourn for reports before deciding on sentence. What people need to read is what the person did, why he did it, and what magistrates did to him.

Malcolm says: 'There's nothing wrong with writing stories straight. Don't strain the facts for a flashy style.' This is his outline of a standard and acceptable opening for a court story:

> A BEREAVED son was ordered to carry out 100 hours of community work for smashing six shop windows.
>
> Magistrates heard that he was trying to come to terms with the death of his mother, who cared for him.
>
> John Dolorous caused £1,600 damage within a minute.
>
> The 47 year old was still holding a brick when police arrested him, the court was told.
>
> After hearing that he had not worked for six years, magistrates decided not to order him to pay compensation.

An alternative (as penned by Malcolm) might be:

> TRAGIC John Dolorous didn't know which way to turn when his mother died.
>
> He ended up under arrest – after smashing six shop windows within a minute.
>
> And that landed shopkeepers with a £1,600 repair bill, a court heard.
>
> When police detained him, the 47 year old was still holding the brick which did all the damage.
>
> But Dolorous will not have to pay for new windows because he has been out of work for six years.

FOLLOW-UPS

It's always worth considering follow-ups. What does the shopkeeper think? His insurance policy could go up and he may think Mr Dolorous has got away with it. What about social services? Was Mr Dolorous known to them and was he getting any help? Social services may not tell you but his neighbours might.

Radio reporters may need to take tape recorders to court. These days many courts allow radio reporters to discreetly record court proceedings as long as there is a prior arrangement that it will not be used for broadcast, and that the taped proceedings will be surrendered to the court at the end of the day. That said, taped interviews are sometimes appropriate after cases, possibly with police officers or victims. Acquitted people may answer questions, too. Even convicted offenders may talk.

Malcolm adds: 'When writing court copy for radio and TV, straight versions should always be used. Some newspapers use journalese like "boozed-up" or "knifeman". These are always jarring to the ear when broadcast.'

NEW POWERS

Magistrates have new powers to try to curb people who commit crime to finance drug-taking. There are now Drug Treatment and Testing Orders which are exactly what they say. Offenders have to submit for checks to ensure they are staying off drugs. Since these are recent additions to magistrates' powers, they are of interest in themselves. Probation officers have to bring the offender back to court if the order is defied. These are heard at what are known as 'breach courts' and can produce good copy.

Magistrates have wide powers in dealing with a range of cases. These may include pollution, factory accidents, welfare benefit fraud and even appeals from taxi drivers who have been banned by local councils.

Stipendiary magistrates are legally trained and paid for the job. These operate in cities but have no wider powers than the unpaid voluntary JPs. However, they are now called 'district judges'.

CROWN COURTS

> The Crown Court can be seen as an imposing institution to reporters starting out in the job. But it is also a source of great stories, making both regional and national headlines. Court reporters have got to be on the ball, proactive and with an eye for the best line in a story.
>
> Rebecca Sherdley
> legal affairs correspondent
> *Nottingham Evening Post*

At Crown Court your shorthand note must again be clear and concise. It is no good telling your newsdesk you can't read your shorthand two minutes before deadline when sub-editors are waiting for your story. Moreover, if there is a complaint, your shorthand is your only real defence. But don't panic. The court system rarely meets the deadline of your newspaper; it's not designed to. Rebecca Sherdley, the *Nottingham Evening Post*'s legal affairs correspondent, says: 'The whole process is far more relaxed and it is rare a case ever gets started on time. Barristers can adjourn cases for days for legal arguments. Witnesses often don't turn up, the defendant decides to plead guilty or the case is adjourned because of unforeseen legal problems.'

BE PREPARED

But when the case does start, be prepared. Research the court list on the Internet at www.courtserve2.net and check each name in the list against your newspaper's archive. Any high-profile cases will be in the archive and it's important to brief your newsdesk about the background to the story. The court also provides a weekly list with the names of defendants due to appear. The names can be checked and diaried, then checked with the more up-to-date Internet list on the day. The court list gives each defendant a case number. Sherdley outlines how, at Nottingham, there is a series of files in the press room containing hundreds of sheets with the name, age and address of defendants and the charges they face. But the charges can change, so always check with the court clerk if you're unsure.

Also think about pictures of the defendant, witnesses and victims, CCTV footage, graphics and artists' impressions. If a man is found guilty of murder following a trial, the judge usually sentences him straight away. Sherdley says: 'A call to the police press office, requesting a copy of his picture before the case, saves a lot of running around later.' In shop robberies, CCTV footage can tell the story far better than anything you write. Graphics are also useful to help chart the course of a dangerous driver or a street mugger who has committed a series of robberies in the same area. With so much information available to include in the story, graphics can help cut down on detail and make court copy a lighter read. Artists' impressions are used in more high-profile cases. They are a colourful addition to any story, especially at preliminary hearings before magistrates and judges, when details about the case can be brief. Cameras are not allowed into a courtroom, while artists can only observe proceedings. The sketch is drawn afterwards but creates a great scene setter for the reader.

HOW IT WORKS

Nottingham has nine criminal courtrooms situated on the middle floor. Court one is the High Court and hears the more serious cases. Each judge has his own courtroom and a clerk, usher and logger assigned to him for the day.

The list of defendants due to appear is split between the judges. Some court-rooms are just assigned to the sentencing cases and others are given a mixture of four defendants or more to be sentenced and two trials. One trial will be called a floater, scheduled in the list as a backup if the first trial is adjourned. If both cases are effective, i.e. they will go ahead, the judge will try to find a colleague to hear the case in their courtroom. Sherdley says:

> Obviously a reporter can't be in every court at once. The most important cases are prioritised, depending on the feedback I get from newsdesk every day. If a story has good pictures and interviews with victims and their families, it's more likely to appear towards the front of the paper. It is also important to be prepared. We have a back-grounder list to ensure, where possible, we have the story ready to run after the court case. This means trying to compile pictures of victims, defendants, the scene of the incident, etc. in advance. This saves time and means the newsdesk knows what to expect. When you are up against other media, it is important to have your back-grounder ready. You may get the exclusive everyone wants and put the opposition to shame.

Most reporters are shown the ropes by a senior reporter or assigned court cor-respondent, who spends much of the day covering cases. The courtroom staff – barristers, clerks and loggers – are much more helpful once they get to know a familiar face. Then there are the 'court watchers', often retired individuals who come to court looking for interesting cases to watch. All are a vital source of information.

STAY ON YOUR TOES

Besides the day-to-day trials and sentencing courts, look out for the bizarre. Sudden outbursts in the courtroom can make riveting reading. Sherdley says:

> On one occasion, I was accompanied to court by an eager group of journalism students after giving a talk to them that morning. We sat in court and they watched the general run-of-the-mill cases. Then, just before lunch, the judge suddenly threw down his wig and stormed down from his bench. We then became aware that one of the bar-risters was in difficulty. He was effectively stranded in his wheelchair because court staff had just been banned from wheeling him in and out of court for 'insurance' pur-poses. Apparently, if they injured their backs, they were not insured. The wheelchair-bound barrister turned to one of his colleagues for help, but they were tied up or simply unaware of his predicament. The judge, who had taught him as his pupil, leapt down and pushed his old friend from the court. His words were: 'It's an absolute disgrace.' Sure enough, the words *absolute disgrace* were the ones which made the front page lead headline the following day. The judge posed for pictures and spoke openly about his friend's situation. We followed up the story with a double-page spread on the new policy imposed by the Court Service and how it would affect other court users.

In another case, a judge handed a cash-strapped shoplifter £5 to get home on the train. His barrister chipped in with the same amount. The reporter spoke to the man afterwards and he obliged with an interview. It turned out the defendant's name was A. Pratt.

CAMPAIGNING JOURNALISM

Court reporters should also be vigilant to cases in which their newspaper is running a campaign. *Protecting Our Children* is an Evening Post campaign that persuaded the Government to introduce tough new paedophile detention laws. Any cases involving child abuse receive high-profile coverage in line with the campaign. Sherdley says: 'It's important to try to develop these cases with the victims, their families and police.'

The vigilance of a court reporter primarily centres on reporting restrictions. In cases involving sexual abuse, the victim and child witnesses cannot be named. Other restrictions are imposed under the Contempt of Court Act to avoid prejudicing a forthcoming second trial involving the defendant. A postponement can also be made at the judge's discretion at any point in the proceedings. Notices of these orders should be posted on the press bench in court and the doors to the courtroom as soon as they are made. Reporters should also check whether or not the relevant orders have been made, if it appears they have not, and keep their newsdesk informed of developments at all times.

It is possible for reporters to challenge the imposition of reporting restrictions in certain cases. Sherdley says: 'We have successfully challenged Section 39 of the Children and Young Person's Act. To name a persistent young offender is a victory for the newspaper and the community which has suffered at their hands.'

INQUESTS

> Coroners, like anyone else, differ in personalities, so try to 'suss' them out gently before expecting any help 'off the record'. It can take time! Once you have trust, you have a big lead over the reporter who doesn't, so never break a confidence.
>
> Stuart Ellis[3]
> North Derbyshire News Agency

Inquests provide a wealth of material for newspapers and other media. They take us behind closed doors in many cases and can make compelling reading. These stories are intrinsically sad, often tragic, sometimes even bizarre. From the reporter's standpoint, they offer the privilege of reporting almost everything that is said without challenge, assuming your account of events is fair and accurate.

The purpose of an inquest is to answer four fairly straightforward questions.

1 Who was the deceased?
2 Where did he/she die?
3 When did he/she die?
4 What were the circumstances of the death?

The coroner's rules specifically state that an inquest is not an opportunity to attach blame to anyone, or absolve anyone from blame. Although it is a court of law, and legal representatives can ask questions of witnesses, there are no parties such as prosecution or defence and no one is on trial.

Inquests are held into only a small number of deaths in each district. Pathologists carry out post-mortem examinations on people whom the coroner suspects may not have died from natural causes. But often the object is to find a cause of death where one is not immediately apparent. Autopsies are routinely held where death occurs within 24 hours of someone being admitted to hospital, but the cause is invariably natural and an inquest is unnecessary.

Stuart Ellis, who has been in journalism since 1979, set up the North Derbyshire News Agency in Chesterfield in the early 1990s. He says:

> In my district, where many people used to work in coal mining, autopsies are held to decide if coal dust exposure contributed to death. If there is evidence of occupational lung disease, an inquest will be held. More 'newsy' of course are inquests into tragic events such as death from hanging, overdose, drowning, gunshot wounds, road accidents, railway line suicides, hospital operation blunders and the like.

OPENINGS

A coroner will hold an 'opening' into each inquest soon after death occurs. This is normally an informal procedure conducted privately at the coroner's own office and the media will only attend if the death is high-profile. The purpose of this opening is to identify the deceased and record the cause of death. The cause is usually supplied by a local hospital pathologist. In the case of a suspicious death, a Home Office pathologist with experience of criminal causes of death will be engaged. The result of an autopsy can be delayed if it requires a second or even third examination by a Home Office pathologist.

The media will usually phone the coroner's staff to get information about the opening and find out the date to which the full hearing has been adjourned. This is usually within a few months, and should not be beyond six months. This date must then be diaried, so tell your news editor straight away. Most newsdesks will phone their local coroner's office every week so they know what is coming up.

LOOK FOR A NEW ANGLE

Most of the more newsworthy events will already have been reported soon after the death, typical examples being car crashes involving youngsters or multiple fatalities. A reporter may have been sent to the home of the deceased to try to interview relatives and collect a photograph. Such photographs may be used again when reporting the inquest.

When an event has already been reported, Ellis outlines how you should look at the initial report and try to get a different angle when you report the inquest. For example, a man killed by a car as he crosses a road. The basic information will be reported soon after the event, so look for another angle from the evidence, such as the fact that the car was speeding or unroadworthy, the driver was drunk, the pedestrian was not looking, and so on. Ellis says: 'Always look out for the possibility of a prosecution arising from the incident. This is sometimes the case in road deaths and industrial accidents. You should be able to get a court date from a police officer at the hearing.'

NO SUSPICIOUS CIRCUMSTANCES

When you are reporting an apparent suicide *before* the inquest, you must not categorically state that the person committed suicide. Police usually use the expression 'no suspicious circumstances' to indicate that no one other than the deceased was involved in the death.

PHOTOGRAPHS

Sometimes your newsdesk may try to get a photograph of a witness arriving at or leaving an inquest. Photographs cannot be taken within the inquest court precincts and you may need to point out the subject to your photographer, telling him which exit the subject is using.

INTERVIEWING WITNESSES OR RELATIVES

You may also be required to approach witnesses or relatives of the deceased after the inquest and ask follow-up questions, possibly arising out of the evidence. Ellis says:

> There may be an issue of conscience here. If you can see someone is clearly distressed, you must ask yourself if it is right to confront them with emotive questions. People will often be prepared to air a grievance but remember that reporting privilege only applies to what is said during the hearing.

Sometimes people comment after the hearing about a terrible personal tragedy in the hope that this will prevent a similar event befalling someone else in the future. This is clearly in the public interest. But it is their right not to answer your questions, and this should be respected. Ellis says: 'If you were the bereaved, you might not feel like walking out of an inquest and straight into a press interview. Do not harass anyone.'

JURY VERDICTS

Most inquests are judged only by the coroner, who will hear the evidence of all witnesses and then *record* a verdict. Sometimes, in cases such as rail deaths and deaths occurring from accidents at work, a jury will sit. Juries *return* verdicts. They will be given help and advice by the coroner on the verdicts they can reasonably return, depending on the evidence. They can, for example, return a verdict of *unlawful killing* if they feel that murder has been committed, or a person or employer has acted recklessly. This verdict was delivered on a car passenger who died in a crash after the inquest heard that the driver – her boyfriend – was drunk and high on drugs at the time of the collision. This had been proved by toxicology – a post-mortem analysis of the driver's blood. Ellis says: 'A jury can make recommendations about better working practices following an industrial accident and this can make an angle for you.'

ALTERNATIVE VERDICTS

Other verdicts which can be recorded are *accidental death*, which is self-explanatory, or *death by misadventure*. Misadventure is similar to accidental death but involves an extra ingredient. It is a deliberate act in which the deceased did not foresee the consequences of his/her actions, for example a drug addict killed by the purity of his cocaine 'fix'. In cases including hanging or overdose, a verdict is often recorded that the deceased took his/her own life. If none of these verdicts fits the circumstances, the coroner or jury is left with only one option – an open verdict.

SUICIDE

Suicide brings into play the key factor of intent. Like a jury in a criminal court, a coroner or inquest jury has to be satisfied beyond reasonable doubt that the deceased intended the result of his/her actions. The fact that someone is found hanged and there is no suspicion of foul play is not sufficient evidence of intent to commit suicide. The deceased must have either left a suicide note, or told someone he intended to kill himself shortly before his death. Without this evidence, an open verdict should be recorded.

But Ellis says: 'Different coroners apply the rules on intent with varying strictness and the verdict you report should be the one the coroner gives!' If the coroner says the deceased 'took his own life while suffering from depression', then that is the verdict – not 'suicide'. On the subject of suicide notes, these are rarely read out during the hearing although the gist of them might be mentioned.

WRITING YOUR REPORT

Once you have all the information from the inquest, you can go ahead and write your report. In general, the introductory paragraph or 'intro' should – as always – contain the most important and/or interesting piece of information. If you do this, the reader will hopefully want to read on. The intro is sometimes derived from comments made by the coroner as he records his verdict. When you are experienced, the rest of the story seems to 'write itself'. You must relay, in a logical and interesting way, the sequence of events and include direct quotes from at least one witness or the coroner. A report without quotes always seems to look 'flat'. Ellis says: 'You must remember to include all the basics too. I have been engrossed in writing reports about really newsy inquests and then realised I forgot to mention the date that the incident occurred!'

There may be technical terms given in evidence that you don't understand, but you will usually find someone after the inquest who can explain them, such as a witness from a professional authority. If you are not sure about anything, you must check it out. As a last resort, don't include anything you are unsure about. Ellis says:

> I rarely use a coroner's verdict in an intro, unless it's something out of the ordinary like unlawful killing. In general, I prefer to tell the story through the key witnesses' eyes as far as possible and end with the verdict and a quote from the coroner. We were told as trainees not to put the verdict at the end in case a sub-editor cut the story from the bottom. But the verdict does round off the report nicely and it would be pretty crass 'subbing' to delete the verdict!

Sometimes the intro can come from outside the inquest evidence, such as a death crash driver who will face prosecution. You can check with police if you think there may be charges and it has not been mentioned in evidence. If there is mention of 'other proceedings', you may find the central witness declines to give evidence on legal advice, in case it incriminates him during a criminal court case. If this happens, the coroner will usually have this witness's statement to police read out. Make sure it is clear whether a witness has given evidence to the inquest in person, or if the evidence is from a statement.

Ellis says: 'I like, but rarely use, the delayed intro approach.' He provides this example of the delayed intro:

> A teenager left home telling his parents he was going out to celebrate his new job.
> Two hours later his decapitated body was found on a railway track.
> An inquest jury failed to unravel the mystery of why 19 year old Jason Jones ...

Ellis says: 'I think this style is OK as an occasional break from the norm. I think it has impact but – until you earn your "stripes" – your news editor will probably prefer a more straightforward intro.' His alternative is:

> A teenager was found dead on a railway track just hours after saying he was going out to celebrate his new job.

According to Ellis though:

> Whatever you write, you have to accept that someone, somewhere higher up the food chain, may decide to alter it. Sometimes they improve your copy, sometimes they make it worse and sometimes they make it inaccurate – in which case everyone assumes it's your mistake! It will not always be possible to use the evidence of all witnesses, so be selective and try not to get bogged down. Evidence is sometimes duplicated by different witnesses and you don't want to be repetitive. Certainly, do not relay their evidence in chronological order unless it happens to work best that way (this rarely happens). Check their names (people don't like seeing their name spelled wrongly) and addresses with a police representative after the inquest.

NAMES MAKE NEWS

Ellis comments:

> It's easy to dismiss the minor inquests like the coal miners I mentioned earlier but remember that these are of interest to readers. Even people who have no interest in the mining industry will be interested to read something about someone they know, or someone they don't know but who lives on their street. Your readers are not only interested in big stories. It's also about getting as many names and addresses of local people in the paper as possible. Readers want to know what people in their neighbourhood have been doing: the good and the bad!

CREATE THE RIGHT IMPRESSION

This obviously applies to all areas of court reporting, not to mention all areas of journalism, but – because of the nature of what goes on there – coroner's courts can be especially sensitive places. So, as in all walks of life, good relations with those who matter will help your cause. You have to earn the trust of people. You can be too pushy, especially if you are new and trying to make an impact, so try not to make the wrong impression. Ellis says: 'Be polite and friendly because, if people like you, they are more likely to help you. Respect the fact that their jobs do not revolve around answering your questions.'

EMPLOYMENT TRIBUNALS

Formerly known as industrial tribunals, employment tribunals operate for people who have a dispute with their employer. Cases can be brought by people who no longer work for their employer, either because they have been dismissed or have left, or who still work for a company.

A case can be brought because somebody thinks they have been unfairly dismissed; discriminated against because of their race, sex or disability; left with no alternative but to resign (constructive dismissal); or been short-changed over wages, redundancy or pensions.

Tribunal cases are run in a similar way to courts but are less formal. Also, remember they are not criminal cases – no one is a *defendant*, there are no 'charges' and no 'sentence'.

There are two sides, usually legally represented, but people can represent themselves. Each side calls witnesses who give evidence, there is cross-examination, a summing up by each side at the end and a judgment given by a panel. Decisions can be given straight away or sent to parties later. The independent panel usually has three people on it, including a legally trained chairperson and two members with either business or union experience.

If they find for the person bringing the claim (usually an employee or ex-employee), their judgments are financial, involving a fine and costs to be paid by the respondent (usually the employer or ex-employer). A tribunal can also direct that a person should be given their job back if they find they've been unfairly dismissed. But Sean Kirby, who has worked for the *Nottingham Evening Post* since 1997, says: 'This is fairly unusual, given the bad feeling between both sides arising from a case.'[4]

It's not common but a company can bring a case against an employee if, for instance, it's felt an employee unfairly brought an earlier tribunal case against the company.

REPORTING TRIBUNALS

Tribunals lists for your area for the week ahead can be obtained from the head tribunals office by calling a pre-set fax number on a Monday. Kirby says: 'Cases are scheduled well in advance and can be dropped on the day of the hearing, so morning checks with the local tribunals office are needed to see what's on.'

Tribunal proceedings carry privilege if they're reported fairly and accurately. The names of both sides, the time and place of the tribunal, and the basis on which it's being brought should be advertised in the tribunal's office reception. Panel chairs now usually direct a witness to give their full name and business or home address. Tribunals have clerks who you can also ask for this information.

Panels can make orders barring the press/public from the room or the reporting of names of certain witnesses. Kirby says: 'This might be done if a sexual discrimination case contains sexual details, or if part of a case involves confidential security or company information.' Sometimes these orders only last until the 'promulgation' of its decision – when the panel's judgment on the case is sent to both parties. But the order can permanently bar reporting names or information, usually in sexual discrimination cases.

Orders can be applied for by either party in the tribunal. However, an order can be challenged. There's no automatic right for a reporter to do this in the tribunal room but a friendly chairperson might allow it. If a panel's decision is deferred to be sent to parties a few weeks later, copies of the judgment can be ordered from the tribunals office for a small fee. But Kirby says: 'It's usually easier to get friendly with one of the sides so they will give you a copy of the judgment when they get it.'

HOW TELEVISION COVERS THE COURTS

> The key thing to remember in reporting courts (and that also includes inquests or tribunals) is to think about how you will illustrate it on television.
>
> Neil Manship[5]
> *BBC Look North*

Neil Manship, who is currently a senior broadcast journalist for *BBC Look North* in Leeds, says the staples of court reporting for regional television are those cases that have previously been covered as crimes, deaths (in the case of inquests) or other incidents. He says: 'On the day of a verdict, it's very difficult to pick up pictures and subsequent interviews unless filming and contacts have been gathered beforehand.'

Murder cases tend to provide the bedrock of the output, but there are many other actions against individuals and companies that are covered. There are no regular court reporters and both television and radio tend to rely on their own system of getting across what's happening as cases progress through the system. Manship says: 'This is usually done by the Home Affairs or Crime Correspondent and our own forward planners.'

Sometimes coroners' officers will tip off media outlets about interesting inquests that are coming up. Quite often a reporter will be dispatched to approach families in order to gather footage and interviews beforehand and to gauge how strong a story it will be. Manship says another good source of tip-offs are bodies such as the RSPCA and Government organisations. He adds: 'They are quite good at pre-warning of newsworthy cases about, for example, cruelty against animals, or breaches of industrial or health and safety laws by companies. They will often provide background material such as still pictures etc.'

There are many interesting stories that go through magistrates' courts but Manship says regional television just doesn't have the resources to keep abreast of all these and is reliant on tip-offs from members of the public, local knowledge or cases that have been previously reported in the local media. He adds:

> Pictures and interviews are our business. Unless you have these, no matter how good the case, it will generally be relegated to a short read with a few seconds of pictures, a straight 'in-vis' read, or dropped altogether. However, if the story is very important and we have no significant source of pictures, we would endeavour at least to do live two-ways with whatever other shots were available to be used during the interview.

HOW RADIO COVERS THE COURTS

> There is no doubt that the local media have a role to play in reflecting the activity of the courts and calling them to account when necessary. Indeed the publication of the identity of those convicted has long been held to be part of their punishment.
>
> John Atkin[6]
> BBC Radio Derby

John Atkin, who is the news editor at BBC Radio Derby, says the greatest challenge for broadcasters in covering court proceedings is obtaining suitable audio material without being able to record what happens in the courtroom. Partly for that reason, many local radio stations and TV programmes appear to be concentrating less on day-to-day court stories and focusing more on larger 'set-piece' trials.

Such trials offer the opportunity to prepare material well in advance, without having to rely on the chance element of being able to interview participants on the courtroom steps. Police forces are increasingly willing to arrange pre-court briefings, at which they will make officers available for interview on an embargo basis.

As cases near the end, it is also advisable to request interviews on a 'what-if' basis, where investigating officers will do two interviews – one assuming conviction, the other acquittal, on the understanding that the appropriate audio will be used at the conclusion of the case. But Atkin says:

> The concept of reporting on courts and crime begs the question of its inherent value to listeners and readers. Beyond knowing who has done what, are they really interested in reading large sections of quotes from prosecuting or defending solicitors? Anecdotal evidence suggests that the audience is far less concerned about the intricacies of crime than many media outlets – broadcast and written – might believe.

In addition, Atkin says journalists should consider whether the reporting of what might be termed routine cases – thefts, muggings, autocrime – can have the effect of increasing the audience's fear of crime over and above that which is realistic. He says:

Particularly relevant in this consideration is the reporting of violent crime, continued increases in which often headline stories, yet which statistically affects mainly a small proportion of society – specifically young males. It is extremely rare that a court case affects many people directly and reports of many cases can be given undue prominence. The breadth of the interest in individual stories should always be considered in deciding where to place them.

HOW ONLINE JOURNALISTS COVER THE COURTS

Nigel Bell,[7] who joined the BBC in 1986, helped set up the Nottingham Where I Live website in 2000. He says that, purely from a regional BBC point of view, news online journalists rarely go to court. They rely on their radio and TV colleagues and use the information they glean in court as a basis for their article. Bell points out one potential pitfall:

The law and the web is still in its early age but what has come to light is the difficulty raised when court cases collapse and a retrial is ordered. Traditionally, nothing is ever taken down on the web. If the search engine is good, you should be able to track down old court reports. This immediately raises the problem of juries potentially reading about the first trial. At first this problem was dealt with like newspapers, i.e. there's nothing to stop people going to their local library and digging out old copies of papers which might have the initial court report. But it has now been decided that in cases where retrials are ordered, all old coverage of the case must be taken off the live server so there's no chance of a website being blamed for influencing a court case outcome.

CHECKLIST

✓ Create the right impression. This is especially important when attending courts and doesn't just apply to the cut of your cloth.
✓ Ask for help. It's definitely worth seeking the expertise of an experienced court reporter the first time you go, and probably on subsequent visits early in your career. Also try to strike up working relationships with as many court officials as possible, from prosecuting barristers to ushers.
✓ Remember your law. This is a must when covering continuing cases.
✓ Remember the basics. Don't forget that you'll need the name of the court, the charge, the plea and the sentence for almost every story. Not to mention the full name and address of the defendant.

✓ Think colour and drama. This can be all too easily forgotten in lots of areas of journalism. It's vital in court reporting.
✓ Think follow-ups. The story doesn't necessarily end with the judge's sentence.
✓ Think pictures and audio. Newspaper and TV journalists may make use of CCTV footage, graphics and artists' impressions. The greatest challenge for radio reporters is obtaining suitable audio material without being able to record what happens in the courtroom.

NOTES

1 All quotes from Rebecca Sherdley taken from author interview, 2003.
2 All quotes from Rod Malcolm taken from author interview, 2003.
3 All quotes from Stuart Ellis taken from author interview, 2003.
4 All quotes from Sean Kirby taken from author interview, 2003.
5 All quotes from Neil Manship taken from author interview, 2003.
6 All quotes from John Atkin taken from author interview, 2003.
7 All quotes from Nigel Bell taken from author interview, 2003.

REPORTING LOCAL GOVERNMENT AND POLITICS

The tips for good council reporting are the same for any other area: know your stuff, be proactive, cultivate contacts, and don't forget *people*.

Caroline Smith[1]
Nottingham Evening Post

'Sexy councillors have unveiled an exciting new blueprint which will transform Trusley in the 21st century.' That's how sex sells – you have to read to the end of the sentence to find out what the hell is going on. But what this example also illustrates is how difficult it can be to make national and local government news interesting. Who wants to read about the machinations of a load of men in suits? And that's often the view not only of many readers/viewers/listeners but also of young journalists who perceive municipal reporting to be sitting for hours on end in council meetings when they could be doing something much more entertaining.

But as Harris and Spark (1997: 125) point out: 'if you work on a local paper … you need to be close to your local council because it is a source of news that cannot be ignored – indeed it must be cultivated.' This chapter will look at the changing shape of local government from the Office of the Deputy Prime Minister downwards to the main parts and roles of the local government system. More importantly, it will look at how most council matters need to be grounded in terms of human interest and how budding reporters need to build up contacts with key members of party groups. The chapter will investigate the reporting of local authorities from the point of view of newspaper, radio and television journalists.

RINGING THE CHANGES

There have been dramatic developments in local government in the last 20 years. Both Tory and Labour governments made much of giving more power to local government. But many would argue that they were just as centrist as each other in exercising control through the purse strings, bearing in mind that local government has to rely heavily on central government for financial support for about 80 per cent of its expenditure. In 1992 a Local Government Commission was set up by the Major Government and, as a result, unitary authorities replaced many of the old traditional counties and districts. Local authorities were encouraged to be 'enablers' rather than 'providers' and compulsory competitive tendering was introduced with the aim of using a (perceived) cheaper private sector to carry out contracts rather than the direct labour force of the councils' own employees. The Conservatives introduced 'capping' to penalise what they regarded as profligate local authorities putting up the council tax beyond what they regarded as reasonable.

THE REGIONS

Under the Local Government Act 2000, all principal local authorities (with the exception of districts with a population of fewer than 85,000) have to choose an executive style of government. The most popular choice of the options available, which includes the right to choose a directly elected mayor, is a council leader with a cabinet. Under these models, councillors outside the executive become backbenchers with more time available for constituency work. The aim was for 'joined-up government', with local authorities consulting and working with other official bodies and voluntary organisations for the benefit of the community. Compulsory competitive tendering was replaced by the concept of 'best value', whereby local government used benchmarking to test the value and cost of their services against that of adjoining authorities. It has been defined in many ways. It is the continuous search by a council to improve the quality, efficiency and the effectiveness of all its activities for the public, at a price people are willing to pay. Capping was allegedly abolished, but held in reserve. New Labour claimed to give more control to local communities yet pulled the strings by ring-fencing specific grants, demanding performance plans and delegating plenty of public spending to unelected quangos.

DEVOLVED GOVERNMENT

New Labour promised devolved government for the regions and set up the Scottish Parliament, which has powers of primary legislation and is able to undertake additional tax raising. The National Assembly for Wales and the Northern Ireland Executive have also been established, but many see them as expensive, glorified county councils. Demand for similar regional government in England has been patchy but the basis was set by the creation of eight Voluntary Regional Boards. Meanwhile, a Bill to empower the regions to hold referendums on whether or not to set up regional governments is under way. If and when they are created, they will be unitary authorities and this will lead to boundary changes and the extinction of some existing councils.

A major change for journalists has been that the Local Government Act 2000 gives councils the power to make decisions in cabinet in secret and keep out the press and public. Local authorities are obliged to inform the press when 'key decisions' are being made and these meetings must be open to the press and public to attend. This power is in addition to the existing power relating to exempt and confidential information.

HOW COUNCILS WORK

Nottingham City Council delivers the full range of local government services which daily touch the lives of its customers – the people who live, work or spend time in the city.

The city council is an all-purpose, unitary authority, which means that it alone is responsible for providing council services in Nottingham. In the rest of the county such services are delivered by two or, in areas with a town or parish council, three different authorities. It became a unitary authority in April 1998, adding education, social services, libraries, transportation, trading standards and other functions – previously run by Nottinghamshire County Council – to its responsibilities, which also include housing, housing benefits, refuse collection, parks, environmental health, council tax collection and planning and development control.

The authority spends around £600 million a year on providing services – pumping millions into the city's economy through its investments, contracts and purchases – while its 14,000 employees include practitioners in everything from architecture to zoology.

Like all local authorities, the city council is a democratic organisation. The city is currently divided into 27 electoral wards and there is an election every four years. Each ward returns 2 councillors except Byron ward, which returns 3, making 55 councillors in all. The councillors meet as a full council every month. A limited number of items of business, such as approving the level of council tax, must be considered by the full council. However, because it is deemed impractical for all 55 councillors to be consulted on every item of council business, the council delegates authority for making its main decisions in several ways. Decisions can be made by:

- the council leader (in other words the leader of the ruling political group) and a cabinet comprising a small number of councillors holding executive powers for services such as education or housing
- the executive board and the resources committee, formal cross-party meetings of councillors in which key decisions on issues such as policy and finance are made
- statutory and regulatory committees which consider issues such as licensing and planning applications
- area committees, which are made up of councillors from clusters of neighbouring electoral wards and consider matters of local interest and concern
- council officers, to whom authority for making day-to-day operational decisions is delegated.

The political composition of all the council's decision-making assemblies reflects that of the authority as a whole. To provide professional guidance and to execute decisions affecting each council service, the authority is divided into ten departments, each led by a chief officer. Officers are obliged to give impartial advice but it is up to councillors to decide whether or not to accept it in making their decision. The departments are those of: the chief executive; city secretary; finance, development and environmental services; housing; leisure and community services; education; social services; Nottingham City Building Works and Nottingham City Contract Works. But don't forget: not all council set-ups are the same. You need to find out about the councils in your area, whether you're studying journalism or starting out as a reporter.

STORIES TO LOOK FOR

We've seen how Nottingham City Council covers a whole range of services. The task now is turning what seem like dry subjects into potentially award-winning stories. Here's a taste of what those 'council functions' might yield.

- **Education:** Initiatives to improve standards at individual schools or educational establishments across the city; moves to tackle persistent truancy.
- **Social services:** A city council (not Nottingham) spending £750 a day delivering meals on wheels by taxi because it couldn't recruit enough drivers; social services bosses criticising the father of two teenagers who 'named and shamed' them on the Internet in an attempt to stop them falling into lives of crime.
- **Libraries:** Stories can vary from closures and (occasional) openings – which obviously affect a lot of people – to book amnesties and the cost of books lost/stolen. Or perhaps something much more interesting like the story of a paedophile who downloaded child porn on a library computer and subsequent moves to prevent it happening again.

- **Transport:** Stories might focus on plans to introduce road tolls or, in the case of Nottingham, a £200m tram scheme which meant traffic headaches, angry traders and a whole host of other stories.
- **Trading standards:** Clampdowns on dodgy dealers at car boot sales or – better still – a gang caught with 100 pairs of fake Calvin Klein underpants with the washing instructions 'fumble dry, remove promptly, use a worm iron'.
- **Housing:** Sales of council stock/changes in right-to-buy discounts; new developments and protests.
- **Housing benefits:** How more people are ripping off local authorities and moves to stop them.
- **Refuse collection:** Many authorities are failing to hit targets set to improve recycling.
- **Parks:** How some are being turned into no-go areas by drug-users or how police off-road motorcyclists are being hired on rest days to catch young-sters speeding through them on quads and scooters.
- **Environmental health:** From rats found in restaurants to traders dumping rubbish behind their shops.
- **Council tax:** Protests over increases; problems with non-payers.
- **Planning and development:** Stories could vary from not in my backyard-type protests over something seemingly trivial to huge developments which may affect thousands of people.

HOW TO GET THEM

So how are you going to get these stories? Harris and Spark (1997: 134) say:

> As in other fields of reporting, confidence in the reporter induces confidences from the contacts. Given this good relationship at each level, the field of politics – ward, munici-pal, constituency, regional and parliamentary – can yield a continuous flow of stories.

In the first instance, identifying your story may come through an agenda for a committee meeting sent by a council. It may be brought to your attention by a reader calling the newsdesk or writing a letter to the editor about some previ-ously undisclosed and – hopefully – newsworthy topic. Over and above that, as Harris and Spark outline, good contacts must be established. At a local level, these can range from councillors and council officers to press officers and the council leader. Cultivating their trust can lead to reporters being tipped off by each and every one of these about a story that may be followed up by the rest of the local – and possibly national – media. Perhaps more importantly, jour-nalists have a responsibility to their audience, as John Turner spells out in Richard Keeble's *The Newspapers Handbook*:

> The journalist occupies a pivotal position between those who make and implement important decisions and those who are often forced to comply with such decisions.

Any democratic system depends on people being well informed and educated about politics by a media which give a full and accurate account of news, encompassing a wide and varied range of political opinion. (Keeble, 2000: 183)

ELECTIONS

The night of a general election can be one of the highlights of a young reporter's career – especially if a long-standing MP is ousted, or there is a huge swing, or the voting is so tight that there has to be a recount. Local elections can also provide high drama. Perhaps a big-name councillor who has represented the area for years (if not decades) is kicked into touch or the council itself sees a shift in power and changes hands to be run by a party that has spent a long time in the wilderness. But great care has to be taken in the run-up to both local and general elections to ensure that balance is maintained.

It may be possible though for national newspapers to back a particular party. Few people will forget the *Sun*'s front page on the day of the 1992 general election. It featured a picture of Labour leader Neil Kinnock's head superimposed on a light bulb with the headline 'If Kinnock wins today, will the last person to leave Britain please turn out the lights?' The crushing defeat for Labour that followed led to the boast that it was 'The Sun wot won' the election for John Major's Conservatives. However, other media are governed by rules that demand balance or, in the case of regional newspapers, usually make sure they avoid accusations of bias by devoting an equal amount of space to each of the main parties.

So how does the theory work in practice? The rest of this chapter is devoted to the thoughts of journalists working at both a local and national level on newspapers, radio and television. It also includes the views of a former city council leader and a press officer who now runs his own media consultancy.

HOW NEWSPAPERS COVER COUNCILS

For many journalists, the thought of reading a council agenda or attending another boring committee meeting fills them with dread. Local government just isn't seen as sexy. But love it or hate it, local politics is a goldmine of potential stories which have all the elements needed to make them great news. They often affect a lot of people (council tax hike), involve a big issue (failing schools), are quirky or humorous (council bans bikinis from public swimming pools on grounds of taste) or provoke strong opinions.

Caroline Smith
Nottingham Evening Post

Caroline Smith, who became the political editor of the *Nottingham Evening Post* in 2001, says the other good thing about covering local government is the sheer variety of stories – hard news, quirky, campaign, tragedy, humour: 'As a local government reporter, you could be in the High Court one day, tramping through the Caves of Nottingham the next or doing a major interview with the Secretary of State for Defence.'

They are all there, you just have to know where to look, and who to talk to. And a council is probably the most open public body there is, with a wealth of information available to the journalist willing to go and seek it. Smith says: 'This is key as it's easy to fall into the trap of being spoon-fed by council press releases, blindly following the PR line, or getting caught up in council processes, rather than focusing on the real issue that readers care about.' But where do you start?

THE COUNCIL AGENDA

Council reports are a really useful source of stories, and once you get used to them, they are easy to decipher. Each council will have its own house style which can vary widely in its clarity and presentation. But, broadly speaking, every council report is constructed in the same way, and once you understand that, they become a lot easier to deal with.

WHAT TO LOOK FOR

Firstly the *heading*, usually followed by a summary or the purpose of the report. This is the bit that should be read first because it provides a succinct synopsis of what the report is about. For instance, councillors at a Nottinghamshire County Council cabinet meeting considered a report about the proposed asylum centre at RAF Newton and its likely impact on local services.

The next bit to look for in a council report is the section called *recommendations*, which sets out what actions the council will take on an issue. In our example, the councillors were asked to note the report. It also agreed that a future report be written to include the cost implications for the council of RAF Newton, plus recommendations for future actions.

The next valuable section is the *background* to the issue being discussed, which usually contains a review of what has happened to date on an issue and is a quick way for a reporter to understand what's going on. In the RAF Newton case, the report explained the Government's plan for a string of accommodation centres up and down the country, plus information about what kind of facilities would be offered for the asylum seekers. It also set out the implications for the wider community, such as the strain on local services and implications for crime.

Also worth looking out for are *comments* from consulted parties. Smith says:

Always check the treasurer or finance director's comments as they are often enlightening. How much is something going to cost? Is the council that is putting up council tax by 10 per cent going to spend £100,000 on a new Rolls-Royce for its council leader? Or on planning agendas, how many people have objected, and on what grounds?

Always check *background papers*. Smith explains:

By law every council has to make available any supporting information which has been used to write a report. A list of background papers should be included on every report, but often they are not listed. This doesn't mean they don't exist, officers often don't bother to put them down, or may conveniently forget if they contain something embarrassing.

In our example, there may be correspondence from the Home Office about the accommodation centre, which might have some scandalous comments about why Nottingham has been chosen etc. Background papers carry privilege, you can use them in stories. If in doubt, ask. If council officers refuse to give them to you, remind them it is an offence to do so under the Access to Information Act.

Finally, on every report it should have a named author and sometimes their extension number. Don't be afraid to ring them, they will often be a useful source of extra information. In our RAF Newton example, the author was the director of social services. He would be able to clarify anything you didn't understand, answer questions and probably be quoted in the story.

So a council agenda is a mine of information and a great source of stories. But they have to be read carefully. Smith says:

Often it may be just one line in the agenda that turns out to be a front-page lead. For instance, Nottingham City Council decided it had to cut tens of thousands of pounds from its leisure services budget. A quick call to the council revealed that it was planning to axe the Robin Hood Marathon, a massively popular event which raises thousands of pounds for charity. It was the next day's splash, and followed by a string of other stories, a local campaign, and finally the council was forced to reinstate it.

Another good tip for dealing with agendas is to develop a good relationship with councillors on the cabinet or committee. According to Smith,

This should include the chairman, council leader and key opposition members. Then, when the agenda lands on your desk, you can ring them and ask what issues of interest are coming up, which reports will interest the readers, and what is likely to be confrontational. Most councillors will be happy to help, and eager to get you to come along to the meeting. This approach, especially by talking to opposition councillors, will help you spot the stories that the council doesn't necessarily want you to find out about.

While key decisions have to be taken in public, other non-key decisions are still a potential source of stories. They are usually taken in private by officers and cabinet members without being circulated publicly. But journalists and members of the public can still find out about them. Smith says: 'Councils have to keep lists of delegated decisions and the reasons why they have been taken. Regular checks are worth doing, just to keep them on their toes!'

Scrutiny reports are slightly different as they do not involve decisions. But the issue being scrutinised is likely to be of public importance, say the closure of a swimming pool or the performance of the housing repairs service. And the report will still be an important source of information. But you will probably get a better understanding of the issue, how it affects people and better quotes by actually attending the council meeting.

One last word on agendas (just to emphasise their importance), former *Derby Evening Telegraph* municipal reporter Kevin Palmer says they can contain as much or as little information as officials want you to know.[2] He adds:

> Often the longest reports, usually on a response to a Government or EU proposal or some administrative item, can be unattractive and lacking in any story for the journalist. But because an item may be controversial, the report can be short or even put into the confidental part of the agenda.

THE COUNCIL MEETING

So you've read the agenda and previewed all the interesting stories in it. The next step is going along to the meeting itself. There are broadly three types of council meeting.

1 **Full council**, attended by all councillors.
2 **Executive or cabinet**, attended by leading councillors, where the decisions are formally taken.
3 **Scrutiny or select committees**, made up of backbenchers, which debate issues of concern but do not have decision-making powers. There will usually be a press bench or area to sit.

Smith says:

> Most decisions made by councils have been taken long before they reach the formal committee or full council stage. They will have been decided in the mythical smoke-filled back room by the ruling political party meeting as a group, or by the elected mayor and his cabinet meeting in private. However, thanks to campaigns by local papers – such as the *Nottingham Evening Post*'s 'Secret Society' – all 'key' decisions have to be seen to be taken in public. It is important to go along.

Council meetings are often long and tedious: there is no getting around it. But regular attendance at City Hall is a vital part of the newsroom diary. There are quite a few benefits of actually going along to a council meeting.

- Councillors like to see reporters there. Smith explains:

  > It shows interest and commitment, and it will pay dividends in the long run. For instance, if councillors and officers know a reporter will be in attendance, they will often seek them out to offer tips, stories, off-the-record gossip, etc. They are also more likely to pick up the phone to you when you ring about stories if they know your face.

- They offer qualified privilege. So if a chief constable tells a council meeting that cannabis should be made legal, you can report it. But if you only find out about the remark after the meeting, you cannot.
- When councillors talk about issues, they often let slip other stories, for example by describing a problem their constituent has with syringes being left in their garden during a discussion on waste collections.
- You will be there to pick up any late reports the council might want to slip onto the agenda. Smith says:

  > Some local authorities like to use this device, also known as emergency items, to minimise publicity for unpopular decisions. For instance, a council which wants to close a secondary school might well mark the report 'to follow' on the cover sheet, and the report is handed out at the meeting itself. This minimises the time the opposition has to look at the report, alert the press and local parents. Sneaky but true.

If you haven't been to a council meeting before, pick up a 'rogues' gallery' sheet with all the councillors' names and pictures on it (most councils will have one) but if in doubt, don't be afraid to go up and ask them after the meeting is over. Smith adds:

> Full Council is also worth attending as they usually have a question-and-answer session, with backbenchers and opposition members asking questions on issues of the day, which can be a good source of stories. Members of the public may be allowed to speak on subjects of concern and petitions will be handed in.

GETTING THE BEST OUT OF COUNCILLORS

Knowing your way around a council agenda and attending meetings is only half the story. Smith highlights the importance of building up contacts:

> Contacts are king when it comes to council reporting as they are elsewhere. The move to cabinet-style decision-making and elected mayors has had a massive impact on the amount and quality of stories coming out of local government. Gone are the days of a dozen decision-making committees, agendas and meetings which offered a wealth of potential stories for local papers.

That system has been replaced by a single decision-making body which has relegated many backbenchers to minor scrutiny roles. As a result, reporters have to work a lot harder to find out what's really going on. Smith explains:

> Most councillors like being contacted by journalists: they may pretend they don't and they may have had the odd bad experience, but by and large they need the media (to get re-elected) as much as we need them (to give us stories).

So always remember that it's a mutually beneficial relationship. That's not to say a reporter will be in the council's pocket. Councillors expect to get hammered every so often; that's what being a politician is all about. But what they expect is fairness, a decent right of reply and, preferably, a reporter who knows something about local government.

They may sometimes want to talk 'off the record' or Chatham House rules. This means they are telling you something you can use in your copy, but under no circumstances should be attributed to them. Smith stresses:

> Do not breach this trust: if in doubt clarify what is and isn't on the record, what is and isn't for use. But never let a councillor off the hook. If he has to respond in public on an issue, then it's your job to make sure he does. It's public money he or she is spending and they are accountable for every penny of it.

GETTING THE BEST OUT OF COUNCIL OFFICERS

With councils becoming increasingly PR-minded, it has become more difficult to get to the actual decision-makers. Press officers should be a reporter's aide, not a barrier to getting to the story. Smith offers the following advice:

> Never deal exclusively with council press officers or you'll never get to the real stories, the ones the council doesn't want you to know about. Press officers should be cultivated like councillors: meet them face to face, take them out for a drink, get them into the office to see how the paper works. They will then be more than happy to help, even when it's a 'bad news story'. But don't become their puppet.

Where possible, speak to council officers instead of press officers. Smith comments:

> The information is always better from the horse's mouth rather than second hand. In an ideal council, a press officer will help a reporter find the right person to speak to and will not impede that process. In the worst case scenario, the council will only let you speak to a press officer. Do not let this happen! If this is happening in your area, cultivate the council leader, the chief executive and the press office. Be clear it will benefit both sides if you are able to speak to senior officers about issues 'for background, information and detail' to ensure accuracy and that a story is fair. They will soon start to see the benefits as they get a better press and you start pulling in some big stories.

Council officers can be a bit prickly until you build up a relationship with them. They may be worried about getting into trouble, speaking out of turn, stealing a councillor's thunder, etc., but Smith says the solution is finding the right approach:

I have found the best way round this is to remember that council officers are generally there to implement policy made by councillors. So if you explain that you will not quote them on policy issues but want to speak to them to get the background facts and figures and ensure the story is factually accurate, then they'll be happy. Senior officers are often fine to be quoted but junior ones may not be allowed to speak to the press, although they may help you with background information. Then go to the councillor for comments for the story. This will keep them happy as they will get publicity, and also they should be the ones put on the spot as they are the elected member and the person taking the decisions. If you make it clear to both sides this is what you're doing, they will be happy and you will get a better, more accurate and fairer story.

POTENTIAL PITFALLS: BUSTING THE JARGON

Many journalists fall into the same trap when they start reporting on councils: they regurgitate council speak and forget about people! Decoding government and council jargon is a skill. In broad terms, if a reporter doesn't understand what the report says, or what the councillor is on about, then neither will the reader. Smith offers some advice:

Don't be afraid to ask them to explain it in easy-to-understand language. Councillors are usually better at doing this. And if you still don't understand, ask again until you do. Then in every story make sure there is no jargon as it's both boring and confusing to the reader. Equally, don't be bamboozled by council PR. This will happen if you rewrite a press release without questioning the statements contained within it. Instead, ask questions, dig a bit and treat all statements with scepticism until proven otherwise!

Former *Derby Evening Telegraph* reporter Kevin Palmer agrees that you shouldn't struggle with masses of figures and jargon:

Get help from someone in the treasurer's department. They are often in the background so much they can be quite flattered if you ask for help. And it is so much better than getting it wrong. Woe betide any journalist who puts the council tax up by more than the council. Or by not enough so that the taxpayers complain heavily when bills arrive!

POTENTIAL PITFALLS: POLITICAL BIAS

If you hold strong political views, it's best to keep them to yourself. Smith explains:

You may get pally with the Labour crew, but the Tories and Lib Dems won't trust you and you will lose respect all round. The problem is compounded if Labour loses power at the next election and the opposition steps into the hot seat.

Balance is crucial in all stories, and this is equally true in council stories, where there are two kinds of balance to remember.

1   Firstly, if the story is anti-council, perhaps it's a piece about protestors criticising the lack of council action over street lighting, Smith says:

> Make sure the council has a reasonable time to respond and their views are accurately reflected in your report – not just the final two paragraphs at the end of the story. Often your article will be stronger with a detailed response from both sides, and it is more likely to be accurate if you have checked the facts properly with the council.

2   Next there is the issue of political balance within a story. Smith comments:

> This is a tricky one as there is nothing more boring than a string of councillors from each political group being quoted in the story. But use your judgement and common sense. For instance, if there is an election campaign in full swing, you must be more sensitive to political balance. The ruling group may be trying to get lots of good news stories out in the hope of garnering headlines. Don't let them manipulate you. Check what the opposition has to say about it. Out of election time, the opposition may be a valuable source of stories, and have some pertinent things to say about X or Y policy but watch for political rhetoric and cheap point-scoring rather than substance.

POTENTIAL PITFALLS: REMEMBER YOUR AUDIENCE

People are key to most council stories. A story that looks good on a council agenda is always much better once you've spoken to the people it affects. Smith gives some examples:

> A nine-month delay in the council's handling of benefits payments translates into a story about a man who tried to commit suicide because he had no money to live on (a true story). A planned housing development on a wildlife haven will take on new life once you have spoken to some of the residents it affects. Don't forget pictures and graphics either, as these can lift a potentially dull council story into something with big impact on the page.

Many of the tips and the general approach outlined above can be used when dealing with any public body, not just councils. According to Smith:

> They apply equally to health authorities, the police authority, parish councils, quangos and the like. But the key difference with councils is that they are likely to be more open than, say, the local hospital board. This is because access to information held by the council is laid down in legislation. So you have the opportunity to challenge the council if it doesn't deliver.

Kevin Palmer has a last word on where you might find stories:

> There are some publications which can be useful – *Local Government Chronicle* has job advertisements which will give the salary of a post when an official may not reveal it. And *Private Eye* can come in very handy. Its 'Rotten Boroughs' section features stories about councillors and officials which sometimes you may not be able to follow up but it can provide useful background information.

HOW RADIO COVERS COUNCILS

BBC Radio Derby news editor John Atkin[3] says the switch to so-called cabinet government forced upon local councils has made the challenge of reporting their activities all the more vital. He says: 'The previous system was – journalistically at least – fairly transparent, in that it was usually obvious which committee would make a decision, and when.' But as we have seen, that system has been replaced with a hierarchy of panels representing council wards, committees, scrutiny committees and the cabinet itself. To counteract that, there is a requirement for local authorities to provide information about their decision-making processes. Key to this is the *forward plan*, a document which rounds up decisions to be made, and gives a date on which that decision will be taken. Atkin comments: 'This is probably the best journalistic tool available to monitor the process of decision-making.'

There have been other side-effects arising from the switch to a cabinet-style system. It appears increasingly to be the case that local authorities are adopting policies that only nominated councillors should give interviews. Atkin views this as a potential problem, 'particularly acute for broadcasters who rely on varied audio – in that, over the course of a week or a month, reporters will find themselves being offered the same interviewee time and time again.' The desire, of course, is to get the information from the horse's mouth – the council officer or employee who is directly involved in the story and who, more often than not, will be briefing a councillor for interview. In the interests of varied coverage, reporters will find themselves having to be robust in pushing for an interview with that individual.

The advantage, though, is that such local authority policies force reporters to think more creatively. It is seldom enough to simply report council decisions; rather, a reporter should seek to examine the effects. Atkin says:

> Being unable, through choice or necessity, to interview a council official forces a reporter to consider other sources of material – community leaders, objectors or, ideally, the members of the public who are directly affected by the decision the local authority spends their council tax on. Ultimately this can only be in the interest of better reporting.

HOW TELEVISION COVERS COUNCILS

> There's no magic formula for getting council stories – it's the same as any other area of journalism. Learn how the process works, get to know the key personalities, and keep your eyes and ears open. A well-stocked contacts book is vital, as is following up previous items.
>
> Neil Manship[4]
> *BBC Look North*

Along with many media outlets, regional television has significantly cut down its coverage of local government matters in recent years. Neil Manship, a senior broadcast journalist for *BBC Look North* in Leeds, says: 'Once every BBC region had a local government correspondent – now there are none.' This is partly due to the perceived lack of interest from the viewers and to the reduction of influence and spending options of many councils. A general consensus is that many council stories are too 'dry' for television. For a medium that relies on visual images for its impact, the details of – for example – a finance meeting can be of limited appeal. Manship disagrees:

> This does not mean there are no stories out there for television outlets. There are lots of good tales involving the personalities and politics of local government. The question is, how do you get at them when there's no formal responsibility for the subject in your newsroom?

Planning stories can be a good source of TV news. Manship says: 'Some of the bigger applications contain CD-ROMs, graphics and other visual aids to illustrate proposals. These sometimes translate well to television so it's worth asking whether these are available.' Planning rows, such as rogue developers building where they shouldn't, create good human stories, especially if it's an ordinary person taking on the might of big business.

Quite often those involved in local politics are characters with bigger ambitions. Some want to become MPs, some like to have power and influence in their communities, and others just like to be in the limelight. Manship points out that 'like everybody else, they make mistakes. Keep an eye on them – they can often create their own stories.' An extreme example of this was the so-called Donnygate scandal in Doncaster, in which corrupt councillors were among those lining their own pockets to push through planning proposals. Several people were jailed in 2002.

Another opportunity for picking up leads is the local papers. Manship says: 'TV sometimes reacts to what's in the morning press and they are generally the bigger issues. But weekly, fortnightly and monthly publications sometimes contain good council stories that are buried on inside pages.'

HOW TO DEAL WITH PRESS OFFICERS

Whichever part of the press and media industry you end up in, the processes and psychology are very similar. It's all about communicating information and contacts and how you work with those contacts. Press officers come in various forms. Many of them started as journalists themselves. If you're dealing with one of those, things should be much easier because they have a similar professional background to you, they understand where you're coming from, and they talk the same language.

If this isn't the case, though, all is not necessarily lost. A number of people enter PR from a variety of backgrounds and some of them are very good. However, if they are people who have just ended up in a press office with no press background and no particular aptitude, it can be difficult. Tim Jones,[5] who developed and managed Nottingham City Council's press and PR team from 1988 to 2002, says:

> There are quite a few civil service press officers like that. They have just been shoved in a press office as part of routine career development and some of them haven't a clue, don't really care, are frightened of journalists and show it by putting up the shutters. There are a few like that in local government too, and other organisations.

The best technique with such people, as with any contacts, is to try to get to know them, win their confidence and trust, and try to demonstrate that you can be helpful to them. Jones says: 'Many people, including some press officers, are motivated or otherwise by the fear of getting their butts kicked. Senior officers are frequently influenced that way.'

Most organisations would like a good image, although some don't realise it. Jones says:

> Good press officers get their bosses to understand that and are proactive, developing a good relationship with the press and media and actually pushing out stories and ideas proactively. And I mean stories that journalists can use, not just free ads for some service or product.

The best journalist/press officer relationships are actually two-way. Tim Jones explains:

> They talk to each other regularly, are aware of each other's needs and constraints, respect each other's position and negotiate the outcomes. Good press officers can be the key to a journalist getting a good story or not. An obstructive press officer can really make life difficult for a journalist.

WHERE DO JOURNALISTS GO WRONG?

Quite a few journalists start off by regarding press officers as the enemy or traitors. There is the mistaken idea among many journalists that colleagues who go into PR are selling out, going into a soft job and earning megabucks. Most PR jobs are anything but soft and all but the lucky few earn little if any more than most journalists. Jones acknowledges this:

> I think it's important for journalists to respect press officers as fellow professionals. They also need to respect the constraints under which press officers have to work. Just because they don't always come back with the answer the journalist wants doesn't mean they are trying to be obstructive. Press officers are middlemen, managing a

dialogue between the journalists and their bosses. They are constantly in negotiation with both, trying to keep both happy. And that can be very difficult. Good bosses can be a dream for both journalists and press officers, with a clearly defined PR policy and practice, always prepared to give an interview or statement or appear on camera. Bad ones can be a nightmare for both! Sometimes, however good the press officer is, there is only so much they can do to help the journalist get the story they want.

Reporters should get their facts right. Most people have more respect for journalists who know what they are talking about and have clearly researched the story before asking for an interview. As Jones explains, 'Senior managers do not react well to being asked challenging questions by people who clearly haven't got their facts right. You're shooting yourself in the foot by doing that.'

Journalists can also help press officers by giving them as much warning as possible of an enquiry, and as much detail about it as possible – organisations can't just magic up answers to a complex statistical enquiry in half an hour. Jones says:

> It's amazing how many journos think they can, or should be able to. Bosses are busy people. They have crowded diaries. In local government, contrary to popular supposition, most senior managers regularly work a 15-hour day, sometimes with virtually wall-to-wall meetings and appointments. Many will try to change their diary to give an interview, but it is very difficult to change, or break into an official committee or some other statutory meeting.

Reporters can also help press officers by being straight with them. If they make a promise and then break it, particularly with regard to a story that is potentially damaging or very important to a press officer's boss, it can seriously compromise the press officer's credibility within the organisation. Similarly, doing daft things like inventing quotes or deliberately trying to embarrass someone because you think they're insufficiently co-operative. As Jones points out:

> You might achieve a very short-term gain but doing this will alienate contacts, which is counter-productive in the long run. So it actually makes good sense for journalists not to screw up press officers, because this could make it very difficult for the press officer to produce the goods next time.

HOW TO DEAL WITH COUNCILLORS

Bob Jones,[6] who was the leader of Derby City Council from 1997 to 2002, was awarded the CBE for services to local government in the East Midlands in 2001. He had regular contact with journalists for more than a decade. This was mainly at local and regional level, but also at national level on a few occasions. The context of the contacts divided into three categories:

1 routine contacts about ongoing council business
2 contacts around 'bad news' stories as far as the council was concerned
3 contact around issues or stories largely generated by the media in question.

Bob Jones says:

> Obviously the categories merged into each other sometimes and the division between the last two was a matter of perception. An example of the second would be the Derbyshire police service losing its official Certificate of Efficiency while I was chairman of the police authority. An example of the third, an extensive newspaper campaign about a taxi which had been sprayed the wrong colour in Derby while I was council leader.

Routine contacts caused him few problems, although he says the amount of documentation generated by a large local authority was a problem for some journalists.

> Clearly journalists like and often require prior knowledge of complex or continuing issues, and this will in my experience be available if the politician trusts the journalist. I never had an off-the-record briefing misused. There is, after all, a mutual advantage in respecting confidentiality. As a system it was most difficult to use when commercial information was involved, or when the local authority was working with other partner organisations.

But Jones says that when the story already existed, the matter was more difficult to deal with:

> Policy decisions in a local authority are mostly complex. What I often wanted was for some of this complexity to be reflected in the media coverage. It was normally difficult to achieve this for two reasons: the journalist had little time to come to terms with that complexity and the media wanted to pursue a story rather than explain an issue.

His main criticism of the media at all the levels at which he had contact with it is its failure to educate the reader/listener/viewer about the background to decisions taken:

> In my experience the relationship between politician and journalist was put under most pressure when the media mounted a campaign on an issue. As an example, there was a concerted campaign by almost all the regional press against the introduction of the leader and cabinet system into local government in the late 1990s. As the press had decided what the story was, the most the politician could achieve was damage limitation. What both parties perhaps have to be realistic about is the paucity of public interest in things which they for the moment are absorbed.

Bob Jones believes journalists should cultivate regular contacts, even if very little comes out of some attempts to elicit information.

> Remember, you may be contacting a busy person at a busy time. You need to be clear about what is on and off the record, and in addition not be too triumphant about a verbal indiscretion which you might make use of. It is after all a two-way relationship for a period of time, and a minor coup here and there is not necessarily going to help.

The former council leader says he was always irritated by being told that privately the journalist agreed with his position – political or personal – but that they had a job to do. He says all that affected him was the coverage which the local authority was receiving in the local press and how fair he felt that was:

> In general I got on well with the local journalists with whom I came in contact, although I had some strong disagreements with their editors on occasion. It was and is a hard time for local councils and no doubt journalists do not all have a taste for municipal affairs and politics. But in a large city most things which determine the future are part of that municipal agenda and both parties have an interest and a role in making them more accessible to the citizen.

THE NATIONAL SCENE

> The well-known case of the regional editor who declared his paper an 'election free zone' in the run-up to the 1992 General Election is thankfully an isolated one. Nevertheless, many papers that are content to run pages of stories about the activities of local councils draw the line at anything that comes out of Westminster and Whitehall.
>
> Paul Linford[7]
> *The Journal*

Paul Linford is assistant editor (politics) of *The Journal*, Newcastle, and has been a member of the parliamentary lobby since 1995. He says politics – and Westminster politics in particular – is often regarded with suspicion by editors and news editors on local and regional newspapers. 'There is a reasonably widespread view that political coverage does not sell papers and is, at best, a necessary evil rather than something that can make a positive contribution to a newspaper's all-round appeal.'

Yet if it is true that 'news is people', and that newspapers have a duty above all to report those things that affect people's lives, then Linford says this neglect of Westminster is hard to justify. 'It is in the very nature of our highly centralised system of Government in Britain that decisions made at national governmental level have by far the greatest impact on our lives.' Not only do some of the biggest stories happen at Westminster – from the rise and fall of governments to the instigation of military conflict – but most major stories that start life elsewhere will swiftly assume a Westminster dimension. Foot and mouth, the Hatfield rail disaster and the Dunblane shootings are particularly poignant recent examples.

WHAT STORIES TO LOOK FOR

As a student journalist or reporter, you may find it useful to consult the following central sources of information when reporting on local government issues:

- annual events at Westminster
- annual Government statistics
- Government funding annoucements
- regional government policies.

ANNUAL WESTMINSTER EVENTS

Every year, there is a series of political events that take place at Westminster that have a direct impact on people's lives. Linford says: 'Some are well-known, like the Budget. There are few papers that would take the view that this does not impact on people and communities, and most papers cover it accordingly.'

Other regular Westminster events are less well known.

- **The Local Government Settlement.** Each November or December, the minister in charge of local government (currently the Deputy Prime Minister) stands up in the Commons and announces the total level of funding for local councils for the financial year beginning in the following April. Linford says: 'This will be accompanied by a breakdown of the central funding going to each council. It is from these figures that local authorities work out their council tax levels. This is therefore an announcement which affects every householder in the country.'
- **The Comprehensive Spending Review.** This happens every two years, but in it the Chancellor fixes spending levels for all the Government departments for the following three years. This therefore covers all spending on areas such as health, education, housing, transport, law and order and regional policy.
- **The Pre-Budget Report.** This takes place every November or December and in it the Chancellor sets out the key themes he or she will follow in the Budget the following spring, sometimes including a few substantive announcements.
- **The Queen's Speech.** This takes place every October or November and consists of the Government's legislative programme for the following year. Linford says: 'Apart from the fact that this will be of general interest to most readers, most Queen's Speeches contain specific proposals that will be of interest to particular regions and communities.'

ANNUAL GOVERNMENT STATISTICS

British politics these days is awash with statistics. Linford says:

The present Government has introduced a panoply of targets and league tables which are regularly made public. Some would say it's a case of lies, damned lies and statistics – but most of the time they also make good stories.

Some of the more important Government statistics which may be of particular interest to local and regional papers are:

- crime figures (source: Home Office)
- unemployment figures (Office for National Statistics – ONS)
- hospital waiting lists and waiting times (Department of Health)
- class sizes, exam results, literacy, numeracy and truancy rates (Department for Education and Skills).

There is also an annual ONS publication, *Regional Trends*, which contains every conceivable statistic about regions and localities from population to the proportion of people who drive a car or own a computer. Nowadays it is only available on the ONS website (www.statistics.gov.uk).

GOVERNMENT FUNDING ANNOUNCEMENTS

The Government regularly makes announcements concerning individual funding programmes which affect local communities. Linford says:

> Almost invariably these will be accompanied by local or regional breakdowns of how much money is coming to a particular locality. Government programmes which tend to be targeted at particular areas include the Neighbourhood Renewal Fund; New Deal for Communities; Sure Start; Education Action Zones; Health Action Zones; Employment Zones; Crime Reduction Partnerships.

There is too little space here to describe all of these initiatives in detail but all are generally aimed at tackling problems particular to certain (mainly deprived) localities.

REGIONAL GOVERNMENT POLICIES

Over the past few years in particular there has been a growing regional dimension to Government policies generally. For instance, the current Chancellor rarely makes a big speech on the economy without some reference to the goal of 'full employment in every region' and narrowing regional economic disparities (now a specific Government target).

Linford comments: 'More specifically, the Government has established Regional Development Agencies (RDAs) in each of the eight English regions to drive forward economic development in their areas, and these have already become an important source of stories for local and regional newspapers.'

There is an increasing drive within Government for more functions to be administered at regional rather than national level and, in some parts of the country, a growing demand for the existing Government regional offices along with the RDAs to be placed under the control of democratically elected regional assemblies.

EXPLOITING THE PARLIAMENTARY PROCESS

Not all journalism is about reacting to events. Newspapers and reporters are increasingly taking a proactive role, and actively seek to influence the political process by highlighting issues of concern to local people and communities. All of the annual political events listed in the preceding section can be a handy focus for local campaigns. Linford says:

> For instance, if a council is making a plea for additional funds to cope with deprivation in their neighbourhood, the Local Government Settlement will be a focus for their efforts. If there is a broader campaign for more education funding, or more funding for deprived areas, then the run-up to the Budget or the Comprehensive Spending Review is a good time to highlight this. At other times there are local tragedies – for instance a spate of deaths caused by dangerous driving – that lead to demands for changes in the law to be introduced in the Queen's Speech. Newspapers may wish to launch such campaigns themselves, or alternatively merely report the fact that such campaigns are taking place within their communities. Either way they are a potentially rich source of copy.

Other tools available to local newspapers for highlighting local issues, usually through their local MPs, include the following.

- **Questions in the House.** These may consist of written questions to departments, for instance finding out what is being done in response to a particular problem, or occasionally oral questions in which the relevant minister – or even the Prime Minister – will be directly challenged at the Despatch Box.
- **Adjournment Debates.** According to Linford, 'These are a particularly useful means of highlighting local problems as the relevant minister will be obliged to give a 10- or 15-minute response at the end of the debate setting out what, if anything, the Government is doing about it.' The debates generally last half an hour and are held either at the end of the Parliamentary day in the main chamber or during the morning in Westminster Hall.
- **Private Members' Bills.** Each year at the start of the parliamentary session in October or November, a ballot of MPs is held for the right to introduce Private Members' Bills. Only the top 15 will have a chance to do so, and in practice only the top two or three stand a chance of their Bills becoming law. Sometimes MPs will choose to bring in a Bill on a major national issue, like fox hunting, but at other times they may choose to focus on a matter of more local concern.
- **Ten-minute Rule Bills.** These are Bills introduced by backbench MPs under the so-called ten-minute rule, which is basically a slot in the parliamentary agenda to enable backbenchers to bring forward legislation. They have no chance of becoming law in their own right, but may occasionally be incorporated in subsequent Government legislation.
- **Early Day Motions.** These are another mechanism used by MPs to highlight particular issues. Although they are never debated, they remain on the Commons Order Paper as long as more MPs are prepared to put their names to them.
- **Petitions.** Occasionally it is possible for a petition on any local or national issue to be presented directly to the Speaker on the floor of the House. This usually takes place at the end of the parliamentary day.

WAYS OF REPORTING POLITICS

Political reporting styles have undergone a revolution. Linford explains:

> In my early days, stories would often appear which solely consisted of some local politician making a set of wild accusations against an opposing party which the opposing party would then seek to refute in similarly extravagant terms. Perhaps thankfully, the newspaper-reading public is now both more sceptical and more discerning, and no self-respecting news editor would today give house room to such routine political knockabout. Most would prefer, if resources permit, to take a closer look at the respective accusations and counter-accusations in order to see who, if anyone, is telling the truth. Even better is for the journalists themselves to set the agenda, by digging out the stories themselves and then going to the politicians for comment.
>
> A common technique for making 'political' stories more interesting to readers is to disguise them as 'human interest' stories, namely by writing them from the perspective of the people affected, rather than the politician generating it. So, for instance, 'Education Secretary Charles Clarke today announced a £1m boost for school budgets in Blogtown' would become 'Parents in Blogtown today urged schools to ensure a £1m Government funding boost is spent on books, not bureaucrats.'
>
> This may at times involve putting the reaction before telling the story, but reporters should not be tempted to treat every political story in this way. When a local MP has been forced to resign his ministerial post because of failing to declare a home loan from a fellow minister, to take a random example, the story is not that his constituents think he is a good fellow who has been hard done by. The story is that he has been forced to resign.

DEALING WITH THE GOVERNMENT MACHINE

Local newspaper reporters are unlikely to come into regular contact with the machinery of Government at the highest levels, but need not be intimidated should they have to do so. There follows what might be seen as a progression of engagement with Government from the lowest-level, departmental press offices, to Downing Street itself.

1 GOVERNMENT DEPARTMENTS

A journalist's first point of contact with the Government machine is often with a press officer in a Government department or the COI (Central Office of Information), which has nine regional offices across England. Linford says:

> When I first started in journalism, Government press departments were by and large helpful to the regional press and would provide the basic factual information you asked for. Nowadays, Governments are far more concerned with controlling the flow of information. So it's unlikely that press offices will actually give out information these days that isn't already in the public domain, usually via either the departmental website or via parliamentary answers. They are given a set 'line to take' from their superiors, or from Downing Street, and will often repeat it ad nauseam no matter how many different ways you attempt to ask a question.

Some Government departments and press offices will helpfully provide regional or even constituency breakdowns to accompany Government announcements, although often you'll have to ask for these. But in general, there is in my experience far less readiness to deal with regional press queries than used to be the case.

2 SPIN DOCTORS

Until ten years ago, all Government spokespeople were known simply as press officers. Then, partly as a result of American influences on British politics, a new and more dangerous species emerged – the spin doctor. What, you may ask, is the difference? Surely they're all just in the game of trying to put the best gloss on Government policy – something governments have always done? Linford says:

As I see it there are two important distinctions – one between the nature of the person, the other between the nature of the role. Press officers are invariably civil servants, and therefore, in theory, at least, politically impartial. Spin doctors *may* be civil servants – Mrs Thatcher's press secretary Sir Bernard Ingham being perhaps the most famous example – but they are much more likely to have come from a party political background or been specifically recruited from the private sector.

The other distinction is one of role. While the job of a press officer is really a defensive role – a back-stop if you like – a spin doctor's is much more proactive, seeking to actively shape and manage the news agenda rather than merely responding to queries.

3 MEMBERS OF PARLIAMENT

Almost all MPs want to have a good relationship with their local paper, and vice-versa. MPs are not only a reliable source of local stories, as people often go to them with their problems, but they also provide a window to what is going on in the wider world of national politics. Linford explains:

The nature of the relationship will really depend on how the MP sees his or her role. If he sees himself primarily as representing his local community, he is likely to be much more helpful and much more emotionally engaged with local issues. If, on the other hand, his aim is to progress through the ranks at Westminster, he is likely to be much more guarded towards journalists in general, and in any case to be targeting his efforts at national newspapers who can give him the national profile he aspires to.

4 GOVERNMENT MINISTERS

Ministerial contact with the regional press can vary wildly, according to the personality and priorities of the individual minister. Linford says:

There is a fairly well-known example of a senior minister who has been known to interrupt international diplomacy to talk to his local paper about the binmen going on strike in his East Lancashire constituency, and who described his local lobby correspondent as 'the most important journalist in the country.'

Such examples are however rare. Generally speaking, the higher a politician ascends up the greasy pole, the less time he will have for the journalists on his local paper.

5 DOWNING STREET

Very occasionally a reporter on a local or regional paper may find it necessary to ring Downing Street. This is perhaps because the Prime Minister is due to visit the area, or because an MP has asked a specific question about a local constituency, or maybe because of a worthy local campaign for which the Prime Minister's support is being sought.

Linford offers some advice:

The lesson is: don't be intimidated. You will actually find that the reverse applies in Downing Street to what normally applies in Government departments. While most departmental press officers are more comfortable dealing with the Lobby, and look down their nose at local 'hicks from the sticks', Downing Street despises the Lobby – including by and large the regional Lobby – and as a matter of deliberate policy from about 1998 onwards has much preferred to deal directly with local papers.

On national papers they get around the Lobby by dealing directly with editors. On regional papers they often deal directly with newsdesks and locally based political correspondents.

CHECKLIST

✓ Contacts are king. Cultivate them. Take them out for a drink. They are vital in most areas of journalism and that's especially true for local government reporting.

✓ Make sure you're getting the most out of agendas. Don't be afraid to ring the author of individual reports for more information. Remember that just one line in a report might turn into a huge story.

✓ Go to meetings. You might occasionally feel like you're losing the will to live but have faith – your presence will pay off.

✓ Avoid jargon. If you don't understand what a report says, neither will your reader, listener or viewer.

✓ Avoid political bias. If you hold strong political views, it's best to keep them to yourself.

✓ Remember your audience. A story that looks good on a council agenda is always much better once you've spoken to the people it affects.

✓ Remember the national scene. Most major stories (and some considerably smaller ones) that start life elsewhere will swiftly assume a Westminster dimension.

NOTES

1 All quotes from Caroline Smith taken from author interview, 2003.
2 All quotes from Kevin Palmer taken from author interview, 2003.
3 All quotes from John Atkin taken from author interview, 2003.

4 All quotes from Neil Manship taken from author interview, 2003.
5 All quotes from Tim Jones taken from author interview, 2003.
6 All quotes from Bob Jones taken from author interview, 2003.
7 All quotes from Paul Linford taken from author interview, 2003.

MEDIA REGULATION

The threat to modern journalism is real, but it comes not just from without but also from within. It comes not just from the manipulations, favouritism and half-truths of the discredited, and partially abandoned, Labour spin culture, but also from the media's disrespect for facts, the avoidable failure to be fair, the want of explanation and the persistent desire for melodrama that are spin's flipside.

Martin Kettle
columnist
Guardian, February 3 2004

Journalism is in crisis. The profession is losing its credibility, its role in society is questioned. Self-regulation of the print press is not always working, while broadcasters – even the BBC – face growing conflicting pressures from Government, the market and the public.

Roman Gerodimos
NUJ Ethics Council Conference in association with *Media Wise*,
December 2004

The entire news media are suspect. The drinks in the Last Chance Saloon have long since been swigged. The glasses are empty. It is closing time and the bill has to be paid.

Bill Hagerty
editor
British Journalism Review, Vol. 15, No. 1, 2004

As information, data and knowledge become increasingly important resources, it is arguable that citizens have come to rely upon the mass media to pass on information and circulate ideas essential to a healthy and vibrant democracy. If one accepts that the media act as public watchdog and fourth estate, then it is essential that they have the freedom to perform this role and equally that the highest professional and ethical standards are adhered to. A network of complex legal provisions constrain many aspects of the work of journalists. In addition, a range of quasi-legal and self-regulatory systems exist to control media ownership and competition as well as media content and the conduct of working journalists.

It is important for the student of journalism to gain an awareness and understanding of this complex regulatory framework. On a day-to-day basis, most working journalists will be concerned to get their story, meet their deadline, and remain within the law and the spirit of any relevant code of conduct. Given the commercial pressures that exist, this rather mechanistic approach to news production is understandable, but the journalist should also reflect upon the competing moral considerations that arise in the coverage of many news stories. Laws, regulations and codes may well have the effect of encouraging and promoting higher standards of journalism, but attention to the ethical reasoning behind a journalist's behaviour and course of action can, arguably, produce better journalism. With this aim in mind, this chapter firstly considers the theoretical rationales which provide a framework for the nature and approach taken to media regulation in the UK. The chapter identifies the range of issues that may need to be addressed through regulation and considers the role of the journalist in this context. Given that the focus of this book is upon the practice of journalism, particular attention is paid to the various regulatory bodies and their codes of conduct. The chapter also invites the reader to consider if regulation acts as a constraint upon media freedom.

THE CONTEXT

A number of rationales exist which seek to justify or negate regulation of the media. These vary in terms of their underlying political, economic and cultural philosophy, but can be said to reflect a contest between two extremes: paternalism and libertarianism. The various approaches reflect a desire to attain, protect and promote certain core values in any given society. In, for example, the libertarian model, these values include the need for and right to the free flow of information and ideas, freedom of speech, cultural and social development, democracy, justice, order, equality and the protection of the vulnerable. These fundamental aims and objectives are clearly of a much wider contextual importance and can be said to reflect the discourse that takes place in debates surrounding the nebulous concept of 'the public interest'. Given the range and influence of the mass media, the same core objectives underpin the justification for and the approaches taken in the regulation, or deregulation of the media. In addition, aims of direct applicability to the media reflect a desire to achieve a high-quality, independent and diverse system of mass communication. It is important to recognise that all rationales of this nature must be evaluated and analysed within the context of the historical period that influenced their formulation, and in the knowledge that different cultures and countries will embrace and promote different theories.

LIBERAL THEORY: A SELECTIVE STUDY

For liberal capitalist societies, the mechanisms of the free market and the free press justify minimal state regulation of the media. The attractions of the free market are based upon a belief that consumer choice is as a result increased and that open competition will create a range and diversity of media products. The marketplace enables citizens to access and be part of such a system through, for example, direct ownership of media outlets or through economic mechanisms such as shareholdings. The 'audience' as consumer, it is argued, is able to have a direct effect upon programme content through the support or rejection of publications and programme output which is reflected in quantifiable ratings or sales figures.

The market model, however, is undermined by a number of concerns. The reality is that diversity of ownership is not an automatic outcome, indeed figures reveal that in the US and the UK there has been a shift to large media groups and concentrations of ownership. Such concentrations may produce benefits in terms of economies of scale, but convergence of ownership may give rise to a reduction in the diversity of ideas and opinions, an advantage to one political viewpoint, an exclusion of minority voices, and an increase in homogeneity of values in culture. Additional anxieties rest upon the impact and influence of advertising bodies, potential contamination by other commercial interests and the tacit recognition that media proprietors have the potential to threaten editorial control, while individual journalists may be unwilling to challenge perceived unethical demands placed upon them for fear of damaging their careers in an uncertain job market.

Libertarian theory also promotes the benefits of a 'free press' and the belief that interference by the state in the activities of the media through laws or state regulation has the potential to undermine their democratic role as public watchdog and source of information. Underpinning these functions is the core value of freedom of expression. Any restraint on this freedom would be perceived as a form of censorship, undermining the democratic process, the independence of the media and its accountability to the public. In the US, this is embodied with a direct reference to the press in the First Amendment to the Constitution. In English law, where there is no similar formal written constitution, the protection of free speech (with no special status for journalists) rests with Parliament, the courts and more recently with the increasing influence of the Human Rights Act 1998.

As with the free-market model, there are obvious drawbacks to relying on such an approach to promote the core values of any given society. The reality is that many journalists and media outlets are far from independent. The commercial constraints and resulting deficiencies in treating news as a commodity undermine the notion of a free press. In addition, the media regularly depend upon the Government directly for certain information and as a consequence can, on occasion, be accused of acting in collusion with the state. Research conducted by the University of Sussex suggests that the public has a growing mistrust of journalists which is fuelled by a belief that much journalism is sloppy, biased, 'dumbed down' and increasingly unaccountable.[1] While there are strong philosophical arguments in support of free speech, there will be times when this interest comes into conflict with other rights such as privacy and the right to a fair trial.[2] These concerns provide strong justification for introducing some means of controlling the content and conduct of the media, particularly to protect the vulnerable members of society. Regulation may also be required to encourage more general access to the media and in that way further promote the notion of free speech and counter the accusation that 'freedom of the press is guaranteed only to those who own one' (Liebling, 1964: 30).

MEDIA REGULATION IN THE UK

Belief in the free market and free press model may support a lighter touch to media regulation. However, concerns relating to the protection of morals and decency, access to and ownership of the media and other cultural considerations mean that the media in the UK remain fairly heavily regulated. Particular concerns of direct relevance to the student journalist also exist relating to the quality of some journalism.

With journalists accused of sensationalism, inaccuracy, bias, trivialisation, deception, entrapment and much more besides, and with a public expectation that the profession should be honest, tenacious, independent and accountable, it is perhaps no surprise that the media in the UK are subjected to a heavy regulatory burden.

The UK currently adopts a patchwork approach to the control of the media. At one extreme a number of laws exist which, while addressing some of the concerns relating to the excesses in journalism, also have the potential to act as a constraint on 'media freedom'.[3] The English law of defamation, for example, which is rationalised on the basis of protecting unjustified harm to others, can be said to have a chilling effect on the work of journalists, and to act as an infringement on freedom of speech. Yet even with such legal constraints, parts of the British press are still driven to distort and sensationalise.

At the same time, the Government can invoke laws ostensibly created to protect national security or confidentiality for its own protection.[4] In addition to the array of laws, a number of statutory, self- and co-regulatory bodies exist in an attempt to balance the needs of industry with the public interest: these have also met with mixed success. Alternative strategies rest, on the one extreme, upon the operation of free market forces, and on the other, in a belief in encouraging and promoting ethical practices. The media, and in particular journalists, may be swift to cry 'foul' and argue that regulation serves the Government and undermines their perceived role as watchdog and fourth estate, yet clearly they too have responsibilities and obligations to society. McQuail (1994) identifies this as a commitment to 'higher goals' such as truth, neutrality, objectivity and accuracy. Laudable though these aims may be, they are however, particularly vulnerable to commercial pressures. The remainder of this chapter focuses upon the regulatory mechanisms deployed in the UK and the reader is invited to consider if they are 'transparent, accountable, proportionate, consistent and targeted' (Ofcom consultation document, 2004: 4).

REGULATION OF THE PRESS IN THE UK

Koss (1981), Ward (1989) and Downing et al., (1995) provide detailed discussion of the historical development of the print media. Such an understanding and analysis are important, for as Negrine (1994) points out, this serves a number of purposes. First, it reflects the notion of the press as a diverse and non-monolithic institution in the last century, as compared to its contemporary status. Second, it enables a deeper understanding of the concept of 'press freedom'. The vitality of this fundamental principle is seen in the early radical press, and explains why the notion of a free press remains a sacrosanct principle for modern-day print journalists. Third, a historical analysis reminds us that political parties and the press are inextricably linked while showing that 'the relationship between the triumvirate of politicians, proprietors and editors ... was never fixed' (Negrine, 1994: 40).

Historically, regulation of the printed medium supports the belief that it served the interests of 'controlling power'. Taxation, stamp charges and duties, fines and even the destruction of printing presses were used in an effort to undermine open discussion that challenged the authority of the 'state'. Manipulation of the press by the state enabled the dissemination of propaganda and misinformation, seen most commonly during periods of war. As history recounts, in post-war 20th-century UK, technological developments and commercial factors influenced a move to deregulation and reliance upon market forces. It is important to remember that this reflects a predominantly economic and political perspective. By the late 20th century, however, concerns over the ability of the market to resolve problems linked to concentration of ownership and journalistic ethics resulted in some legislative provisions to deal with mergers and cross-ownership, and a move to a more formalised system of self-regulation.

The print media in the United Kingdom have been able to resist statutory control and retain a system of self-regulation, despite concerns that perceived vested interests undermine the attainment of aspects of non-public policy objectives. Governments have regularly threatened to set up a statutory press council in response to growing concerns that the systems in place to regulate print journalistic conduct are ineffective. On each occasion, the industry has vociferously resisted such a development and indicated a willingness to get its house in order. In 1953 a General Council of the Press was created in response to criticism contained within the first Royal Commission on the Press.[5]

From its inception and during the years that followed, the General Council and subsequently the Press Council were subject to increasing levels of criticism. Despite the introduction of changes following reviews in the 1960s, 1970s and 1980s, complaints concerning the perceived behaviour of the British press and the ineffective nature of the Press Council had increased to such a level that a further public inquiry was set up.[6] The committee, chaired by David Calcutt, considered the options for maintaining standards in the press and recommended that a new voluntary body be created to regulate the press. However, it warned that if this failed to provide effective and appropriate regulation, then a statutory Press Council would be established.

In January 1991, as a direct response to the report of the Calcutt Committee, the Press Complaints Commission (PCC) came into being and replaced the Press Council. At the time of writing, the PCC continues to provide a mechanism for the regulation of the print media in the UK. Since its inception it has undertaken a process of continuous review of its membership, processes and Code of Practice. In its annual report (2003) the chairman stated that:

> I believe that it is essential for the long-term health of the PCC that it evolves constantly – not for the sake of it, but in its own interests and in those of the ordinary members of the public who complain to us in their thousands. It would be both complacent and wrong to assert that all the criticisms levelled at the Commission in the past have been baseless. Yet the PCC need not be afraid of embracing change in order to take account of legitimate and constructive criticism.

Despite the willingness to 'embrace change', many remain critical of the PCC and argue that self-regulation is ineffective and that despite being told that the industry is 'drinking at the last chance saloon', the 'press and its owners have been able to exploit the reluctance of government to be seen to interfere with free speech in a democracy' (Gibbons, 1998: 279).

THE PRESS COMPLAINTS COMMISSION (PCC)

> The success of the Code in raising journalistic standards is something that many within the publishing industry have acknowledged in recent years. At the same time, it is a claim dismissed in some quarters as wishful thinking.
>
> Les Hinton
> chairman of the Code Committee
> *PCC Annual Report 2003*
>
> *(Continued)*

(Continued)

It could be argued that ... the PCC is a blatant piece of window dressing to protect the press from statutory control.

Professor Roy Greenslade
Guardian, November 2004

Despite the fact that respect for the principle may be tempered with some cynicism, the independence of the media remains an ideal to be invoked in resisting what the press may regard as censorship.

Gibbons, 1991: 24

Established in 1991, the PCC provides a system of self-regulation for the newspaper and magazine industry. The PCC has resisted any form of statutory control, arguing that this would undermine the freedom of the press. It is committed to the belief that self-regulation provides an efficient, accessible and cheap means of dealing with complaints.

The PCC is financed by the industry it serves and its composition includes an independent chairman who is not engaged in the print industry even though he is appointed by them. The chair is supported by 16 Commission members, the majority of whom are lay appointments (public members) with the remainder made up of individuals holding senior positions within the industry (press members). Critics argue that the reality is that members are drawn from too narrow a pool and that the effectiveness of the PCC would be enhanced by the inclusion of working journalists as Commission members. The public members and press members are appointed by an independent Appointments Commission. The cost of the PCC is met by the print industry, which pays a fee to the Press Standards Board of Finance (Pressbof), which in turn funds the Commission.

The Code Committee, currently made up of 14 editors from the print industry, produces a Code of Practice which is ratified by the PCC (see www.pcc.org.uk). Advocates for this approach argue that as the Code is produced by the industry for the industry, there is an inherent interest in making it work. The current Code of Practice, which is reviewed on an annual basis, consists of 16 clauses, 7 of which are subject to a public interest consideration override.

On initial consideration, the Code appears to be fairly brief, particularly when compared to those produced for the broadcasting industry. Closer scrutiny reveals an underlying approach which acknowledges that it is not possible to provide a definitive set of statements on the appropriate standard of conduct required, given the variety of activities and events that can make up a journalist's normal and not so normal working day. Instead the Code seeks to identify a set of general guidelines for working journalists which strive to promote the highest professional and ethical standards. The Code has, in addition, been developed with an awareness of the practical realities associated with the world of journalism and a firm commitment to the duty placed upon journalists to act in the public interest. The PCC notes that 'it is essential that an agreed code be honoured not only to the letter but in the full spirit' and that it is the responsibility of editors to ensure that the Code is observed by their staff. The duty to abide by the Code is increasingly included within individual contracts of employment as an additional incentive to ensure compliance.

The Code offers guidance on a wide range of issues and currently includes clauses under the following headings:

- accuracy, privacy, harassment, children, children in sex cases, hospitals, reporting crime, the use of clandestine devices and subterfuge (these are subject to the public interest exception clause)
- opportunity to reply, intrusion into grief or shock, victims of sexual assault, discrimination, financial journalism, confidential sources, witness payments in criminal trials and payment to criminals.

The Code states that there may be exceptions to some clauses (as identified above) where they can be demonstrated to be in the public interest.

The Code defines the public interest as:

Including, but not confined to:

i)   detecting or exposing crime or serious impropriety
ii) protecting public health and safety
iii) preventing the public from being misled by an action or statement of an individual or organisation.

The Code also asserts that:

There is a public interest in freedom of expression itself.

Whenever the public interest is invoked, the PCC will require editors to demonstrate fully how the public interest was served.

The PCC will consider the extent to which material is already in the public domain, or will become so.

In cases involving children under 16, editors must demonstrate an exceptional public interest to over-ride the normally paramount interest of the child. (PCC Code of Conduct, 2004)

The PCC only receives and deals with complaints that fall within its Code of Practice. It normally requires such complaints to come from individuals involved directly in the story, although they can be received from the general public in very limited circumstances. It is arguable that this complaints-based approach fails to provide an effective system for regulating broader issues such as discrimination and stereotyping and, as a result, misses an opportunity to do something to drive up editorial standards.

Details of how to make a complaint against a newspaper, magazine or journalist are detailed on the PCC website, but there is also a helpline telephone number available and specialist facilities for the blind, visually impaired, deaf and hard of hearing. Complainants are initially invited to explore a resolution directly with the relevant editor, but if they are not satisfied with the response received, they can then begin a formal process by putting their complaint in writing to the PCC. Complaints should be made within two months of the publication or within two months after the close of correspondence with the editor of the publication concerned.

If the issue raised comes within the terms of the Code, then the Commission will either deal with the matter immediately, or undertake a full investigation. The Commission can conclude that there has been no breach, or that action taken or offered by the publication was a sufficient response or that the complaint is upheld. Sanctions include a requirement for the offending newspaper or magazine to publish any adjudication with due prominence. The PCC does not have the power to award compensation or impose fines. It is also only able to act after the event and has no power to prevent publications or restrict further publications.

The PCC website provides a useful set of statistical materials which detail the number of complaints received, how they were resolved and makes available individual adjudications in full. For students of journalism, the site is well worth a visit. The statistical information gives an interesting insight into the number and nature of complaints received year-on-year. The actual adjudications also supply a wealth of information as they highlight the range of very different situations with which journalists are confronted on a daily basis. The adjudications make available a body of examples that provide guidance and a potential ethical framework to assist journalists when handling often contentious and sensitive situations.

As already noted, the PCC Code is fairly short and based on a number of core principles. In one sense this makes it easier for journalists to remember and act upon them, indeed some editors advocate an even briefer version. The difficulty is that the principles in the Code provide a means of measuring behaviour and assessing journalistic standards, but the practicalities and realities that arise from each different situation and set of circumstances mean that individuals will invariably make different decisions in similar cases, as indeed will the PCC in its adjudications.

An examination of a three-month period of activity by the PCC illustrates many of the issues raised in this chapter. The quarterly report, October to December 2003, notes that:

134	complaints were outside the remit of the PCC
139	had no case under the Code
490	were resolved directly and otherwise not pursued
54	were deemed to have had sufficient remedial action taken or offered by the publication
6	were adjudicated, with 5 claims rejected and 1 upheld.

Of the six cases requiring adjudication, four involved claims concerning accuracy. The single case that was upheld by the Commission also related to an alleged breach of Clause 1 of the Code (accuracy). The complaint against the publication *Luton on Sunday* was that an accurate report on the increasing problem of prostitution on the streets of Luton in 2003 was illustrated by a photograph that had been altered in a misleading fashion. The image had been created by putting together two separate photographs. There was no indication that the picture had been constructed in this manner and the complainant suggested that the intention was to alarm and dismay and that the publication had wilfully used an invented image to achieve this aim.

This example is an interesting one to consider. It illustrates that the PCC does not simply deal with the national press, indeed a large proportion of its cases concern local and regional newspaper and magazine output. The circumstances are also interesting to reflect upon. The journalist had a strong local public interest story, but was presumably also under pressure to get a good image to sit alongside the copy. Did it matter that the images had to be manipulated to illustrate what were, after all, verifiable facts? If journalists are required to maintain the highest standards of accuracy, doesn't that also apply to images? The PCC in upholding the complaint noted that it was not a grave example. They used the case, however, to reinforce what was an important ethical principle and to remind editors that they must make it clear if any images used in publications have been altered or artificially assembled.

So how effective is the PCC and is it a flagship for the self-regulatory model? You may wish to consider this question by researching the statistical information and considering the adjudications supplied on the PCC's website. It would also be worthwhile taking those statistics and reviewing a week of local and national print publications. At the time of writing, critics suggest that print journalism is one of the least-respected professions. This view might be reflected in falling newspaper sales and the perception that ethical standards remain low in some publications. The concern is that self-regulation is ineffective, that the evidence suggests a rise in the number of complaints; that many breaches of the Code are repeated again and again; that spurious activities are often 'justified' as being in the public interest; and that complaints to the PCC are often defended by arguing that the letter of the Code hasn't actually been broken. The fact that the PCC is not able to fine publications or award damages to the victims of a breach of the Code suggests that the body responsible for maintaining standards and meeting the expectations of the public is in effect toothless. This has also strengthened the image of the press as an unaccountable power in the UK.

It is not surprising that the PCC defends its record and argues that self-regulation is the most effective means of maintaining and raising standards while ensuring the protection of ideological principles such as freedom of speech and the defence of democratic freedoms. As previously noted, the view is that the self-regulation model has enabled the development of a coherent, responsive, flexible and realistic Code which 'belongs' to the industry and is tailored to its needs. The complaints system is speedy, inexpensive for the end user, of no cost to the taxpayer and, so the PCC argues, effective. Any increase in the number of complaints is not an indication of a lowering of standards, but evidence of the heightened visibility of the PCC and its function. With a raft of legislative provisions which already impose numerous restrictions on the activities of working journalists, the concern is that state regulation of the newspaper and magazine industry would undermine the PCC's role as public watchdog.

BROADCASTING REGULATION IN THE UK

Just as a historical evaluation of the role of the press provides an explanation of the approach taken to its regulation, a similar analysis of the development of broadcasting in the UK affords an account of the more closely regulated and monitored system currently in place. As with the press industry, technological, historical, political and commercial factors all play their part in the creation and regulation of the broadcasting industry in the UK. Television in particular had an 'immediacy, universality and placing within the domestic environment' (Ward, 1989: 68) which created anxieties about its potential to influence behaviour and standards.[7] The limited number of frequencies, or 'spectrum scarcity', combined with manufacturing considerations, created an early broadcasting industry with a distinctive monopolistic form, based on the notion of public service. The Peacock Committee identified a number of concerns related to concentration of ownership, technical standards, distribution, access, conduct and content.[8] The difference, however, was that due to the perceived special nature of broadcasting, higher levels of restriction were required to ensure that the principles were attained. The advent of commercial television, technological advances and structural changes brought about a reappraisal of the role of broadcasting in British society. Whilst consumer choice appeared to increase with privatisation, deregulation and an increase in the number of television channels, the reality was that market censorship took hold. Concerns relating to the impact upon the public sphere raised questions about how the industry *ought* to be regulated and whether or not public service broadcasting deserved special protection.

Broadcasters, like their counterparts in the press industry, are subject to numerous legal provisions, but history shows that with the inauguration of commercial television, 'all radio and television [was] subjected to a regime of institutional censorship, with rules and guidelines of powerful effect' (Robertson and Nichol, 1992: 594). The apparent deregulation of the industry through the Broadcasting Acts of 1990 and 1996 arguably meant *more* regulation. More recently, up until the introduction of Ofcom in December 2003, the system of broadcasting regulation operated on three levels to provide an institutional system of censorship at considerable cost to the taxpayer. The Independent Television Commission (ITC) and the Radio Authority (RA) existed to award licences and to punish any broadcasts that contravened their various codes. The Broadcasting Standards Commission (BSC) acted as a second tier to police the process. Finally, a third tier existed (and still exists) in the form of statutory provisions, which in the opinion of many journalists present a set of hurdles and barriers to restrain their activities.[9] The concern was that this 'light touch' served the Government's interest and posed a severe constraint on media freedom. Numerous examples exist to illustrate that the regulatory processes, which lacked an appropriate appeals system, combined with special ministerial powers, indirect pressure from politicians and commercial considerations, caused programmes to be banned, edited or, worse still, not even made.[10]

At the time of writing, the student of journalism and practitioners alike are faced with a period of radical change in broadcasting regulation. The Communications Act 2003 has created a new, single, all-powerful organisation to oversee the media industry. Ofcom, which came into existence in December 2003, has taken up the work of five pre-existing agencies[11] and has a broad remit which covers issues relating to media ownership, public service broadcasting, spectrum allocation and content-related considerations. Many of these matters fall outside the sphere of this chapter, which focuses upon the regulation of journalistic conduct. However, it is important for the reader to be aware of the wide range of Ofcom's functions. Over the next five years it is reasonable to anticipate that most students on journalism or media-related courses will find that they are confronted with a project or essay which requires them to consider how effective Ofcom has been in meeting its ambitious aims. These changes create difficulties in providing a definitive summary of the current system of broadcast content regulation. Ofcom was committed to producing a new Broadcasting Code for use by the industry, practitioners and the public by 2005. A consultation document containing Ofcom's proposed Code, comprising 146 meaty pages, was published on July 14 2004, with a deadline for responses of October 5 in the same year. In the period between the creation of Ofcom in 2003 and the publication of its new Code in July 2005, guidance was provided through the so called 'legacy Codes' of the ITC, RA and BSC. With this health warning in mind, the chapter will proceed by providing a brief résumé of the relevant pre-Ofcom agencies and their 'legacy Codes'. It will then proceed to outline the composition and jurisdiction of Ofcom and introduce the reader to the new Code.

THE INDEPENDENT TELEVISION COMMISSION (ITC)

The Broadcasting Act 1990 replaced the Independent Broadcasting Authority (IBA) and the Cable Authority with the Independent Television Commission (ITC). This body had broad licensing powers and was also under a duty to monitor and regulate broadcasting. The BBC, a public service broadcaster, was not subject to ITC licensing or its Programme Code. The following two ITC Codes remain in force and at the time of writing represent Ofcom's current policy for editorial standards within commercial television services in the UK:

- The Programme Code
- The Code of Programme Sponsorship.

THE RADIO AUTHORITY (RA)

The Radio Authority also came into existence as a result of the Broadcasting Act 1990 with a remit to award licences and regulate radio programming and advertising. Radio Authority Codes included:

- The News and Current Affairs Code
- The Advertising and Sponsorship Code
- The Programme Code.

THE BROADCASTING STANDARDS COMMISSION (BSC)

The Broadcasting Act 1996 brought together the Broadcasting Complaints Commission and the Broadcasting Standards Council to create the BSC. This statutory body was responsible for standards and fairness in television and radio. This included commercial broadcasters, the BBC as well as text, cable, satellite and digital services. Its three main tasks were to:

- produce codes of practice relating to standards and fairness
- consider and adjudicate on complaints
- monitor, research and report on standards and fairness in broadcasting.

The BSC, made up of 13 commissioners appointed by the Secretary of State for Culture, Media and Sport, considered complaints relating to standards and fairness. Anyone who was concerned about the portrayal of violence, sex or other issues of taste and decency was able to make a complaint directly to the BSC. Individuals with a direct interest in a broadcast also had the right to lodge a formal complaint if they felt they had been treated unfairly or that there had been an unwarranted infringement of their privacy.

The BSC produced a:

- Code on Standards
- Code on Fairness and Privacy.

At the time of writing, these Codes represent Ofcom's current policy on standards and fairness across the broadcasting industry.

THE BRITISH BROADCASTING CORPORATION (BBC)

> Parliament looms over the BBC like a cloud of unknowing – it is a preoccupation and a permanent source of irritation and threat. Like an ageing rich aunt suffering from a long drawn-out disease and incessantly changing her will, Parliament's very presence nags at the BBC.
>
> Anthony Smith
> *TV and Political Life*

Established by Royal Charter in 1926, the BBC holds a unique position in that it is the main public service broadcaster in the UK. It is funded by the state by means of the licence fee, although it also raises funds through a range of commercial activities. The BBC is accountable to Parliament, licence fee payers and audiences. The Board of Governors, who are appointed by the Queen in Council, monitor the BBC's standards against set objectives. The Governors also appoint the BBC director general, who is responsible for the Corporation's management.

BBC services are regulated by the Royal Charter and accompanying agreements which recognise the BBC's editorial independence. The Charter requires the BBC to maintain standards, and to this end the BBC publishes a code of ethics for programme makers, called the *Producer Guidelines*, within which all its staff, journalists and management must operate. The Guidelines provide advice on upholding standards in a range of matters including accuracy, impartiality, fairness, taste and decency, violence, election broadcasts and children. The Guidelines also include useful summaries on general legal matters such as contempt and defamation.

Complaints are handled by the BBC's Programme Complaints Unit, which produces a summary of decisions in the *Programme Complaints Quarterly Bulletin*. This document, along with the Producer Guidelines, can be found on the BBC's website at www.bbc.co.uk. At the time of writing, the BBC is reviewing its complaints procedures and is drawing up a new Code of Practice which will be monitored by a new Complaints Management Board.

OFFICE OF COMMUNICATIONS (OFCOM)

With technological and transfrontier convergence and as infrastructures merged, regulatory issues overlapped and it became apparent that there was a strong case for a single system of control. The Communications Act set out an ambitious programme for change with a move to a single 'light touch' regulator. The newly formed Office of Communications (Ofcom) is tasked with a number of duties and aims to create a regulatory framework which will enable the UK media sector to compete more effectively in the global marketplace.

In terms of content regulation, Ofcom aims to ensure a wide range of high-quality television and radio services whilst ensuring that the public is protected from potentially harmful or offensive material. Ofcom's view is that the old system of content regulation was confusing, expensive, had unnecessary levels of duplication, and ran the risk of different decisions being made by the various regulatory bodies on the same issue.

Ofcom operates with a Unitary Board structure, which at the time of writing has nine members appointed from industry and government. A Consumer Panel exists to advise Ofcom on consumer issues and a Content Board has delegated and advisory responsibilities for a range of content-related matters. Three key Ofcom divisions have been created to deliver the organisation's aims and objectives and are currently grouped under the following headings:

- Strategy and Market Development
- Competition and Markets
- Content and Standards.

The Content Board is made up of 13 members, including lay representatives and individuals with experience in broadcasting. It operates a three-tier system of content regulation under the following headings:

- protecting audiences, referred to as 'negative content regulation'
- ensuring creative diversity
- broadcasting as a public service.

The handling of fairness and privacy complaints has been delegated by the Content Board to a Fairness Committee. This body consists of four members, three of whom are also members of the Content Board, with the fourth taken from a panel of external advisors.

As previously noted, until Ofcom produced its new Broadcasting Code in 2005, it used the 'legacy codes' to deal with content-related complaints. These included the:

- Advertising and Sponsorship Code (RA)
- News and Current Affairs Code and Programme Code (RA)
- Code on Standards (BSC)
- Code on Fairness and Privacy (BSC)
- Programme Code (ITC)
- Code of Programme Sponsorship (ITC).

STANDARD COMPLAINTS

Individual complaints are forwarded to a contact centre and assessed by a case officer and a standards team to determine if there has been a breach of the relevant code. Complaints can be held to be either out of time, resolved, upheld in part or in total, or not upheld. Sanctions include a requirement not to repeat the broadcast, publication of the adjudication, on-air corrections, fines, and the power to shorten or revoke a licence. The power to shorten or revoke a licence is not applicable to the BBC, Channel 4 or S4C. Appeal opportunities are available through the case officer's line manager and in limited circumstances to the Content Board. Copies of all adjudications are available in a *Programme Complaints Bulletin*, which is accessible on Ofcom's website (www.ofcom.org.uk).

COMPLAINTS RELATING TO FAIRNESS AND PRIVACY ISSUES

Complaints regarding fairness and privacy should normally be generated by those directly involved in the case. If the circumstances are straightforward, the complaint will be considered by the Executive Fairness Group, who can decide if it is to be upheld, upheld in part, or not upheld. There is the potential for these decisions to be reviewed by the Fairness Committee. Sanctions available are as outlined above under the section covering standard complaints. A summary of the Executive Fairness Group/Fairness Committee adjudications are provided in the monthly *Programme Complaints Bulletin*, but a separate more detailed *Fairness and Privacy Adjudication Report* is also available on Ofcom's website.

THE OFCOM BROADCASTING CODE

The Code, with which all Ofcom television and radio licensees as well as the BBC (with some exceptions) and Sianel Pedwar Cymru (S4C – Channel 4 Wales) have to comply, sets out a number of core principles and associated rules. Drafted in light of the Human Rights Act and in line with relevant legislation, the Code retains many of the existing regulatory rules whilst omitting others and introducing new provisions. The aim was to produce a new single source that is accessible and easy to understand. Sections cover:

- Protecting the Under-18s
- Harm and Offence
- Crime
- Religion
- Due Impartiality, Due Accuracy, and Undue Prominence of Views and Opinions
- Election and Referendum Reporting
- Fairness
- Privacy

- Sponsorship
- Commercial References and Other Matters.

OFCOM AND PRIVACY: AN ILLUSTRATION

The section covering privacy provides a useful illustration of the approach adopted by Ofcom in the drafting of its new Broadcasting Code. The section, which contains rules that Ofcom expects broadcasters to observe, begins with an opening Principle which aims to help broadcasters understand the particular standard objective. Its stated aim is: 'To ensure that broadcasters avoid any unwarranted infringement of privacy in programmes and in connection with obtaining material in programmes.'

There then follows a set of rules and 'practices to be followed' which provide a framework for journalists to enable them to make appropriate judgements in individual cases. Rule 1 asserts that 'Any infringement of privacy in programmes, or in connection with obtaining material included in programmes, must be warranted'. The remaining rules cover issues relating to:

- private lives, public places and legitimate expectations of privacy
- consent
- gathering information, sound or images and the re-use of material
- suffering and distress
- people under the age of 16 and vulnerable people.

Feedback during the consultation process indicated that the section is welcomed, although aspects were criticised for having a tendency to be woolly and lacking a clear set of definitions of the public interest.

It will be interesting to watch the development of Ofcom, but at this stage it is hard to reconcile the flood of consultation documents and the size of the Broadcasting Code with the notion of a 'lighter touch'. The notion of a single code is attractive to some quarters that see this as making it simpler for the public and those in the industry to use. It should also, arguably, reduce the associated administrative costs. Others argue that the Code lacks media-specific detail and that it is already littered with 'exceptions' identifying sections that will not apply to the BBC. The draft Code was criticised for using highly contentious language and being overlong. Supporters, however, believe that the Code will be easy to understand and will create a new era of co-regulation which will promote the public interest while supporting the work of broadcast journalists and assisting them in making the difficult decisions that they face on a daily basis in the coverage of news and current affairs.

CONCLUSION

This chapter has attempted to highlight the complexity of the issues surrounding media regulation. The debate will turn endlessly on the nature and extent of such regulation. However, such a framework is essential because of the special nature of the media as mediators in society and the acknowledgement that regulation provides an opportunity to promote the public interest. For these reasons it is too important to be left to the Government, the market or the industry alone. Education and continuing professional training also have a crucial role to play in maintaining ethical and responsible journalism. The challenge is to find an appropriate system of checks and balances upon commercial, political and media interests which will, in turn, preserve and protect society's fundamental core values.

NOTES

1 The Mass Observation Archive, 2004, University of Sussex.

2 See Chapter 7.

3 See Chapter 6.

4 See the *Spycatcher* fiasco: *A-G v. Guardian Newspapers Ltd.* (No 2) [1988] 3 All ER 545.

5 Royal Commission on the Press, Cmnd. 7700 (1949).

6 Home Office, *Report of the Committee on Privacy & Related Matters* (1990) Cm. 1102.

7 An ITC survey in 1995 stated that the prime source of world news for the public was 71 per cent TV, 16 per cent newspapers and 11 per cent radio.

8 *Report of the Committee on Financing the BBC*, Cmnd 9824, 1986.

9 See Chapter 7.

10 For example, the following programmes were 'banned' by the BBC. 1979 *Solid Geometry*; 1977 *Brimstone and Treacle*; *The Naked Civil Servant*; 1978 *Scum*; 1985 *Brass Tacks* (following representations by Scotland Yard); 1992 *Panorama*. See also Alastair Campbell's speech to the Fabian Society on February 9 1999, in which he called for broadcasters to let 'democratically elected politicians speak for themselves, free and unedited.'

11 The Radiocommunications Agency, Independent Television Commission, Radio Authority, Oftel and Broadcasting Standards Commission.

GLOSSARY OF LEGAL TERMS

Absolute discharge   The defendant has been convicted but is discharged without penalty.

Accused   The person accused of a criminal offence, also called the defendant.

Act   Act of Parliament, also referred to as a statute.

Actus reus   The physical act which constitutes a crime.

Acquittal   Failure to prove a criminal allegation following a trial results in acquittal. Discharge is also used.

Adjourn   Put off to another date.

Admission   A special written acceptance by the defendant of the facts in a case.

Advocate   A barrister or solicitor, who speaks for his client.

AEO   Attachment of earnings order.

Affirmation   A witness has a right to 'affirm' that he/she will tell the truth.

Allegation   Term used before conviction.

Antecedents   Details of the offender's background. Given after conviction and before sentencing.

Arraignment   A defendant is 'arraigned' before the jury in the Crown Court and 'charged' before a Magistrates' Court.

Arrest   Detaining someone or depriving them of their liberty.

Bail   Conditions attached to the accused's right to be free pending trial.

Balance of probability   The standard of proof in civil cases.

Bench   The entire body of local magistrates, or the magistrates sitting.

Beyond reasonable doubt   The standard of proof in criminal trials.

Binding-over   A legal order requiring the person to be of good behaviour.

Charge   An alleged offender is either 'charged' or 'summonsed'.

Chief clerk	Title of clerk to the courts (Crown/county).
Child	A person below the age of 14.
Circuit judge	Working mainly in the Crown Court and dealing with criminal cases, circuit judges can also hear some civil actions, in these circumstances they are referred to as county court judges.
Cite	Lawyers 'cite' law reports or Acts of Parliament, as examples to support their argument.
Claim form	Formerly known as a writ. The document that is used to start a civil action.
Claimant	Formerly known as the plaintiff. The individual or organisation bringing an action in a civil case.
Co-accused	Persons charged jointly with another regarding the same offence.
Committal	Procedure when a case is committed from the magistrates for trial or sentencing to the Crown Court.
Common law	Law derived from judicial precedents or custom.
Community service	Unpaid work in the community.
Compensation	To be paid by the defendant to the victim.
Complaint	A document which gives details and starts civil proceedings.
Concurrent sentences	Two or more sentences of imprisonment. The individual convicted serves the longer period.
Consecutive sentences	Two or more sentences of imprisonment, one to follow the other.
Contempt of court	Interference with the judicial process. Disregarding the authority of the court.
Copyright	The exclusive right to control the production of copies or certain original works.
Coroner	A coroner, often a doctor or a lawyer, holds inquests to determine the cause of death in certain cases.
Corroboration	Supporting testimony or facts.
Costs	Costs incurred by one party can be paid by the other side.
Counsel	Barrister.
CPO	Chief Probation Officer.
CPS	Crown Prosecution Service.
Cross-examination	Asking questions of a witness by the other side.
CSO	Community Service Order.
CST	Consent to summary trial.
Decree absolute	The final order of divorce.
Decree nisi	The first stage of a formal divorce.
Discovery	The formal exchange of lists of documents in civil actions.
Dismissed	'Case dismissed', where the prosecutor fails to prove a criminal case. Also used in civil proceedings.

DPP	Director of Public Prosecutions.
Duty solicitor	Rota solicitor.
Either-way offence	An offence triable either summarily or at a Crown Court before a jury.
Ex-parte	An application to the court, but only one side is present, now known as 'without notice'.
Examination-in-chief	Questions put to a witness by the party who calls him/her.
Exhibits	Things put in evidence.
Expert witness	A professional who gives evidence in his/her field of expertise.
Foyer	The entrance hall to a court is often called a 'foyer'.
In camera	Public and press are kept out of court.
In chambers	Proceedings of the court held without the media and public being present. Now known as 'In private'.
Indictable offence	Triable before the Crown Court.
Indictment	A formal written statement of the charges faced by the accused.
Information	The document used for the basis of the allegation.
Injunction	A court order which instructs the other party to do/not do something.
Inter-partes	Both sides are heard.
JP	Justice of the peace (magistrate).
Jurisdiction	Power or authority.
Justification	An absolute defence of truth in a defamation action.
Juvenile	A young person under 18 years on a charge.
LCD	Lord Chancellor's Department.
Legal Aid	State-aided system to fund legal advice.
List	The list of cases to be heard in a court or courtroom on a particular day.
Malicious falsehood	An untrue statement made recklessly that has caused some financial loss.
Mens rea	The guilty mind in a criminal case.
Mitigation	Argument in favour of a lesser penalty or sentence.
No case to answer	The defendant is discharged.
Oath	To swear to tell the truth on a holy book.
Parties	Those directly involved in proceedings.
Plaintiff	See claimant.
Pleadings	Now known as 'Statements of case'.
Precedent	Previous judicial decisions of authority.
Precincts	The area surrounding the court.
Prima facie	At first sight.
Private prosecution	A prosecution brought by a private individual.
Proof of service	It may be necessary to prove that a summons has been served.

Queen's Counsel (QC)	Senior barrister.
Recorder	An assistant judge.
Remand	Awaiting trial, on bail or in custody.
Retirement	Adjournment by magistrates to discuss a case.
Setting down	The pleadings in a civil case are complete and the case is put on the court list.
Sit/sitting	Magistrates 'sit' in court.
Small claims court	Civil court for dealing with claims under £5,000.
Statute law	Acts of Parliament.
Stipendiary	A salaried professional magistrate.
Subpoena	A witness summons.
Summary proceedings	The case is dealt with by magistrates.
Summing up	The judge sums up the arguments for the jury at the end of a case.
Summons	An order to attend the court.
Testimony	Evidence in person from the witness box.
Tort	A civil wrong, e.g. defamation.
Ultra vires	Beyond the powers.
Usher	Court official, usually identifiable from their black gowns.
Ward	The court acts to protect a minor or incapable person.
Warrant	Search warrants, warrant for arrest, etc.
Without notice	Formerly known as ex-parte.
Writ	Now known as a 'claim form'.
Worships/Your Worship	Traditional form of addressing a magistrate. Now more common to use Sir/Madam.

GLOSSARY OF JOURNALISM TERMS

Actuality	The live or recorded sound of an event or interview on location, i.e. as it 'actually' happens.
Angle	Main point or points of a story.
As-live	Item pre-recorded to sound as if it is happening live.
Audio	Literally, sound. Material from an interview or a live or recorded voice piece that provides an aural illustration of what is happening.
Bed	Recording of music or actuality played under speech to provide continuity or atmosphere. For example, many commercial radio stations use a 'music bed' to play under news bulletins.
Bi-media	Describes any operation that involves radio and television.
Brief	Instructions given to a reporter, usually by the news editor, on how the story should be covered.
Broadsheet	Now a dying breed: those big newspapers that get in the way when you try to read them on the bus. Previously regarded as more serious newspapers than the tabloid newspapers.
Catchline	Word at the top of a script that identifies the story or item; also known as a 'slug'.
Check calls	Calls made to the emergency services on a regular basis to monitor any breaking news.
Clip/cut	Extract from an interview or other recording.
Copy	Written news story. In broadcasting, copy stories do not have any audio or visuals.
Cue	Written introduction read by a newsreader that links into audio or video.
Cutaway	Shots used in a picture sequence to illustrate what is being talked about and/or to mask an edit.
Demographic	Profile of a radio station's average listener based on age, gender, race, profession etc. This is very important to advertisers who wish to target a particular audience.

Desk	Control panel in a studio that mixes different sources for transmission.
Dissolve	Where one picture is faded out as another is faded in.
Drive	To drive a desk is to operate the studio desk.
Dub	To make a copy of a recording from one source to another.
Duration	The length of time to the nearest second of a programme item. Written items for broadcast are timed at three words per second.
Embargo	Used to delay the publication of information.
ENPS	Electronic News Provision Service. The computerised newsroom system used by the BBC.
Exclusive	Story that is (supposedly) unique to a particular media source.
FX	Sound effects.
GV	General view. Shot that shows the entire scene to establish the location of a report.
Hack	Slang for a newspaper reporter.
Intro	First paragraph of a newspaper story, or the cue to a broadcast piece.
ISDN	Integrated Services Digital Network. A system of providing high-quality digital audio signals through telephone lines.
Lead	Main story in a radio or television bulletin, or the main story on a newspaper or online page.
Level	Volume of recorded or broadcast sound as registered on a meter. Also a pre-recording check on a speaker's voice, known as a 'level check'.
Link	Any speech between items on radio or television that introduces or sets up the next item.
Noddies	Shots of the reporter nodding or listening to an interviewee, used to mask edits.
OOV	Literally 'out of vision'. Where pictures appear and the presenter is not shown on camera.
Package	A recorded item for broadcast, combining interviews, links, and/or music and effects, prepared for broadcast with a cue.
Popping	Distortion caused by the rush of air in 'p' and 'b' sounds, usually caused by the microphone being in the wrong position.
Prospects	List of news stories expected to be covered that day.
PTC	Piece to camera, also known as a 'stand upper'. Where the reporter talks directly to the camera.
Q&A	Literally question and answer. An item where the presenter interviews the reporter who has been following a particular story.
RAJAR	Radio Joint Audience Research. The body owned by the BBC and the Commercial Radio Companies Association which measures audiences for all radio stations in the UK.
Running order	The planned order of items in a programme.

Set-up sequence A collection of four or five set-up shots. These are single shots of varying length that can easily be edited together in order to give the reporter space over which to introduce the interviewee in the script.

SOC Standard out-cue. An agreed form of words used by a radio or television reporter at the end of a report, e.g. 'James White, IRN, London'.

Sound-bite Brief extract from an interview.

Standfirst The bit between the headline and a feature which explains what the story is about and often includes the name of the author.

Stringer Freelance journalist.

Sub-editor Person responsible for writing headlines, checking stories and designing pages.

Tabloid Those handy-sized newspapers which used to be thought of as down-market but now include the *Independent* and the *Times*.

Talkback Intercom system used to talk to reporters on location or in other studios.

Two-way Another name for a Q&A. An interview between a presenter and a reporter to provide information about a story.

Voice piece Scripted report of a story by a reporter, used with a cue read by the newsreader.

Voice-over Commentary recorded over pictures.

Vox pop Literally, 'voice of the people'. A series of responses from people in the street, edited together in a continuous stream.

Waveform Visual display of sound on a computer in digital editing systems.

Wild track Recording of background noise or ambient sound on location, used to provide atmosphere or continuity on recorded packages.

Windshield Foam 'sock' used over microphones to prevent wind noise on recordings.

BIBLIOGRAPHY

Allan, S. (1999) *News Culture*, Buckingham: Open University Press.

Bagnall, N. (1994) *Newspaper Language*, Oxford: Focal Press.

Barnard, S. (2000) *Studying Radio*, London: Arnold.

Beaman, J. (2000) *Interviewing for Radio*, London: Routledge.

Bennion, F. (1978) *Statute Law Obscurity and Drafting Parameters*, British JLS 235.

Boyd, A. (2001) *Broadcast Journalism: Techniques of Radio and Television News* (5th edn), Oxford: Focal Press.

Christmas, L. (1997) *Chaps of Both Sexes? Women Decision Makers in Newspapers: Do They Make a Difference?* London: BT Forum/ Women in Journalism.

Cottle, S. (ed.) (2003) *News, Public Relations and Power*, London: Sage.

Crone, T. (2002) *Law and the Media,* Oxford: Focal Press.

Davis, A. (2003) 'Public relations and news sources', in S. Cottle (ed.) *News, Public Relations and Power*. London: Sage.

De Burgh, H. (ed.) (2000) *Investigative Journalism: Context and Practice*, London: Routledge.

Delano, A. (2000) 'No Sign of a Better Job: 100 Years of British Journalism', *Journalism Studies* 1(2): 261–72.

Downing, J., Mohammadi, A. and Sreberny-Mohammadi, A. (1995) *Questioning the Media*. London: Sage.

Evans, H. (1986) *Editing and Design: Newsman's English*, London: Heinemann.

Fleming, C. (2002) *The Radio Handbook* (2nd edn), London: Routledge.

Galtung, J. and Ruge, M. (1981) 'Structuring and Selecting the News' in S. Cohen and J. Young (eds), *The Manufacture of News* (revised edn), London: Constable.

Gibbons, T. (1998) *Regulating the Media*, London: Sweet & Maxwell.

Gibson, O. (2004) 'Tidings of Online Comfort', London: *Media Guardian,* November 29 2004, p. 13.

Gitlin, T. (1980) *The Whole World Is Watching*, London: University of California Press.

Greenslade, R. (2004) 'Why the Web is Friend and Foe', *Guardian*, November 15 2004.

Hall, S. (1981) 'The Determinations of News Photographs' in S. Cohen and J. Young (eds), *The Manufacture of News*, London: Constable.

Harris, G. and Spark, D. (1997) *Practical Newspaper Reporting* (3rd edn), Oxford: Focal Press.

Hennessy, B. (1997) *Writing Feature Articles* (3rd edn), Oxford: Focal Press.

Hicks, W. (1998) *English for Journalists* (2nd edn), London: Routledge.

Keeble, R. (2000) *The Newspapers Handbook* (2nd edn), London: Routledge.

Koss, S. (1981) *The Rise and Fall of the Political Press in Britain* London: Hamish.

Liebling, A. (1964) *The Press*, New York: Ballantine Books.

Manning, P. (2001) *News and News Sources*, London: Sage.

McQuail, D. (1994) *Mass Communication Theory*, London: Sage.

Negrine, R. (1994) *Politics and the Mass Media in Britain*, London: Routledge.

Nichol, A., Millar, G. and Sharland, A. (2002) *Media Law and Human Rights*, London: Blackstone Press.

Robertson, G. and Nichol, A. (1992) *Media Law*, London: Penguin.

Schudson, M. (1996) 'The Sociology of News Production Revisited', in J. Curran and M. Gurevitch (eds), *Mass Media and Society* (2nd edn), London: Arnold.

Sellers, L. (1985) *The Simple Subs Book* (2nd edn), Oxford: Pergamon.

Tuchman, G. (1975) 'The News Net', in O. Boyd-Barrett and C. Newbold (eds), *Approaches to Media*, London: Arnold.

Ward, K. (1989) *Mass Communications and the Modern World*, London: Macmillan.

Welsh, T. and Greenwood, W. (2001) *McNae's Essential Law for Journalists* (16th edn), London: Butterworths.

Williams, K. (1998) *Get Me a Murder a Day: A History of Mass Communication in Britain*, London: Arnold.

Wiseheart, K. (1922) 'Newspapers and Criminal Justice', in R. Pound and F. Frankfurter (eds), *Cleveland Foundation Survey of Criminal Justice*, Cleveland, Ohio: The Cleveland Foundation.

INDEX

Lightning Source UK Ltd.
Milton Keynes UK
UKHW031844111218
333820UK00006B/562/P